BECKETT AND BION

BECKETT AND BION

The (Im)Patient Voice in Psychotherapy and Literature

Ian S. Miller

with contributions by Kay Souter

KARNAC

First published in 2013 by
Karnac Books Ltd
118 Finchley Road, London NW3 5HT

British Library Cataloguing in Publication Data

A C.I.P. for this book is available from the British Library

ISBN 978 1 78049 147 9

Edited, designed and produced by The Studio Publishing Services Ltd
www.publishingservicesuk.co.uk
e-mail: studio@publishingservicesuk.co.uk

Printed in Great Britain

www.karnacbooks.com

CONTENTS

PART II: AN INTERPRETATIVE CONSTRUCTION
OF BECKETT'S LITERARY DEVELOPMENT AND
BION'S LATER CLINICAL THEORIES

ACKNOWLEDGEMENTS

Because there are two of us, acknowledgement must begin with the stimulation, productivity, frustrations, confrontations, and working through of the pair, engaged in thought. Linked to Beckett and Bion, working with each other has been an exercise in continuously finding the Other, as well as serving as the Other's Other, and, most of the time, "good enough". The challenges of international collaboration have been mitigated by technology, but, at bottom, it still comes down to voice and presence.

There are other Others, as well, to thank, beginning in New York with Annette and Zach, Laura, and Gil, whether encouraging or tolerating the passions of such enquiry. Continuously present in Melbourne, a shout out to Allan. And in Ireland, Conor and Judy, Christine and James J, leading to Sam at TCD.

Finally, often present, however absent, is the influence of my late teacher, William Grossman, MD.

I also acknowledge the following:

Cambridge University Press: extracts from *The Letters of Samuel Beckett*, Vol 1, 1929–1940 (2009), edited by Martha Dow Fehsenfeld and Lois More Overbeck, © The Estate of Samuel Beckett 2009, published by Cambridge University Press, reproduced with permission.

Faber and Faber Ltd: permission to reproduce extracts from *Molloy* and "The End", by Samuel Beckett.

Grove Press: excerpts from "The End", "Texts for Nothing", "First Love", "The Calmative", "The Expelled", and "One Case in a Thousand" from *The Complete Short Prose 1929–1989*, copyright © 1995 by the Estate of Samuel Beckett; excerpts from *Molloy*, English translation copyright © 1955 by the Estate of Patrick Bowles and the Estate of Samuel Beckett; excerpts from *The Unnamable*, English translation copyright © 1958 by the Estate of Samuel Beckett; excerpts from *Company* copyright © 1980 by Samuel Beckett; excerpts from *Worstward Ho* copyright © 1983 by Samuel Beckett; excerpts from "Proust" from *Poems, Short Fiction, Criticism (Vol IV)*, copyright © 2006 by the Estate of Samuel Beckett; excerpts from *Watt*, copyright © 1953 by the Estate of Samuel Beckett; excerpts from *Waiting for Godot*, copyright © 1954 by the Estate of Samuel Beckett; excerpts from "Endgame", English translation copyright © 1957 by the Estate of Samuel Beckett; excerpts from "Bram Van Velde" from *Disjecta*, copyright © 1984 by Grove Press, Inc, used by permission of Grove/Atlantic, Inc.

ABOUT THE AUTHORS

"Do you take your work home with you?" had been a question often asked by patients in over thirty years of Ian Miller's clinical practice as a psychologist and psychoanalyst. Very surprisingly, as he listened one evening to Conor Lovett's Gare St Lazare Ireland performance of Beckett's *First Love*, the answer seemed to be a resounding "yes". That resonant experience was the beginning of this project.

Ian's undergraduate education at the University of Pennsylvania focused on historical analysis of ancient manuscripts. His Doctorate in Clinical Psychology was followed by psychoanalytic training at the New York University Postdoctoral Program in Psychotherapy and Psychoanalysis. He is currently based in Dublin, where he maintains a psychotherapy practice. He is a member of the Irish Forum for Psychoanalytic Psychotherapy.

Kay Souter's experience has mirrored Ian's, with emphases reversed. She is a literary critic and educator, and has taught English literature at universities in Australia for over thirty years.

In the 1980s, she decided to learn more about psychoanalysis, and promptly found herself introduced to the work of W. R. Bion, whose extraordinary approach not only resonated for her, but also allowed her to explain Samuel Beckett to the drama students she was working with at the time. She has published widely on psychoanalysis and representations of the family, and in recent years her work on Bion has allowed her to focus on learning space development. She is based in Melbourne, where she works at Deakin University. At the weekends, she works in the small family vineyard in the foothills of the Australian Alps.

Introduction

This reading of Beckett and Bion is not simply interpretative, but a construction that has arisen from a very dynamic process, full of hypothesis and surprise. Far from negating other readings, it only adds density to the textured understanding of these two brilliant thinkers, each formally in different lines of work, but joined through what Bion himself might call a "reciprocal perception" of psychoanalysis. It is reciprocal because Beckett transformed psychoanalytic thinking into a literary genre while Bion transformed psychoanalytic thinking into process understanding. Each utilised the same object, but with different attentions to different ends.

Our collaboration began fortuitously, over a bottle of Souter Vineyard cabernet, after meeting at an international conference in Melbourne where Kay was a keynote speaker and I gave a paper. Somewhere approaching the lees, we got to talking about Beckett and Bion. Ian had recently seen Conor Lovett perform in *First Love*, and had a strong intuition about the narrative's clinical underpinning. He had begun reading Beckett biographies as well as psychoanalytic papers about the Beckett–Bion relationship. Kay's interest in Bion had long informed her teaching and writing (Souter, 2009).

Each agreed that something had gone missing in scholars' under-standing of the Beckett–Bion relationship. Most glaring to us, as we began a second bottle, was a lack of critical thought concerning both the nature of Bion's Tavistock training at the time of Beckett's therapy and what, from the standpoint of now current theory, seemed to be Bion's violation of therapeutic boundaries in inviting his patient to dinner and a Jung lecture in October 1935.

Additionally, Beckett's own documented and prolific reading in psychoanalysis seemed nowhere to have been noted as a potential resistance to psychotherapy. In fact, it seemed to us as if the commu-nity of Beckett scholars, while mindful of psychoanalysis, had approached it as a theory alone rather than as an experiential clinical practice, and that the community of psychoanalysts, while mindful of the Bion–Beckett linkage, had insufficiently documented the terrific shifts in psychoanalysis, theory and training, both informing this early psychotherapy and subsequent developments in the field.

We agreed to collaborate on what was initially, to be a paper; so the work began. Biographies were invaluable, especially Knowlson's brilliant *Damned to Fame*, which allowed us to hypothesise about the young Beckett's emotional situation. Crucial to our research were Fehsenfeld and Overbeck's recently edited compilations of Beckett's correspondence. Reading them chronologically provided a rich resource in tracking Beckett's emerging thought and emotion, over time. Especially interesting to us were the many letters written during the period of Beckett's psychotherapeutic encounters with Bion. These provided an extra-therapeutic window on the treatment, from which, together with biographical materials, our changing hypotheses might be extended.

Reading, on the psychoanalytic side, the classic papers of Simon and Anzieu on the Beckett–Bion relationship provided a fine jumping-off point. Bion-related scholarship by Bléandonu and Conci was invaluable; as was Dicks's history of the Tavistock Clinic. The tran-scripts of Jung's 1935 Tavistock lectures provided not only important contents, but also much context about the institutional life of Tavistock at that historical moment. Certainly, we are also indebted to psychoanalytic scholars, from Breuer and Freud onward, whether of Freudian, Kleinian, or Middle persuasions (including ego-psycholo-gists, interpersonalists, and relationists) for the wisdom they have imparted to us via theory, supervision, and personal psychoanalysis.

My reading of a footnote in Anthony Cronin's biography of Beckett opened up another fruitful avenue. It led to discovery of an unedited, taped interview of Beckett's lifelong friend, Geoffrey Thompson, in the Dublin archives of Ireland's national radio broadcaster, RTE. Thompson's interview provided much detail about the period of Beckett's psychotherapy—especially about the Jung lecture. This allowed us to reshape our hypothesis, deepening it with both complexities of institutional life and the possibility of creative solution to a therapeutic impasse.

Beckett's correspondence carried us forward in the Beckett–Bion relationship and provided a segue for the continuation of Beckett's transference to Bion through the war years to the novellas and the trilogy. At the same time, a chronological reading of Beckett's work, together with works by McGreevy and Aldington, were helpful in generating other threads in relation to Beckett's social world and evolving literary style.

My linkage of the novellas and the trilogy to *Studies on Hysteria* in preparation for a talk at Trinity College, Dublin, in February 2012, was a bridge to our understanding of Beckett's literary transformation of free association. This hypothesis received support as we read about Beckett's own interests in generating a post-Joycean, post-Proustian, personal literary voice. In addition, we were strongly mindful of Beckett's own struggle with debilitating panic and the familial stressors leading to Geoffrey Thompson's referral to psychoanalysis in 1933.

The decision to read Ernest Jones' writings of the 1920s, which formed a substantial portion of Beckett's study, was invaluable. Jones' evocative descriptions are critical elements in thinking about Beckett's transformation of psychoanalytic concepts in literature.

Perhaps most exciting was our recognition that Beckett's use of the reader shifted several times during the period immediately prior to his writing *Waiting For Godot*, and we were only reading in the English, leaving the back and forth of translation from French to English aside. From this, we were able to trace Beckett's own literary working through in fiction relative to the internalisation of Bion as analyst, especially within the trilogy. We hypothesised that development in Beckett's depictions of the dyadic relationship facilitated his own shift from novel form to drama through innovative and controversial use of the reader. Unwittingly, the reader participates in the author's examination of internalised objects and, in so participating, also engages with a new and dynamic form of modern literature.

Our interest has been in understanding Beckett's translation of his own therapeutic experience into art. This extends the psychoanalytic contribution to Beckett studies beyond the psychoanalytically inflected contents of Beckett productions to the use of experience within the clinical practice of psychoanalytic psychotherapy as a conscious or unconscious vehicle that powerfully affects the experience of apprehension by reader or audience.

In approaching Beckett's creative development in relation to his psychotherapy with Bion, we also enquired into Bion's work subsequent to his engagement with Beckett. Just as Beckett's internalisation of Bion as a transference object would power his own creativity, we recognised the probability of Beckett's significant influence on Bion, long after they had last met in 1935. We conclude our work in turning to Bion's subjective use of Beckett as the Patient Zero of his own post-Kleinian developments.

The structure of the book is divided into two parts. Part I is a variation upon the case study. It documents the context and events of Beckett's psychotherapy with Bion. Part II rests upon this initial presentation in an interpretative construction of both Beckett's literary development and Bion's later clinical theories.

Chapter One presents a biographical introduction of Samuel Beckett. It sets the tone for Chapter Two, a discussion of Beckett's early metapsychological monograph, *Proust*. Chapters Three and Four present Beckett's two years in psychotherapy, 1934 and 1935, while Kay's contributions in Chapter Six discuss Wilfred Bion's history and background.

Beginning Part II, Chapter Seven addresses Beckett's radical use of free association as a literary form. Chapters Eight and Nine examine Beckett's novellas; Chapters Ten and Eleven discuss "the trilogy". Chapter Twelve examines Beckett's creative transition from prose to drama, and Chapter Thirteen, another significant contribution of Kay, discusses Bion's theoretical use of his work with Beckett.

PART I

THE CONTEXT AND EVENTS OF BECKETT'S PSYCHOTHERAPY WITH BION

Presenting problems

Recalling his lifelong friend, Samuel Beckett, the London psycho-analyst Geoffrey Thompson noted in a 1976 radio broadcast that an understanding of Beckett's relation to his mother, May, was fundamental to any understanding of the renowned writer (Thompson, 1976). While this reference to maternal difficulty suggests a simplified psychoanalytic shorthand, Thompson could not have been more correct in relation to Beckett's psychological situation during his twenties. Indeed, it was the tormented struggle to separate from his family of origin, while simultaneously affirming his identity as a writer, that framed Beckett's path to psychoanalytic psycho-therapy with Wilfred Bion in London between 1933 and 1935.

For Beckett, his twenties was a decade of contrast, both rich and painful, resulting in the development of literary acquaintances and accomplishment as well as the experience of suffering great anguish. These contrasts took Beckett close to the limits of tolerance, but would ultimately empower him to individuate from the adhesive power of his family, played out through the "savage loving" (letter to Thomas MacGreevy, 6 October, 1937, Fehsenfeld & Overbeck (2009), hereafter cited as TM, followed by the date of the letter) between May Beckett and Sam, the younger of her two sons. Before achieving this psychological consolidation, Beckett would endure almost a decade of personal challenge in struggling to affirm his adult identity as a writer. Complicating his distress was the underlying suffering of painful physical symptoms and panic attacks.

It was a decade in which Beckett would practise a continuous circuit of separation and return, both specifically from his family's Foxrock home, Coolindragh, and generally from Dublin, his spiritual home (O'Brien, 1986). Beckett's own oscillations, "a series of physical flights from one spectacle of suffering after another" (Knowlson, 1996, p. 159) foreshadowed his character Molloy's continuous psychological departure and return to his own mother, initiating the first novel of Beckett's "trilogy" (Beckett, 2006b). Indeed, Beckett's own path paralleled what he would describe in his psychological notebooks as "the vicious cycle of psychogenic illness: disappointment of desire, aggression, fear of results, object of desire turned into something terrifying, repudiation, disappointment, etc." (Feldman, 2006, p. 110) until achieving acceptance of a firm and actionable recognition that "I am what her savage loving has made me, and it is good that one of us should accept that finally" (TM, 6 October 1937).

Samuel Beckett began his undergraduate education at Trinity College, Dublin, in 1923, at the age of seventeen. While secondary school classmates at the Portora School in Enniskillen had recognised his tendencies towards moodiness, withdrawal, and introspection, these were to develop, over the period of his time as a Trinity undergraduate, into the difficult triad of superiority, contempt, and depression (Knowlson, 1996, p. 79). The development of physical symptoms, beginning in 1926, would include the diagnostic markers of panic attack including insomnia, heart palpitations, night sweats, and fear of madness (American Psychiatric Association, 1994).

Throughout this period of emotional turmoil, Beckett was able to maintain and burnish his extraordinary capacity for critical reading and writing. In terms of emotional balance, he demonstrated a determined and reliable capacity for intellectual activity, often reflected in his early writing, through his extensive use of dictionaries, etymologies, foreign languages, and literary allusions, which was strikingly at odds with his psychological disarray. His highly focused writing, including the extensive composition of letters and "notebooks" on literature, philosophy, and psychology contrasted sharply with the maddening distraction of emotional suffering. Writing functioned as an intellectual buoy, a "psychic retreat", in providing a reliable refuge from the experience, the near-despair, of personal suffering (Steiner, 1993). Beckett's typed notebooks on the subject of psychoanalysis reached 20,000 words, primarily drawn from his reading of Ernest Jones' extensive *Papers on Psycho-analysis* (1948) and *Treatment of the Neuroses* (1963) (Feldman, 2006, p. 100). Unlike the encyclopaedic quality of Beckett's notes on philosophy, his "Psychology notes" suggest that Beckett used them as intellectual adjuncts in finding his way through personal suffering (Feldman, 2006, p. 96).

Late in 1935, and in attendance with psychiatrists Wilfred Bion and Geoffrey Thompson, Beckett would hear Jung argue that a writer's characters develop autonomously from the unconscious experience of a personality's symptom complexes. Jung's comments both underlined and suggested the mobilisation of what Beckett had already studied in Ernest Jones' guide for physicians in the treatment of neurosis. Jones defines "complexes" as

> a group of connected ideas, invested with a strong body of emotion and having a definite conative tendency (wish, longing, etc). In actual practice it is found that such localized groups of ideas always present some propensity towards dissociation, the extent of which varies considerably in different instances; consequently there is generally some portion of the complex that is repressed in the unconscious. (Jones, 1963, p. 36, fn 1)

"Conation" is an early twentieth century psychological term referring to the mental precursor of thought as desire or aversion (McDougall, 1918, p. 29). The implementation of Jung's suggestion would involve Beckett's own narrative mobilisation of the conative, in articulating wishes and longings that were conventionally repressed in polite society, but which are aggressively resonant as currents of love and hate beneath the conventional surface of daily interactions.

It was in the exploration of this unconscious world, itself lived within every man's daily life, that Beckett's writing would also secure him a special kind of psychic retreat, wherein his own considerable sufferings might inform productive creative pursuit. "In a secret way", according to Jung, the writer's use of himself would narrate his own "indefinite, because unknown, number of complexes or fragmentary personalities" (Jung, 1968, p. 81). Not only would Beckett's characters articulate these fragmentary personalities, but the written record of their narratives would also provide Beckett with a self-generated study of his internal world, enacting it for the author "in order to witness it" (Beckett, 2006b, p. 297).

Two psychic retreats, then, emotional outlets functioning together, the first providing emotional distance through clear intellectual activity and the second providing literary externalisation of the author's unconscious "complexes", would help to stabilise Beckett's turmoil within the pain and suffering of emotional conflict. In writing, Beckett would also create a powerful and creative space between writer and reader, facilitating his own psychological growth through the joint action of producing and reflecting upon objects of his mind.

At Trinity, Beckett flourished under the mentorship of Thomas Rudmose-Brown, a "teaching professor" of Romance languages, who not only encouraged Beckett's love for contemporary French poetry, but also encouraged his creative writing, saying, "every one of us must strive, unflinchingly, to be himself" (Knowlson, 1996, p. 66). A similar Delphic message had probably been communicated to Bion from his supervisor, J. A. Hadfield (Feldman, 2006, p. 95). Yet, however over-determined this classical sentiment by teachers and mentors—both of Beckett and Bion—its practical achievement would be another matter altogether.

Understood from within this context, Beckett's painful struggles as a young adult were on this road to discovery of his mature adult identity. Conflicted, he was both appreciative of his mentor's continuing support and care, but could also be cruelly destructive and rejecting of it, as in his mocking characterisation of "Ruddy" as the grotesque "Polar Bear" in *Dream of Fair to Middling Women* (1992) and *More Pricks Than Kicks* (1970) (Knowlson, 1996, p. 66).

Beckett's mother, May, was a complicated, often anxious and preoccupied woman. The circumstances of her original meeting with Bill Beckett, the writer's father, doubtlessly heightened her own anxieties in what she took to be her younger son's lack of direction, midway through his undergraduate study at Dublin's Trinity College. May had been a capable and business-like young nurse during Bill's own brief psychiatric hospitalisation, following the termination of his earlier engagement to marry (Knowlson, 1996, p. 33). Their subsequent courtship had been brief, and, while there is no biographical record of future emotional turmoil for Bill, May's own traits of high-strung rigidity and internal focus were prominent (Bair, 1978; Knowlson, 1996).

The tone of her behaviour towards Sam is most famously suggested in a vignette from *Company*, written late in Beckett's life. The images in *Company* suggest an emotionally pregnant screen memory, a psychological situation reflecting profound and deep latent content. It describes the exit of mother and son from Connolly's Store in a town very similar to Beckett's home of Foxrock. The boy attempts to engage his mother on the subject of the distance of the sky from earth, an almost universal interaction in the lives of latency age children and their parents, but the boy's curiosity and desire for response is met with his mother's sharp rebuke (Beckett, 1996, p. 6). An earlier iteration of this incident, penned a half-century before in *The End*, reflects an even more traumatic outcome. There, the mother's response to her son's question is a terse, "fuck off". It is followed by a sentence suggesting the shock and trauma of this moment with a direct allusion to non-nutritive caring, "I suddenly remembered I had not thought of asking Mr Weir for a piece of bread" (Beckett, 1995a, p. 81). The adult memory of traumatic childhood experience in seeking maternal nurturance continues to haunt adult behaviour, hampering this fictional character's ability to secure caring from another.

Such harsh treatment is redolent of Fairbairn's comments on the failure of mothers to convince their children of their love through conveying aspects of both possessiveness and indifference (Fairbairn, 1952, p. 13). Just as possessiveness and indifference might alternate confusingly for a child, Beckett's narratives, too, contain confusing levels—some more accessible than others. The non-nutritive example of Mr Weir, for example, suggests Ernest Jones' 1920 comments on the Weir Mitchell treatment of hysterics, which had evolved to the bed rest and isolation from which the narrator in *The End* was being driven (Jones, 1963, p. 24), but which also included the overfeeding of which Virginia Woolf complained (Poirier, 1983). For the narrator in *The End*, nourishment is absent. Like the multi-levelled relation of consciousness and unconsciousness, Beckett's own allusions slide between the openly shocking and a different shock, just beneath the surface.

This pairing of maternal indifference and over-concern is profoundly difficult for children to overcome, and frequently eventuates in the development, for the child, of schizoid characteristics, including a pronounced internal focus and deep sense of aloneness (Fairbairn,

1952). Beckett's own fabled memories of prenatal life within May's womb were associated with similar claustrophobic feelings of painful entrapment.

This same felt inability to escape the confines of his mind probably marked Beckett's coming of age, during his early years at Trinity. It was there, studying for scholarship exams at age twenty, that he first experienced and sought medical attention for what today would be classified as panic attacks. The disorder is described in the American Psychiatric Association's *Diagnostic and Statistical Manual* (*DSM-IV*, 1994, p. 402) as including:

> multiple panic attacks with persistent concern about more attacks and worries about implications of attacks (going crazy, etc.)

with at least four of the following symptoms, developing abruptly and peaking within ten minutes: palpations and accelerated heart rate; sweating; trembling or shaking; shortness of breath or sensations of smothering; feeling of choking or abdominal distress; dizziness or feeling unsteady; de-realisation, feelings of unreality; or depersonalisation, feeling detached from oneself; and the fears of losing control, going crazy, or dying, as well as numbness, tingling chills, or hot flushes. Beckett's characters' sense of perennial dying, unreality, de-realisation, deterioration, and pervasive fear clearly show how such experience of panic might provide experiential ground for authorial character development.

Beckett persevered in his studies, and was awarded the College Scholarship. Against the background of panic, this occasioned an early version of his characteristic inability to go on, triumphed over by his perseverance: "I can't go on, I must go on, I'll go on" (Beckett, 2006b, p. 407). Yet, it was later during that same year of graduation and success, 1926, that his propensity to panic blossomed into a larger psycho-social condition, broadly recognised and familiar to many late twentieth-century collegians as an "identity crisis". The identity crisis emerges in the transition from adolescence to adulthood as a confusion of roles in which young adults struggle to "find themselves" in solidifying a cohesive sense of ego identity. Erikson's description of identity (1959, 1970) integrates an individual's subjective and observable sense of personal sameness and continuity and extends to choices in living, including occupation, friendships, mentors, values, and first sexual encounters.

The formal beginning of Beckett's identity crisis can be dated to a family argument concerning Sam's plans for the future, during the Christmas holiday of 1926–1927 (Knowlson, 1996, p. 81). At the time, the young Beckett reflected profound disinterest in future professionalism. His father, Bill, seemed able to tolerate Sam's reticence. May, however, felt things differently. Her first son, Frank, who had also graduated from the Portora School and Trinity, had opted for conventional security. He had joined the Beckett family business of quantity surveying. Sam, however, was another matter.

It is likely that a combination of Sam's recent panic attacks, coupled both with his ambivalence about the future and with his self-consciously studied nonchalance, modelled on Dante's character Belacqua, deeply disturbed her. Perhaps she dreaded a possibility of her second son's future hospitalisation, paralleling in her fearful imagination a linkage with Sam's father. Perhaps her identification was more personal, identifying within Sam her own emotional struggles. In any case, in demanding a concrete plan of action, her behaviour towards Sam externalised her own anxiety. In the mutual dance of unspoken communication called projective identification by psychoanalysts, where the receiver enacts, and so confirms, the other's extruded anxieties, Sam responded to May's sharp attack with equally sharp rebuttal. The battle was on.

Sensitive to experiential states of emotional entrapment, Beckett reacted quickly and pragmatically to his mother's demand for certainty. Pressed for an answer to affirm May's insecurity, Sam found a plausible escape into something he knew well, academia. He agreed to discuss the possibility of future academic life with his academic adviser and mentor, Thomas Rudmose-Brown, who was predictably thrilled with the decision. The route would lead Beckett conveniently away from the fights at Coolindragh through productive academic flight, a prestigious and yet private career path into which his parents could not follow him. Rudmose-Brown charted a course for his scholarship-winning student, beginning with the position of exchange lecturer in English at the École Normale Supérieure, in Paris. This would lead later to an assistantship in modern languages under Rudmose-Brown's watchful eye, back home at Trinity.

The only difficulty was Beckett's profound ambivalence about this course of action. Certainly, it solved the problem of his mother's persistent and intrusive interest in her son's vocation, but it set up another in that Beckett was setting a course which both interested and exasperated him. Like all young people in that situation, he was thrilled to have what would be an extended moratorium, a rich intellectual period away from his family, and in Paris. It was even more productive than he could have expected. It was there that he would meet Thomas MacGreevy, the previous exchange lecturer, and, through MacGreevy, be introduced to James Joyce and the vast circle of Anglophone expatriate intellectuals in Paris.

In terms both of his emotional support and his practical actions, MacGreevy would facilitate Beckett's entry to the world of letters. Thirteen years older than Beckett, MacGreevy must have seemed a worldly-wise role model. A fellow Irishman from Kerry and a twice-wounded lieutenant in the Great War (Knowlson, 1996, p. 98), his social facility seems, too, to have made him what social network theorists would later term a "connector", a vitally social individual linking others who might not otherwise participate in wider social networks (Gladwell, 2000).

Erikson stresses that part of the resolution of the identity conflict is the development of "fidelity", a sense of genuineness, sincerity, and loyalty, to others. Beckett's friendship and reliance upon MacGreevy would reflect not only MacGreevy's gracious and giving nature in introducing Beckett to a life in literature, but also the younger man's fidelity and esteem for his mentor. The socially retiring Beckett was fortunate in finding this friend and, significantly, Beckett's biographers mention no symptomatic recurrence of panic during this period in Paris.

On the other hand, while outward bound for Paris, Beckett was also profoundly uninterested in the teaching vocation implied by the Paris position. This was reflected both in his first teaching post at Campbell College in Belfast in 1928, where he sardonically referred to the students as "the cream of Ulster, rich and thick" (Knowlson, 1996, p. 88) and in his subsequent misery on return to Trinity after the liberating Parisian sojourn. Beckett's pragmatic promise might have temporarily placated May, but it also created a tension between the fictive pursuit of the academy and his emerging desire to pursue creative writing.

The delicate peace thus created between Beckett and May did not last long. Even before his departure for Paris after the summer of 1928, sparring continued between May Beckett and her twenty-two-year-old son (Knowlson, 1996, p. 92). This time the provocative issue, just like the question of Beckett's future vocation, also occurred in the context of a young man's slow separation from the anchorage of his family. It concerned another element of the Identity Crisis as described by Erikson: the dawning of Sam's sexual interests.

The object of Beckett's desire was his cousin, Peggy Sinclair. Multiple interpretations of May's distressed concern have been noted by Beckett biographers. Was the issue simply the generalised sin of a son's sexual interests? Was it that Peggy, as Beckett's cousin was too close a family member for consideration as a girlfriend? Might it have been that potential intercourse could lead to the complications of pregnancy? Might it have been that, uncomfortably for May, Peggy's father was Jewish?

The result of the blowup between mother and son was that Sam left his mother's home precipitously, in the first of two expulsions from the family home, deeply felt, and subjectively experienced by him as maternally driven. Staying briefly with a friend in Dublin, Sam next worked his way to France and proceeded on to see Peggy, who lived with her family in Germany. Faced with May's discomfort, he acted nevertheless, in his own interest, but at considerable emotional cost. Two years later, he would annotate a copy of Proust's *A l'ombre des jeunes filles en fleur* with the inscription, "Mail boat, August 1928", reflecting on this painful separation. In Beckett's case, the shadow of flowering young women also threatened loss of maternal love and expulsion from the suburban Eden of home at Foxrock.

Beckett's relationship with Peggy would ultimately break up by late 1929, when quarrelling and disagreement supplanted intimacy (Knowlson, 1996, p. 115). However, Peggy would remain central in Beckett's affections, and her untimely death in 1933 would also serve to unsettle him both en route to psychoanalysis and after. From this German sojourn with Peggy, Beckett finally arrived at the École Normale Supérieure in Paris, to bask in MacGreevy's continuous companionship, facilitation of the little details of everyday life, and encyclopaedic knowledge. It is hard to imagine that all of this would not have greatly impressed the young Beckett, especially as MacGreevy was also a literary man, a writer of poetry, essays, and literary criticism (Knowlson, 1996, p. 98).

MacGreevy's introductions to the world of English arts and letters in Paris were invaluable to Beckett in providing entry into a world of expatriate artists and establishing the intellectual foundations of an identity very different from that of university lecturer. While MacGreevy's introduction of Beckett to Joyce is prominent in the Beckett's biographies, it is probable that in his larger stewardship of Beckett's nascent life as a writer, MacGreevy figures even more significantly in concrete steps taken toward resolution of Beckett's identity crisis. It was MacGreevy who encouraged Beckett's composition of *Whoroscope*, Beckett's first prize-winning literary attempt, elevating him to prominence among the Parisian expatriate literati (Knowlson, 1996, p. 116), and from *Whoroscope*, MacGreevy facilitated Beckett's career one step further.

This step, however, was monumental. In one generous act, MacGreevy paved the way for multiple solutions to Beckett's dilemma in growing up. Having begun his post at the École Normale with the intention of writing a PhD on Joyce and Proust, Beckett had hesitated in his academic production. MacGreevy was aware that this inaction would place the younger man's Trinity appointment in jeopardy, as Trinity expected at least a master's thesis from Beckett on his return to Dublin. At the time, MacGreevy was embarking on the writing of several monographs for a literary series overseen by his friend, Richard Aldington. Like MacGreevy, Aldington was a war veteran, and had recently published a novel centred on the wasteful and tragic deaths of British young men during the First World War, *Death of a Hero* (Aldington, 1929).

Mindful of Beckett's academic interest in Marcel Proust, MacGreevy nominated his friend for the composition of a monograph on Proust's work. Having already won a prize sponsored by Aldington, MacGreevy reckoned that, were the application successful, Beckett might earn a bit of money and also have the basis of an acceptable academic thesis for Trinity. MacGreevy suggested that his young protégé Beckett might profitably follow the same successful methodology as he had with the Cartesian *Whoroscope*, but now in relation to Proust. This would involve close reading and summarising of the writer's work as a basis for a work of literary composition. MacGreevy recognised it as an extended repetition of an earlier task that his protégé had performed admirably.

Beckett's application was successful, and, notably, the monograph qualified for his master's thesis—meaning that Beckett's Parisian year would be seen by Trinity as a significant step in his academic ascent, should that become Beckett's desire. Supporting Beckett as an author,

MacGreevy was also making certain that doors of opportunity remained open for Beckett—at a time when Beckett's own emotional turmoil might have closed as many doors as it opened. In this act, MacGreevy showed himself to be a thoughtful and caring friend. Beyond his considerable efforts in linking Beckett to Parisian society and culture, his profound care for the younger man must have been palpable and deeply moving to Beckett. MacGreevy not only facilitated connections, but also thought about Beckett's psychological needs and acted generously. Like Rudmose-Brown, MacGreevy supported Beckett not only through possibilities of concrete action, but also by thinking about the development of Beckett's own thinking. MacGreevy would continue to figure as a profound support for Beckett, and Beckett's regular correspondence with MacGreevy informs much of what we know of Beckett's life, especially during the period of his psychoanalysis with Wilfred Bion.

Despite the academic brilliance of Beckett's monograph on Proust, which will be discussed more fully in the next chapter, Beckett was profoundly ambivalent about the work during its composition. He grumbled continuously about Proust in letters to MacGreevy, as if Proust had directly presented Beckett with personal insult (TM, 7 August 1930; TM, 25 August 1930). Yet, it is clear that MacGreevy grasped the significance of Beckett's thinking about Proust. In the epigraph to his own monograph on Richard Aldington, MacGreevy quotes Beckett's *Proust*. This the first formal citation of Beckett's work, but it is also a good friend's acknowledgement of Beckett's depth as a thinker:

> Yesterday is not a milestone that has been passed, but a daystone on the beaten track of the years and irredeemably part of us, within us, heavy and dangerous. We are not more weary because of yesterday, we are other, no longer what we were before the calamity of yesterday. (MacGreevy, 1931)

Returning home to Dublin from Paris, Beckett's physical symptoms again troubled him. The first sign was an outbreak of a facial rash, treated dermatologically. His letters to MacGreevy reflect his deep sense of emotional discomfort, recognising that home-life was redolent with false kindness, "pumped" into him, he said, at "high pressure" (Knowlson, 1996, p. 123). Depressed, he complained to MacGreevy in March 1931 about a whole range of ramifying symptoms: his aching teeth, eye trouble, bronchial trouble, and continued panic. He inter-preted his hallucinations and dreams to be the "edge of madness" (TM, 11 March 1931). Self-medicating his panic with alcohol, Beckett wrote that he would sometimes "booze my heart quiet" (TM, 22 September 1931).

As with his dissatisfaction in teaching earlier at Campbell College, Beckett seemed unable to keep his disaffection under control at Trinity. Famously, he performed a prank in the delivery to the Trinity Modern Language Society of a paper on "Concentrism", a subject he had wholly fabricated (Knowlson, 1996, p. 125). Nevertheless, a student's notebook of Beckett's lectures reflects another dimension of Beckett as teacher. Extending his psychological refuge in the serious-ness with which he undertook scholarship, despite his conflicted behaviour, his lectures reflect a thoughtful study of modern French literature with the unique precision of interpretation he had earlier presented in *Proust* (Beckett, 1931; LeJuez, 2008).

During spring vacation, Beckett returned to see the Sinclairs in Germany and also visited Paris. He returned to a Dublin for summer term, only to develop pleurisy at the end of May. Recovering at home in Foxrock, the simmering tension between mother and son exploded yet again. This time, the tinderbox was May's discovery of, and shock at, her son's writing. Possibly, she had come across either a love letter to Peggy Sinclair or sexual content in an early draft of *Dreams of Fair to Middling Women*. Disgusted and horrified, May again expelled her son from Coolindragh (Knowlson, 1996, p. 131).

However, unlike Beckett's future characters in *First Love*, *The Expulsion*, and *The End*, Beckett was not physically homeless. He was able to retreat to his quarters at Trinity. From there, two weeks later, he and his brother again visited France, returning to Dublin at the end of July. It is likely that Beckett remained apart from his mother through November, but was comforted through his father's continu-ous emotional support in the provision of a weekly Turkish bath and dry martini (Knowlson, p. 135), two expensive instances of cosy masculine indulgence.

Knowlson writes that during this period, in the composition of *Dreams of Fair to Middling Women*, Beckett "deliberately cultivated and explored his isolation, like the depths of some dark, familiar pool" (Knowlson, 1996, p. 135). Extending his interest in the vicissitudes of psychology first described in *Proust*, Beckett would write, the mind at last its own asylum, disinterested, indifferent, its miserable erethisms and discriminations and futile sallies suppressed; the mind suddenly reprieved, ceasing to be an annex of the restless body, the glare of understanding switched off. (Beckett, 1992, p. 44)

This was Beckett's first description of the mind itself as a psychic enclosure. As its own asylum, it was an insular, compartmentalised sanctuary of self-contemplation, detached from both interpersonal contact and bodily awareness. Together with this schizoid depiction of inner withdrawal, Beckett would also describe, in his poem "Eneug", a projection of inner devastation on to the external world.

Throughout this depressed period of self-induced expulsion from home, Beckett both read widely and visited the National Gallery. His critical capacities, despite his self-judgement to the contrary, appeared unimpaired. In fact, his capacity for structured, intellectual thought during a period of intensive psychic pain reflects the productive use of a psychic retreat in the stabilisation of deep distress. It was not only the immediate situation with his mother that troubled him, but, more fundamentally, his bad faith with Rudmose-Brown, in representing himself as interested in a career in teaching and research when he was not. Crucially, it is this clarification of personal interest and values, of an honest reckoning of self with personal choices, that initiates the resolution of the identity crisis. Beckett realised that flight from Dublin, Trinity, and teaching would be a complex matter.

His self-condemnation of bad faith extended not only to Rudmose-Brown, but also to his parents. For each of these significant others, father, mother, and academic mentor, Beckett saw himself as a disappointment. Thinking of his father, he saw himself as fleeing from adult responsibility. Thinking of his mother, he saw himself reflected in her eyes as a "washout".

Still, choosing flight, he again decamped to Germany on Boxing Day, 1931. He spent a month with the Sinclairs in Kassel before travelling to Paris. Despite his elective self-liberation from Trinity, Beckett was negativistic and unsure. Bleakly, he told MacGreevy, "I'll probably crawl back with my tail coiled round my ruined poenis" (TM, 20 December 1931). Even here, within his grim prediction of failure, Beckett signalled MacGreevy with what seems to have been a literary allusion. Beckett's turn of phrase echoes a passage from Richard Aldington's 1929 novel, *Birth of a Hero*, certainly known to

MacGreevy as Aldington's biographer, in which the character, George Augustus, attempting self-definition as a writer, "had a hell of a time with dear Mamma when he went home with his tail between his legs" (Aldington, 1929, p. 64). Indeed, Beckett was later to employ George Augustus's exact words on his own failed return to Dublin (Knowlson, 1996, p. 159).

Immediately before leaving for Paris, Beckett had been involved in a serious car accident. He was unhurt, but another potential and unrequited love, Ethna McCarthy, who had been his passenger, was seriously injured and hospitalised. Peggy, now engaged, was also ill. Writing furiously, he remained in Paris from February 1932 through the summer. The result, *Dream of Fair to Middling Women*, later deconstructed into *More Pricks Than Kicks*, is described as a work of "self-conscious fiction" with different rules for author and reader. Knowlson writes, "It is as if he were playing a game with the reader, talking to him, teasing him, even taunting him, and he actively relished dismantling the props and supports of the conventional novel" (Knowlson, 1996, p. 145).

As in Beckett's previous compositions on Descartes and Proust, he made extensive use of obscure references, weaving hundreds of allusions and quotations from dictionaries, reference books, and literature, philosophy, and theology, into the novel. When *Dream of Fair to Middling Women* was finally published in 1992, a reviewer likened it to an uphill climb—as to Calvary—requiring the reader's knowledge of foreign languages, the *Oxford English Dictionary*, a good encyclopaedia, and Job's patience (Knowlson, 1996, p. 145).

Running out of funds and keen to be working again, Beckett travelled to London in the summer of 1932. He was unsuccessful both in finding work and in having *More Pricks Than Kicks* published. Feeling himself unable to work creatively, he read extensively in the British Museum none the less. By now, Ethna McCarthy had recovered and was engaged to Beckett's friend, Con Levinthal. Alone, disappointed, and humiliated in his lack of success, he wrote to MacGreevy that, as he had earlier predicted, "I crawled home with my tail between my legs", confirming his initial scepticism about this attempt at auto-emancipation (Knowlson, 1996, p. 159).

Beckett again commented on the faux kindness of his family in Dublin, writing, "Father real. Mother comico-real. My need for anaesthetic of caress comico-real" (Knowlson, 1996, p. 159), his jokiness nevertheless making his deep connection to his mother abundantly clear. His loneliness and alienation were, likewise, real. There was nothing comical about it. Still, Beckett felt the emotional support of his father, and, despite having mocked Rudmose-Brown in his writings as the "Polar Bear" as well as having rejected his generous offer of a Trinity post, the older man secured him translation work. MacGreevy, Rudmose-Brown, and Bill Beckett remained Beckett's supporters.

However, his health problems began again, beginning with a neck cyst, a "deep seated septic system", that plagued the twenty-six-year-old from December 1932 to May 1933, as well as surgery on a hammertoe. His depression was heightened by tax difficulties. Then Peggy Sinclair died unexpectedly of tuberculosis in May 1933, leaving Beckett "horrified and depressed". A month later, on 26 June, Bill Beckett died of a heart attack. His son's encomium, written to MacGreevy, provides eloquent testimony to how real his father seemed to his son:

> He was in his sixty first year, but how much younger he seemed and was. Joking and swearing at the doctors as long as he had breath. He lay in the bed with sweat pea all over his face, making great oaths that when he got better he would never do a stroke of work. He would drive to the top of Howth and lie in the bracken and fart. His last words were "fight, fight, fight" and "what a morning" . . . I can't write about him. I can only walk the fields and climb the ditches after him. (TM, 7 July 1933)

Like his dying father, Sam Beckett had also been fighting, for the consolidation of his own adult identity for seven long years. The period was marked by three departures from Dublin to Germany and then to Paris, and two expulsions from his mother's home, each the confluence of self-generation and his mother's bitter intolerance. Yet, he had consolidated a fledgling sense of himself as a writer; and his *Whoroscope* and *Proust* had been critically received quite well. Having proceeded in a compromised path toward teaching, he had broken definitively with academia and proceeded to dedicate himself to writing. But throughout—at least while he was resident in Dublin—panic attacks, self-doubt, and fear of an unsuccessful and impotent return home undermined him. This was the portrait of the artist as a young man. The deaths, one after the other, of Peggy Sinclair and his father proved to be too much to bear.

Beckett's own description of what came next is terse and unadorned. He says,

> After my father's death, I had trouble psychologically. The bad years were between when I had to crawl home in 1932 and after my father's death in 1933 (when I was in London). I'll tell you how it was. I was walking up Dawson Street and I felt I couldn't go on. It was a strange experience. I can't really describe. I found I couldn't go on moving. So I had to rush in to the famous pub in Dawson Street, Davy Byrne's. I don't know where I was going, maybe up to Harcourt Street (station). So I went into the dearest pub and got a drink – just to stay still. And I felt I needed help. (Knowlson & Knowlson, 2006, p. 67)

Having just collapsed, and now fortified both with drink and a literary allusion to *Ulysses* via Davy Byrne's, Beckett then walked the ten or so blocks to his friend, Geoffrey Thompson's surgery on Lower Baggot Street. Although Thompson worked as a cardiologist, he had made plans to begin his psychiatric residency in England. Beckett waited for Thompson to arrive. Thompson's prescription for Beckett was immediate. "When he got there, I was standing by the door. He gave me a look over, found nothing physically wrong. Then he recommended psychoanalysis for me" (Knowlson, & Knowlson, 2006, p. 67).

Because psychoanalysis was not then allowed in Dublin, according to Beckett, Thompson "tried to get it arranged so that I could go to the man he was going to see". That man was J. A. Hadfield, the senior psychodynamic supervisor at the Tavistock Clinic and, as it happened, the sometime therapist and supervisor of the newly qualified psychiatrist, Wilfred Bion. Beckett was formally on the road to psychoanalysis.

Beckett's terse recounting of the inability to go on was followed by his going on, facilitated by the outstretched hand of his friend, Geoffrey Thompson. Like MacGreevy's earlier attention to a Beckett about to stumble in Paris, having completed neither book nor Master's thesis, Thompson's attentions to the fallen young man echo a critical historical moment from an earlier era in Beckett's life. When Beckett was a schoolboy, he had had an experience when, as in Dawson Street after his father's death, he found that could not go on. On that occasion, Beckett had forgotten his tram ticket back from Dublin's Harcourt Street Station to Foxrock and had decided to walk the eight miles home, laden with a heavy bag of cricket equipment. One mile from home, the boy had collapsed under the bag's weight. He was discovered later that night by Bill Beckett who, shouldering the cricket bag, walked his son home, supportively. No word needed to be said. Predictably, once home, the worried and frantic May was punitive, sending her son to bed hungry. His father brought Sam food. Bill Beckett had modelled endurance for his son, teaching him to go on when going on was impossible, teaching him that supportive male assistance would be at hand (Knowlson, 1996, p. 51).

In *Worstward Ho*, Beckett writes,

> Hand in hand with equal plod they go. In the free hands – no. Free empty hands. Backs turned both bowed with equal plod they go. The child hand raised to reach the holding hand. Hold the old holding hand. Hold and be held. Plod on and never recede. (Beckett, 1996, p. 93)

After the collapse at Davy Byrne's, Sam grasped Geoffrey Thompson's outstretched holding hand to help him in his going on, and Geoffrey recommended psychoanalysis, Anna O's talking cure.

CHAPTER TWO

Proust as metapsychology

B eckett's monograph *Proust* was his second Parisian literary production. It had been written in 1930 under the watchful eyes of Thomas MacGreevy, the instigator and prime force behind Beckett's submission of his recent prize-winning poem, *Whoroscope*. Richard Aldington, who had awarded that prize, had arranged next to produce a series of literary monographs, published in London by Chatto & Windus. MacGreevy was also writing a monograph on a modern master for the series, T. S. Eliot, and he would later write another on Aldington himself. It had been MacGreevy's thought that if *Proust* were accepted, it would provide Beckett with much needed pocket money for his continuing stay in Paris. Additionally, it might qualify as Beckett's now neglected Master's thesis, necessary for his return to an academic assistantship at Trinity College in Dublin (Knowlson, 1996, p. 116).

Though *Proust* has been called, "an intellectual justification of unhappiness" characterised by "an ostentatious display of learning and its extravagant style" (Knowlson, 1996, p. 122), its writing came at the conclusion of a relatively stable period within Beckett's tumultuous decade of identity conflict. MacGreevy and the École Normale Supérieure had been portals to a rich literary life among the Parisian circle of James Joyce, and during this period Sam had been free from panic.

Originally, Beckett had undertaken the reading of Proust's sixteen volumes in anticipation of a doctoral dissertation on Joyce and Proust. This lofty intellectual project was abandoned, but, within a year, by the summer of 1930, Beckett had completed his full reading of Proust (TM, 25 August 1930). Beckett's initial comments to MacGreevy about Proust were balanced between the cogently intellectual and the cur-mudgeonly, reminding the reader of a younger edition of Beckett's future character, Krapp. Beckett noted both Proust's skilful balance between equilibrium and stasis, as well as the continuously repetitive nature of the work—perhaps preparing Beckett for later toleration of the ramblings and returnings of psychoanalytic free association. Beckett also cultivated an almost personal relation to Proust—as if to a disagreeable colleague.

Hardly a man to shirk from complaining on his own account, Beckett complained loudly about Proust's unhappiness. He found in Proust "a maudlin false teeth gobble-gobble discharge from a colic-afflicted belly", even equating his writings with the act of defecation, dreading "to think that I have to contemplate him at stool for 16 volumes" (TM, Summer 1929, pp. 11–12).

Beckett also complained mightily to MacGreevy about his own writing of the *Proust* monograph, which he had completed in two months over the summer of 1930 (TM, before 5 August 1930, p. 35; TM 7 August 1930). By late August, fortified through the beneficence of Black and White Scotch whisky, Beckett pushed himself to com-plete the work. *En route* to the composition of a highly scholarly work under the multiple pressures of family, school, identity form-ation, and economics, the twenty-four-year-old's comments to his friend, MacGreevy, are cutting and irreverent: "I don't know whether to start at the end or the beginning – in a word, should the Prous-tian arse-hole be considered as entrée or sortie" (TM, 25 August 1930).

Within this studied anal preoccupation, Beckett would both retain and expel aspects of Proust, transforming "maudlin false teeth gobble-gobble" into a distinctly Beckettian literary world view. The creative act of digestion, both aggressive and retentive, is also transformative, and finally arrives at Beckett's own useful understanding and identi-fication with Proust's literary psychology.

Five years later, reflecting on such moments to MacGreevy, Beckett would relegate his derogatory and dismissive attitudes as "the fatuous torments which I had treasured as denoting the superior man" (TM, 10 March 1935). Yet, together with his rigorous intellectual work in composing *Proust*, Beckett's correspondence with MacGreevy reflects a jocular and free intelligence, if one more profoundly attuned to the negative than to the positive.

Proust, Beckett's first published monograph, is an essay in literary metapsychology. It represents a statement of the young Beckett's philosophy of mind, his thinking about individual psychology couched in the literary production of Marcel Proust. As metapsychology, *Proust* presents an idealised view of human cognition and emotion, and suggests Beckett's own concerns through self-examination years before both his extensive reading in psychoanalysis and his own experience of psychoanalytic psychotherapy.

The beginning of *Proust* is anachronistic in terms of psychoanalytic theory, an object relational meditation upon internalised interpersonal relations some twenty years before the mature theorising of object relations. Beckett contemplates the enduring presence of significant others within individual thought. Citing Proust, he observes people as "occupying in Time a much greater place than so sparingly conceded to them in Space". He recognises that the internalisation of others endures long beyond the actual time elapsed in their presence, and that their internal presence within the mind continues to exert its pressures on the evolution of an individual's thoughts.

Recognising Beckett's own relatively happy moratorium in Paris when freed from the pressured Dublin interests of May Beckett and Thomas Rudmose-Brown, and while simultaneously engaged in the recent and new social and intellectual experiences of MacGreevy, Aldington, Joyce, and other acquaintances, one can almost visualise a mental cavalcade of particular moments in time, occupied by images of people newly significant to Beckett. Like "Proust's creatures", Beckett's own thoughts must have teemed with what he termed "this predominating condition" both as the weightiness of others within life's emotional baggage and in the transformational possibilities resulting from individuals now occupying his new, Parisian literary world.

The effects upon the individual of others across different moments of time permanently change human experience. These internalised personifications not only operate upon one's present thoughts, but are also a psychic reservoir available within consciousness to remind the individual of now-gone yesterdays. Tragically, however, Beckett focuses not on the liberating possibilities of internalising the new, but on the deadly weightiness of the old, from which there is no escape. People, and how we have known them, remain within us.

Through this reading of Proust, Beckett was composing a developmental object relations psychology which emphasised the enduring effect of significant others in psychological change. He cast this development as a necessary deformation of prior experience, in that "yesterday has deformed us, or been deformed by us" (Beckett, 1931, p. 2). Such deformation suggests departure from an original, idyllic formation through the recipience of others' uncaring and unmindful acts.

Thomas MacGreevy would also resonate with this idea of internalised, mutative experience. He acknowledges Beckett publicly, quoting a paragraph from *Proust* as the epigraph to his own monograph, *Richard Aldington, An Englishman*. The deep respect shown by MacGreevy's act cannot have been lost on Beckett, whose psychological dependence and productive use of MacGreevy's continuous support was instrumental in the consolidation of his adult identity as a writer. MacGreevy continued to be present in Beckett's life, both physically and through their continuing correspondence, through many difficult years.

While experience in Paris provided a heady literary roadmap away from the vocational *cul de sac* of Dublin, Beckett's words are resonant with the enduring psychological effects of others' actions in shaping our experience. It is likely that May Beckett's demand for both her son's vocational certainty and censure of his sexual interest in Peggy Sinclair lay beneath his psychological reading of Proust, as he wrote,

> Yesterday is not a milestone that has been passed, but a daystone on the beaten track of the years, and irredeemably part of us, within us, heavy and dangerous. We are not merely more weary because of yesterday, we are other, no longer what we were before the calamity of yesterday. (Beckett, 1931, p. 3)

Together with the heaviness and danger in the wake of yesterday's calamities—those engagements of self with others in the environment—there is also hope in Beckett's metapsychology. Poetically,

Beckett's thinking aligned with William James' stream of consciousness in its transformative flights and settlings of thought (Miller, 1987). Just as James had forty years earlier highlighted the latent thought-stuff of "sciousness" in its emergence into knowable thought or consciousness—literally "with" sciousness—Beckett would soon play with the idea of ongoing experience as a condition he termed "gress" or action, knowable in reflection as progress or regress (letter to Nuala Costello, 27 February 1934).

Suggesting a nascent, dynamic reading of Proust even before his reading of Freud's *The New Introductory Lectures* (1933a) and the works of Ernest Jones (Feldman, 2006), Beckett writes that reality and significance exist only in the world of latent consciousness. This is a world teeming with passionate desire, of changing motivation led by momentary aspiration. Beckett would recognise a shift in human desire as yesterday's wishes, existent as "valid for yesterday's ego, not for to-day's", which must necessarily fall short of today's aspiration. Rather, today's ego emerges as the product of yesterday's state of mind and aspirations, together with imperfect satisfaction. In this process, we are changed. Just as our internalisation of others changes how we see the world, so do our desires and their consequences.

Even under the most successful of outcomes, the attainment of desire—which Beckett recognises as "identification of the subject with the object of his desire"—must disappoint. Its highest achievement is not identification but the movement of the individual from one ego state, which Beckett designates "Subject A", to another, as the individual is transformed through actions across time, to "Subject B". In this necessary life-giving transition from yesterday to today, Beckett writes, "the subject has died – and perhaps many times on the way" (Beckett, 1931, p. 3). This is the first formal statement of what will become a Beckett literary signature, the continuity of an individual's ongoing death, through the necessity of engagement in living.

Beckett writes that even if, by miracle, Subject A's object of desire is achieved, the very fact of temporal advance transforms what was formerly uncertain into the inevitable. Tragically, even under the most perfect conditions, "all conscious intellectual effort to reconstitute the invisible and unthinkable as a reality being fruitless"—that is, experiential revisitation of yesterday's now-passed psychological states—"we are incapable of appreciating our joy by comparing it with our sorrow". Complete satisfaction is, therefore, illusory, because goals must be weighed according to the same self that sets the bar, and in pursuit of those goals, that self is forever altered. Therefore, Beckett concludes that satisfaction "is as illogical as to expect one's hunger to be dissipated by the spectacle of Uncle eating his dinner" (Beckett, 1931, p. 3).

Beckett argues in *Proust* that our experiences of internalised others and in pursuit of our daily aspirations both change us and cause us to be who we are. Recognisable within his later writing is the ongoing change of loss represented as death, a condition of life continuing without cease. From within *Proust*, Beckett argues that we daily die in living, and are different subjects each day. Pushed to its limit, the metapsychology suggests both multiple, unlinked states of mind and states of mind linked through disappointment and loss. Beckett's reading into Proust reflects a discontinuity as profound as the movement from normal experience into the dread of a panic attack. Individual psychology shifts from relative stasis to catastrophe.

Like psychological continuity, voluntary memory also fails us. While the effects of time change us in the modification of character, we become aware only involuntarily, and in retrospect. Arguing from Proust, Beckett establishes the authenticity of Freudian free association in articulating the Jamesian stream of consciousness. Involuntary emergence of thought provides the platform for reflection. Poetically, he suggests that

> The individual is the seat of a constant process of decantation, decantation from the vessel containing the fluid of future time, sluggish, pale and monochrome, to the vessel containing the fluid of past time, agitated and multicoloured by the phenomena of its hours. (Beckett, 1931, p. 5)

As if commenting upon the action of psychotherapy or upon the understanding of a fictional character by author or reader, Beckett writes that "the observer infects the observed with his own mobility". William James recognised this observational dilemma and named it "the psychologist's fallacy", wherein the mind, however observing of its object, can know only itself (James, 1981). Beckett's own location of this phenomenon is individual, similar to Freud's and, later, Klein's, who recognise that prior to the ego's introjection of the external world, it apprehends the external world from within its own experiential viewpoint and colouring. Together with Freud and Klein, Beckett agrees with James that the observer cannot escape his own experiential shaping of the thing observed.

The dilemma, for Beckett, is reflected in his reading of Proust and is compounded when two individuals meet. Here, Beckett presciently and somewhat uncannily anticipates the mature writing of the man who will become his own psychotherapist only three years later, Wilfred Bion. Bion will one day reflect that when two individuals meet in the enterprise of psychotherapy, their contact precipitates an "emotional storm", the finest resolution of which is the attempt to understand (Bion, 1994, p. 322). Beckett, drawing on Proust, writes that in

> human intercourse, we are faced by the problem of an object whose mobility is not merely a function of the subject's, but independent and personal: two separate and immanent dynamisms related by no system of synchronization. (Beckett, 1931, p. 7)

Beckett himself would later realise, within his psychoanalytic work together with Wilfred Bion, that this is no mean feat. Years later, after many years of clinical experience (and without specific reference to Beckett), Bion would link the therapeutic work of enduring this emotional storm to battle.

> In war the enemy's object is so to terrify you that you cannot think clearly, while your object is to continue to think clearly no matter how adverse or frightening the situation. The underlying idea is that thinking clearly is more conducive to being aware of "reality", to assessing properly what is real. But being aware of reality may involve being aware of the unpleasant because reality is not necessarily pleasing or welcome. This is common to all scientific inquiry, whether of people or things. We can be in a universe of thought, a culture, or even a temporary culture, of such a kind that we are sure to suffer the pain of feeling that our universe is not conducive to our welfare. To dare to be aware of the facts of the universe in which we are existing calls for courage. (Bion, 1994, p. 322)

Beckett's coolly reasoned reflection on Proust foreshadows the white heat of psychoanalysis observed by Bion. Within its relational field, not only do the two participatory subjects daily shift from A to B as a function of their ongoing interaction, but also daily engage actively in what the mature Bion would describe as a frightening "emotional storm" in which, as the young Beckett recognises, exist "two separate and immanent dynamisms related by no system of synchronization".

Later, this would be reflected in Beckett's own correspondence during psychotherapy, where squabbling, disagreement, and displeasure with the other's responsiveness would occupy his thinking. At one moment, Beckett's own sense of Bion might be the friendly "covey", a chum-like bloke, and at another, a callous presence—not unlike May, perhaps—uninterested in his pain (TM, 22 September 1935). Still, with time and reflection, even the rough oscillation of this emotional storm shifts in memory, as the involuntary yield of mutual enquiry broadens the capacity for experience.

So it was that in the months following Beckett's parting from Bion, the young writer experienced renewed panic and suffering together with a fierce assessment of what he termed "the London Torture". Yet, a year later, in Germany, he would send Bion a Christmas card and receive Bion's wish to re-engage therapeutically (TM, 22 December 1936). Later still, in his writing, Beckett would review the therapist's presence with fear and hatred, characterising his presence as "without opening his mouth, fastening on me his eyes like cinders with all their seeing" (Beckett, 2006b, p. 292).

Later still, this would reverse to thinking of him "with more felicity and understanding than ever" (Beckett, 1995, p. 333).

Such movement in relation to significant others—of experience, disintegration, and reintegration—is foreshowed for Beckett in *Proust* as he writes, "at the best, all that is realized in Time (all Time produce), whether in Art or Life, can only be possessed successively, by a series of partial annexations – and never integrally and at once" (Beckett, 1931, p. 7).

This partial series of annexations, never of one piece, and involving continuous change, represents psychological progress at its best. It represents progress from Winnicott's state of unintegration or from Klein's paranoid–schizoid position, to the integrated achievement of the depressive position. This emergence, located by Beckett in *Proust*, is opposed by Habit, "the guarantee of a dull inviolability" (Beckett, 1931, p. 8). Just as the individual represents a succession of different individuals, so successive moments of individuality generate a succession of habit, the generic term for the countless treaties concluded between the countless subjects that constitute the individual and their countless correlative objects. The periods of transition that separate consecutive adaptations (because by no expedient of macabre transubstantiation can the grave sheets serve as swaddling clothes) represent the perilous zones in the life of the individual, dangerous, precarious, painful, mysterious and fertile, when for a moment the boredom of living is replaced by the suffering of being. (Beckett, 1931, p. 8)

The young Beckett, here, elevates the nobility of suffering—as if resonant with the mature Bion. He recognises that the productive action of lived suffering is necessary death because "the old ego dies hard". Beckett construes the self, bound by convention as a " a minister of fullness" and "an agent of security", cowering before the possibilities and imperatives of the new

when it is opposed by a phenomenon that it cannot reduce to the condition of a comfortable and familiar concept, when in a word, it betrays its trust as a screen to spare its victim the spectacle of reality, it disappears, and the victim, now an ex-victim, for a moment free, is exposed to that reality – an exposure that has its advantages and its disadvantages . . . The old pact is out of date. (Beckett, 1931, p. 10)

His example is in Proust's sleepless narrator, tortured by the dimensions of an unfamiliar room. Beckett reads into this anguish as a psychological condition. He asks and answers,

What is taking place? The old pact is out of date. It contained no clause treating of high ceilings. The habit of friendship for the low ceiling is ineffectual, must die in order that a habit of friendship for the high ceiling may be born. Between this death and that birth, reality, intolerable, absorbed feverishly by his consciousness at the extreme limit of its intensity, by his total consciousness organized to avert the disaster, to create the new habit that will empty the mystery of its threat – and also of its beauty. (Beckett, 1931, p. 11)

Absorbed in reading Proust, Beckett locates a proof-text of psychological self-absorption, an aspect not so much of habit, but of characterological defensiveness. Beckett's own absorption is reflected in the closeness of his reading, and his location in *Proust* of the need for "total consciousness" in aversion of disaster. The habit described by

Beckett via Proust suggests a terrified soul's promise of momentary calm at significant emotional cost. It resounds biographically in the defensive rigidity of Beckett's mother, so frightened about her son's absence on that day years ago, after Sam's collapse on the Foxrock road, that, in her own anguish, she punishes him further by denying him his dinner (Knowlson, 1996, p. 51).

Beckett's experience of catastrophe here parallels Bion's, whose psychoanalytic articulation of it would occur twenty-five years after Beckett's *Proust*, just as *Proust* occurred forty years after James' stream of consciousness and thirty years after Freud's free association. Yet, the mutual and independent acquaintance with catastrophe, first articulated by Beckett in *Proust,* would silently link Beckett and Bion throughout their published works.

Beckett resonated deeply with Proust's suffering, as when habit dissipates and the individual himself meets the change with indifference, another psychological dynamic present in the later Beckett. Here, Beckett links his earlier discussion of the individual's evolution from one moment of personhood to another. What happens when risk is undergone and the resultant self could not care less? How tragic

> when the alchemy of Habit has transformed the individual capable of suffering into a stranger for whom the motives of that suffering are an idle tale, when not only the objects of his affection have vanished, but also that affection himself. (Beckett, 1931, p. 13)

The result is an individual who becomes lost to himself, a condition of the modern. Beckett's example from Proust is in individual awareness of "his own absence", when his habitual relation to the other shifts. In psychoanalytic psychotherapy, this occurs regularly in recognition of personal distortions within the transference to the therapist. In Beckett's own novellas and "trilogy", these are represented, from time to time, through narrators' atomistic reflections on transference. For Proust, it is in awareness that the grandmother of one's habitual tenderness exists only in one's mind, conditioned by personal history as, unfeelingly,

> he realizes with horror that his grandmother is dead, long since and many times, that the cherished familiar of his mind, mercifully composed all along the years by the solicitude of habitual memory, exists no longer, that this mad old woman, drowsing over her book,

overburdened with years, flushed and coarse and vulgar, is a stranger whom he has never seen. (Beckett, 1931, p. 15)

Ironically, given Beckett's future therapeutic experience, his Proustian description might as well depict a moment of psychoanalytic self-awareness of the other, as much freeing as it is terrifyingly new in the shift from an enduring perception to its later, emotional clarification.

The risk of suffering Beckett describes is also the risk within psychological enquiry, "in a perpetual adjustment and readjustment of our organic sensibility to the conditions of its worlds" (Beckett, 1931, p. 14). In the dissolution of habitual distortion, suffering, for Beckett, allows the clarification of the "real". This is also the yield of effective psychoanalysis. Its opposite is the neurotic condition, located in Proust by Beckett as habitual boredom, "the most tolerable because the most durable of human evils" to which individuals and society become anaesthetised.

Beckett observes that Proust's attention focuses upon the process of association leading to involuntary memory. Beckett stresses that Proust cites twelve or thirteen such incidents, including trains of thought initiated by thinking about cobblestones and cutlery in *Remembrance of Things Past* (Beckett, 1931, p. 24). Stylistically, this observation underwrites the idea of discrete thoughts giving rise to associations or linked thoughts, subjectively construed, the basis of Freud's technique of free association. Beckett's enumeration of incidents in Proust's writing also parallels Josef Breuer's similar citations of Anna O's symptomatic relationships to her psychological situation in *Studies on Hysteria* (Freud (with Breuer), 1895d).

While Proust celebrates the value of involuntary associative memory in saving life from the perpetual boredom of habit, Beckett returns to a recurrent fear: indifference. Proust provides an example of the meaning-giving nature of associative thought in relation to the example of a buttoned boot. Beckett describes the Proustian character as

he stoops down – cautiously, in the interests of his heart – to unbutton his boots. Suddenly he is filled with a divine familiar presence, once more he is restored to himself by that being whose tenderness, several years earlier, in a similar moment of distress and fatigue, had brought him a moment's calm. (Beckett, 1931, p. 27)

Beckett would later return to a similar image of boot buttoning in *Watt*; but there, rather than memory's supplying meaning, memory itself would signal the possibility that an indifferent act be imbued with significance through an act of human relatedness to another. Beckett subverts Proust's potential comfort in memory in that the self's future edition may be indifferent to the comforts and meanings of the now transformed past. Redemption is momentarily possible only in the other's recognition.

For Beckett in *Watt*, the central motif of conveying a memory of boots buttoned offers not personal calm, but a desperate need to connect one's own solitary experience to another's. Watt attempts to explain the buttoning of Knott's boots to Sam. He wants Sam to know, deeply, his experience, and so to "know" him. He writes,

> But he could not bear that we should part, never to meet again (in this world) and I in ignorance of how Mr Knott put on his boots, or his shoes, or his slippers, or his boot and shoe, or his boot and slipper, or his shoe and slipper, when he did so, when he did not merely put on a boot, or a shoe, or a slipper. So, taking his hands from my shoulders, and laying them on my wrists, he told how Mr Knott, when he felt the time had come, taking on a cunning air would begin to sidle up to the boots, up to the shoes, up to the boot and shoe, up to the boot and slipper, up to the shoe and slipper, sidle sidle little by little with an artless air little by little nearer and nearer to where they lay, in the rack, till he was near enough, pouncing, to secure them. And then, while he put on the one, the black boot, the brown shoe, the black slipper, the brown boot, the black shoe, the brown slipper, on the one foot, he held the other tight, lest it should escape, or put it in his pocket, or put his foot upon it, or put in a drawer, or put it in his mouth, till he might put it on, on the other foot. (Beckett, 2006a, p. 343)

Here, Beckett creatively amplifies the Proustian concept of involuntary memory. For Watt, memory affords not rest but emptiness absent its affirmation in relationship by another— a character having the same containing relationship as a therapist or containing maternal figure. The Proustian character, "after years of fruitless solitude" has lost interest in society. Watt, dependent upon the understanding of another, extends to society, in the person of a single significant other, one more chance. Within his own evolving metapsychology, Beckett pushes past involuntary memory as human salvation. However momentary it might be, salvation's necessary condition is reciprocal human affirmation. Here, it is strikingly described as if in a mother's "good enough" containment of her child's anxiety, described by such psychoanalysts as Winnicott and Bion.

For Beckett, in *Proust*, we find the first intimation of this character to come, his name translated from the French for a conductor on an electric railway—"wattman"—-cited in a Proustian epiphany of memory.

> Crossing the courtyard he stumbles on the cobbles. His surroundings vanish, wattman, stables, carriages, guests, the entire reality of the place in its hour, his anxiety and doubts as to the reality of life and art disappear, he is stunned by waves of rapture, saturated in that same felicity that had irrigated so sparingly the desolation of his life. Drabness is obliterated in an intolerable brightness. (Beckett, 1931, p. 52)

Not so for Beckett's Watt, whose momentary farewell is the same boot buttoning, dependent, so dependent upon another, against the possibility both of his own indifference and another's.

For Beckett in *Proust*, what affords hope is involuntary linkage as the "essence of any new experience" when

> by accident, and given favorable circumstances (a relaxation of the subject's habit of thought and a reduction of the radius of his memory), a generally diminished tension of consciousness following upon a phase of extreme discouragement. (Beckett, 1931, p. 53)

Conceptually, Beckett might be describing a moment of movement between Klein's paranoid–schizoid position and the depressive position, when experience split into opposing aspects of good and bad becomes integrated as new experience. Productively, the catastrophic "phase of extreme discouragement" preceding this psychological leap, and corresponding to the heightening of a habitual good–bad split, has shifted. Beckett locates within Proust's writing, the phenomenological correlate of Freud's "working through" of resistance (Freud, 1914g).

Beckett also learns from Proust about a writer's innovative presentation of characters. Absent a third person narrative framework, Proust's characters "state" themselves directly. Their psychological worlds become "apprehended" by the reader through the immediacy of this " indirect and comparative expression of indirect perception" (Beckett, 1931, p. 67).

Beckett writes that

> The rhetorical equivalent of the Proustian real is the chain-figure of the metaphor. It is a tiring style, but it does not tire the mind. The clarity of the phrase is cumulative and explosive. One's fatigue is a fatigue of the heart, a blood fatigue. One is exhausted and angry after an hour, submerged, dominated by the crest and break of metaphor after metaphor; but never stupefied. (Beckett, 1931, p. 67)

Here, Beckett observes the exhausting demands upon the reader of Proust. His own correspondence reflects acquaintance with this state of mind, wondering via anatomical metaphor, which end is up (TM, 25 August 1930). But Beckett observes that, despite the demand in the writing, Proust does not stupefy the reader. The reading of this Proustian demand underpins Beckett's own later readings, testing of the reader's capacity to endure beyond such exhaustion, to remain unstupefied. While extending the demand upon the reader, Beckett's future literary assimilation of free association would push past the author's use of metaphor to the jagged and jarring narrative use of direct expression. Discovering the use of free association as literary device, both in the novellas and in the "trilogy", Beckett pushes the reader past "blood fatigue" to stupefication.

Reading Beckett's metapsychology, one is struck, beyond poetic language, by its solid mid-century picture of dynamic psychological function with footings in early modernism, from William James to Freud. While *Proust* articulates the twenty-five-year-old Beckett's theory of psychology, it is a psychology reflective not only of human thought but of human behaviour, reflected in literature as both product and underlying process. It is worthwhile to review its numerous points.

Beckett begins with consideration of individual embeddedness in interpersonal relations. Others' actions upon us shape us. In Beckett's language, they "deform" us, permanently changing how we approach the world as the effects of interpersonal action endure in our psyches far longer than our actual exposure to these enduring moments in real time. His is a traumatic view of human interaction through the intrusion by others upon the individual's stream of consciousness. It is itself reflectively knowable as the object of analytic thought.

Life, then, is shaped by the necessity of passionate change from moment to moment as earlier mental states die, through progressive and inexorable transformation. Because we are forever evolving, we are incapable of experiencing either a perfect reliving of past experience, or in satisfying earlier desires. While this constancy of change causes us to become who we will become, it also entails the continuous probability of catastrophic disruption. Unspoken, but correlated with Beckett's own experiences, is the young writer's core dread: that static states of normal equilibrium may be punctured at any moment by catastrophic panic.

For Beckett, our understandings of what we undergo are elusive. Voluntary memory fails us. The constancy of involuntary memory affords a continuous reservoir for contemplation as experience moves through the present from hopeful future anticipation to the deformation of experienced past time. Not only are we incapable of precise, rational, thought, but also the observer's own psychological viewpoint influences the way in which he observes the world. Our viewpoint is always subjective and cannot be otherwise. This radical subjectivity is heightened in the discontinuity of meanings and perception in the interactions between individuals. Both within individual moments of successive experience and between individuals, linkage or connection is continually threatened by indifference. Not only is psychological progress located within the constant movement of partial shifts in personal viewpoint, but it is also blocked through the resistances of habits, generated to ensure a sense of security under different circumstances at different moments of our lives. In this way, our own defensive desires for security deflect the pain of necessary accommodation to the emergent new, as well as the clear communication of meaning to self and other. Analogous discontinuities of communicated meaning become the subject of Bion's mature thinking in "Attacks on linking" (Bion, 1959).

For Beckett, the endurance of suffering is a precondition for human growth. The associational process, however, in which memory productively surfaces, is insufficient by itself, as personal gratification. To become meaningful, communication must occur through one individual's containment or holding of another's meaning. Beckett finds warrant in Proust for the writer's imposition of suffering upon the reader, who connects to the narrator's solitary associations in a psychological act of apprehension, at the cost of deep emotional engagement—even becoming drained or angry—with the act of reading.

Significantly, the dynamics described by Beckett outline, first the struggle within a single individual necessary to understand the self's emergent experience, second, the necessary and impossibly painful hurdle of an individual's experience receiving validation in the containment of another's listening, and third, the location within the writer's relation to the reader in which to situate this fundamental interpersonal engagement as a vital enterprise within the field of literature.

Proust is Samuel Beckett's early blueprint for the courageous contemplation of repetitive acts of thought, both satisfying and frustrating, both coherent and incoherent, that will occupy his literary career. The congruence between his literary metapsychology and the emergent dynamic psychology of twentieth-century psychoanalysis—especially in the narration and listening implicit in the emotional storm of the clinical psychoanalytic process—will later function as his experiential correlate for experimentation in the literary relationship between author and reader. Dread, non-meaning, and indifference are continuous possibilities in the living through of life, as they are in the relationships between individuals.

Rather than reflecting a necessary outcome of psychological growth, indifference suggests a particular form of psychological catastrophe. Indifference suggests the implosion of narcissistic grandiosity and omnipotence—the defensive inflation of self—into its opposite, the sense of nothingness implied by narcissistic deflation (Bach, 1994). Here, Beckett's identification with Proust's thickly self-referential interests reveals itself to defend against the nightmare that so much intellectual work is ultimately worthless, except in attempting to build a dyke against a sea of meaninglessness and confusion. This particular form of indifference, located by Beckett in *Proust*, but clearly apprehended by Beckett himself, leads to catastrophic panic and its unknowns in fear of heart attack and madness, those symptomatic precursors of his psychoanalytic experience.

CHAPTER THREE

The first year of treatment: 1934

There is no explicit record of who said what to whom in Beckett's psychotherapy. Indeed, parallel accounts of psychotherapy from the perspective of patient and analyst are extraordinarily rare. Instead, the psychotherapeutic convention provides for the writing of case studies by psychotherapists. These, however, are shaped by one-sidedness and the many distorting conventions of professional presentation, including tendentiousness, are aimed at elucidation of one or several clinical developments, and usually also at professional advancement. This has been so since *Studies on Hysteria* (1895d) and Freud's foundational dream of Irma's Injection in *The Interpretation of Dreams* (1900a).

Perhaps closer to the experiential moment, at least from the therapist's point of view, is the clinical diary, or ongoing narrative of the therapist's experience. However, these are almost always kept as private case notes, rarely seen in the public sphere. Written either to aid in case presentation to a supervisor, or to examine aspects of the clinical approach, these are generally closely held and personal study tools. Ferenczi's *Clinical Diaries*, for example, were written specifically because of his own awareness that new clinical approaches warranted close study and consideration (Dupont, 1988).

What patients say about their therapy is heavily influenced by the momentary situation of the patient relative to the therapist. Reflecting the changing perspectives of transference as the vehicle of external projection, such opinion varies from the withdrawn and persecutory to the more or less resolved, shifting continuously and subject to the dominant current issues in the patient's internal life. Often, it is a retrospective judgement, far in the future of what took place, and suffers from the distortions of time and post-therapeutic contingency. As the mature Beckett would write, almost fifty years after his work with Bion,

> A voice comes to one in the dark. Imagine.

> To one on his back in the dark. This he can tell by the pressure on his hind parts and by how the dark changes when he shuts his eyes and again when he opens them again. Only a small part of what is said can be verified. (Beckett, 1996, p. 3)

Peering into one's inner dark, supine on the analytic couch, opening and shutting one's eyes, aware of the analyst's voice as well as one's own internal promptings, little can later be empirically demonstrated and verified. Therapeutic action happens within and between individuals, and inheres within individual experience.

Certainly, there is no verifiable record of this therapy from Bion's perspective. Yet, this is not wholly so in Samuel Beckett's case. Whatever their functional impact upon the therapeutic process, Beckett's habitual letter writing to friends and acquaintances during his therapy placed his psychotherapeutic work with Bion front and centre as a communal object of contemplation. No matter that, necessarily, much—almost all—detail goes missing. The form and rhythm of the letters highlight Beckett's ongoing momentary interpretations of therapy as it proceeds over a period of two years. The letters reflect Beckett's own censorship, his own decisions about those intimacies that are publicly knowable, even to select individuals. As such, they are an approximation to his experience, filtered through considerations of self-presentation and personal privacy.

Approximating experience, these letters are the literary equivalent of the manifest dream, with the latent dream equivalent in unverifiable therapeutic interaction. But what dreams! Recognisably the reflections of an engaged patient, they provide today's readers, familiar with the dynamics of psychotherapy, with a sense of power-ful therapeutic engagement. Reading into the letters, considering their composition and effect, the contemporary reader imagines how the same quality of reasoning and discourse affected Bion both in his par-ticipation and observation. The Bion known to Beckett, however, was not the iconic psychoanalytic Bion. Beckett's Bion was an unseasoned psychiatrist at Tavistock. As yet unanalysed himself, his practice was by any measure not yet successful: it would take him almost a decade to exceed a census of two patients in private practice. It was a time before Bion would consider that "my contact with patients was profit-able for them and was helping me and them to open my mind too" (Conci, 2011, p. 77). Bion, at the time, was a reluctant student of a training supervisor he did not respect. Writing years later about his formal psychoanalysis with John Rickman, Bion provides an ambiva-lent retrospective view of his training even after the period of Beckett's psychotherapy. "I thought Rickman liked me . . . But there was some kind of emotional turbulence, with its high and low pressure areas, which extinguished the analysis. . . . It stopped" (Bion, 1985, p.46).

Yet, Bion declares that the effect of his initial psychoanalytic training was that it "extinguished in me any spark of respect" for the wisdom of his pre-analytic training model during the period of Beckett's psychotherapy. If, from this interim moment, after his work with Beckett but before his experiences during and after the Second World War, Bion had lost respect for his earlier manner of psychother-apeutic influence and conduct, then what, of constructive therapeutic value, might have been conveyed to his patient? Was this disdain entirely retrospective? Was the spark of respect still flickering warmly during the earlier period?

Bion had served throughout the First World War as a tank com-mander in the machine gun corps. His actions had been heroic, and for them, he had been recommended for the Victoria Cross and had received the Distinguished Service Order. He had also withstood the rigours of psychiatry training. He literally knew how to soldier on. While he would eventually conjure up the image of battle as a metaphor for psychotherapy, he would also apply the analogy of gardening. Even if therapy presented an emotional storm between its participants, patients were, nevertheless, to be nurtured by it, like seedlings in a thunderstorm (Rickman, 2003, p. 39). Minimally,

Beckett had taken the hand of a therapist who, true to Hippocrates, would try to do no harm. He was also a therapist whose own tough characteristic stance would mirror a requisite dimension of psycho-dynamic therapeutic efficacy. By nature and training, Bion was tough, and was available to survive and keep thinking about any and all of the patient's projective expressions of both love and hate, while actually under psychic fire.

Beckett's letters trace his course of psychotherapy, through multiple viewpoints, extending well beyond its two-year duration. Together with his metapsychological monograph on Proust, his psychological notebooks tracing his extensive reading in psychoanalytic texts (Feldman, 2006), and his biographical reminiscences from late in life (Knowlson & Knowlson, 2006), Beckett's correspondence about his experience of dynamic psychology and psychoanalysis leaves a rich impression of studied experience, illuminating his future writing.

This work treats Beckett's therapy with Bion in this chapter and Chapter Four, each representing a single year of psychotherapy. By the midpoint of therapy, at the end of the first year, Beckett has described a difficult therapeutic course that nevertheless suggests his internalisation of Bion's therapeutic presence, together with a heightened acquaintance with Beckett's own private, internal sense of isolation. During the second year, Beckett seems to comply with the formal requirements of Hadfieldian reductive analysis—the limited form of psychoanalysis then practised by Bion—and also, under the fragmenting pressures of therapy, seeks containment supplemental to the therapeutic dyad in the friendship and support of another psychiatrist, Beckett's childhood friend, Geoffrey Thompson.

Year 1: 1934

Beckett's letter to his cousin, Morris Sinclair, of 27 January 1934, portrays Beckett's therapeutic situation through the hopeful and idealising vision of an enthusiastic patient, one month into therapy. Perhaps momentarily discrepant for the contemporary reader is that Beckett's view of the psychoanalytic course of treatment is in months, rather than the years that would become the late twentieth and early twenty-first century psychoanalytic norm. The period of Beckett's psychoanalysis corresponded to a moment in psychoanalytic development when an earlier focus on symptom remission was evolving into a focus on the entire personality, requiring longer periods of time (Ferenczi & Rank, 1923; Strachey, 1934). Even in the early days of psychoanalysis, however, the length of treatment varied. Winnicott's psychoanalysis with James Strachey, for example, spanned a decade, beginning in 1923. Freud wrote both that "psycho-analysis is always a matter of long periods of time, of half a year or whole years – of longer periods than the patient expects" and that he did "not bind patients to continue the treatment for a certain length of time; I allow each one to break off whenever he likes" (Freud, 1913c, p. 129).

Beckett's work with Bion lasted for two years, finishing in December 1935. While Beckett's late-life reminiscence reduced the length of his therapy to six months, it probably reflects memory's distortion of fact (Knowlson & Knowlson, 2006). It might also reflect the former patient's earlier wish for a more compressed therapeutic course. It might also have served, late in life, to underplay the significance both of psychoanalysis and psychoanalytic experience within Beckett's later literary work.

In his first letter about psychoanalysis, Beckett expresses great relief. He tells his cousin that three times each week "I give myself over to probing the depths with my psychiatrist". Noting that his nightly panics have become less frequent and acute during his first month in therapy, he writes that it has already "done me some good". Therapy has begun, and, as with most patients, its "honeymoon" period has been positive. Beckett then signals a shift from his straightforward description to Sinclair, as if projecting himself into his cousin's thinking. He attempts to clarify his position, as if apologetic elaboration were necessary. Writing that he regards himself as fortunate "to have been able to embark on" psychotherapy, he writes to Sinclair that his intention is not to complain.

The idea of complaint stands out as discrepant. The letter fairly dances with relief. It seems unimaginable that Sinclair would receive his cousin's news with anything but empathic resonance. Beckett's disclaimer signals a complexity otherwise missing from the letter. Though seemingly elated by his new experience, perhaps he is also embarrassed or humiliated by a disability requiring such remediation? Though certain of Sinclair's continuing support and solidarity, does he also project a more generalised sense of external judgement? Beckett's disclaimer adroitly avoids such questions as it moves the letter forward. Yet, it suggests a sense of unease, together with his glowing report on therapy's first weeks.

Beckett next describes his therapeutic attentions in that "it is the only thing that interests me at the moment, and that is how it should be, for these sorts of things require one to attend to them to the exclusion of virtually anything else" (letter to Morris Sinclair, 1 January 1934, hereafter cited as MS, followed by the date of the letter).

Of course, this would not have been strictly the case; there would be many other interests and distractions competing with therapy's exclusive claims on Beckett, most notably, the patient's own capabilities in stabilising himself through academic research and reading. Even when suffering from serious writer's block, compounding his ever-ready sense of despair, Beckett was able to right himself through scholarly reading and criticism. As he earlier told Thomas MacGreevy, he could both "gallop" through classical literature and "booze my heart quiet" at the same time (TM, 22 September 1931).

During the course of his therapy, Beckett's interests beyond the experience of psychotherapy would extend his encyclopaedic philosophy notebooks with 20,000 words on fifty-four typed pages about psychoanalytic psychology. Anchored in Woodworth's 1931 *Contemporary Schools of Psychology*, his reading included works by Freud, Jones, Adler, Rank, and Karin Stephen, as well as gestalt psychology (Feldman, 2006). These texts represent Beckett's curriculum in psychological self-education, encouraged by Bion and parallel to the experience of therapy. They elaborate Beckett's own prior metapsychological framework, derived from the study of Proust, and link the principles underlying applied clinical psychology with Beckett's understanding of psychology within literature.

As a consolidation of psychological understanding under his own control during the potentially destabilising work of psychotherapy, Beckett's studies seem also to have represented a protective bulwark against the paralysis of frightening emotion. It is to this defensive or resistant aspect of study during the conduct of psychoanalysis that theorists turned in concern about "the degrading of the analysis into a mere pedagogic measure, that is, to depriving oneself of all the possibilities of the exploration of the unconscious" (Ferenczi, 1926, p. 38).

Arguing against such intellectual armament, Freud would write,

I dislike making use of analytic writings as an assistance to my patients; I require them to learn by personal experience, and I assure them that they will acquire wider and more valuable knowledge than the whole literature of psycho-analysis could teach them. (Freud, 1912e, p. 120)

Indeed, for Beckett, this period allowed an intellectual consolidation of literary metapsychology, academic psychology, first-hand acquaintance with the conditions of psychiatric hospitalisation, and personal experience of the relation between the patient and his psychotherapist. All would become "grist to the mill" of his literary productivity, beginning with the novel *Murphy*, begun while he was in treatment with Bion. Nowhere in his letters does Beckett indicate any concern—whether his own or Bion's—that this literary use of psychoanalysis might function not only as experiential learning to be assimilated creatively in writing, but also in the capacity of therapeutic resistance. Bion's own psychoanalytic tradition, however, would later affirm the earlier observations of Ferenczi and Freud, "that if analysis becomes education in psychoanalytic concepts, or suggestions based on theories, it may be admirable but it is not psychoanalysis" (Segal & Britton, 1981).

Feldman (2006) amply illustrates the breadth of Beckett's extra-therapeutic psychological study, quoting extensively from Beckett's psychology notebooks. Beckett ranges from contemplation of diagnostic entities such as hysteria, anxiety neurosis, and obsessional neurosis to the dynamics of introjection and projection within literary "puppets", such as those he cites in *The Unnamable*,

I shall not be alone, in the beginning. I am of course alone. Alone. That is soon said. Things have to be soon said. And how can one be sure, in such darkness? I shall have company. In the beginning. A few puppets. Then I'll scatter them to the winds, if I can. (Beckett, 2006b, p. 286)

Beckett details the depressive's turning aggression upon himself and notes Karin Stephen's descriptions of anal aggression in *Psychoanalysis and Medicine: A Study of the Wish to Fall Ill* (1933):

overwhelming quality of infantile excretory processes, so that they are both dreaded & desired by the subject. They constitute a diffuse form of orgasm, taking control of the organism & carrying themselves through to a crisis independently of volition. This type of sensation of excretion before sphincter control has been established. The child punished for lack of control may grow up dreading loss of control on various planes, excretory, genital, etc., resulting in constipation, frigidity, etc. The sheer terror of being run away with by a bodily function. (Feldman, 2006, pp. 99–100)

Tellingly, he would also write in his notebook, following Ernest Jones, that to terminate

the analysis before the fundamental aberration is elucidated is like presuming to cure a riddling abscess by tapping superficial pockets of pus instead of thoroughly laying open & draining entire system of connected cavities (free from necrotic areas). (Feldman, 2006)

The analogy to Beckett's own earlier draining of a physical "septic system" must have resonated deeply. Yet, in the context of the analytic experience, especially given the workings of transference, how does the patient know when "the fundamental aberration is elucidated"? Despite Beckett's academic study of psychoanalysis, his own experiences would determine his behaviour in treatment.

Beckett's intention, written to Morris Sinclair, to maintain focused analytic attention, goes beyond a simple declaration of personal resolve. It also paraphrases an instruction given by psychoanalysts to their patients in the early stages of therapy. Patients are advised to refrain from decision-making based on what might seem good ideas in the developing contexts of psychoanalytic dialogue, but turn out to be figuratively half-baked for the purposes of enactment in action beyond the consulting room. Returning to Beckett's letter, we might then read his curious disclaimer to Sinclair in a different context

I am not complaining, I regard myself as very fortunate to have been able to embark on it, it is the only thing that interests me at the moment and that is how it should be, for these sorts of things require one to attend to them to the exclusion of virtually anything else. (MS, 27 January 1934)

Beckett's odd negation of complaint actually highlights its opposite. He is complaining! But the complaint is not, of course, directed to Morris Sinclair. Rather, it is an implicit complaint, unspoken but loudly embedded in Beckett's paraphrase of the analyst's formulaic communication to the patient—to attend to the treatment to the exclusion of virtually everything else. Beckett seems to bridle at the idea that psychoanalysis itself must become paramount during the period when the patient begins therapy. That is, that the psychotherapeutic experience must be attended to rather than the more familiar activities of writing or academic study of psychoanalysis, potentially distracting from the therapeutic process.

Beckett's first letter about psychotherapy suggests what might have otherwise occurred for him within the action of psychotherapy, but, as a critique, it is displaced into a non-therapeutic context. Had Beckett's complaints been brought to the therapy as his therapist's directions for conduct during the course of therapy had indicated they might have been, their concerns might have been folded into the therapeutic process. Instead, an aspect of the therapeutic process—here, the veiled complaint—is exported via a letter to an individual who is unable to identify Beckett's underlying meaning.

Upon reading, Sinclair would be left with an important, if enigmatic, aspect of a deeper communication. The unarticulated complaint would remain safely guarded from enquiry in the possession of someone unable to link it with the analytic process. Later, Beckett would formally adapt this practice within his creative writing, placing uncontextualised and atomistic comments about psychoanalysis throughout the novellas and the "trilogy". Encountering these disjointed allusions without a clue or working hypothesis about their significance, the reader might discount them as so much incoherent babble, of possible significance only to the narrator. Yet, just as in Beckett's letter to Sinclair, his written allusions to psychotherapy would represent, rather, a displacement of important contents, latent within very different manifest contexts.

Yet, even this parallel to dream construction is formally erroneous because Beckett's references are anything but unconscious. Rather, like the author's extensive literary and philosophical references embedded in his earlier novels, they are conscious signifiers, personally meaningful puzzles for anyone who understands. As such, just as the younger Beckett described his own emotional condition in the language of a work by Richard Aldington, addressed to Thomas MacGreevy, Aldington's own biographer, who would surely understand the allusion, Beckett's references mirror the complex depths and

confusions of interpersonal communication. In this way, their embeddedness in text might not only provoke a question as to their possible
meanings, but also confirms Beckett's conviction from *Proust* about
the tremendous difficulty of one individual's accurate understanding
of another. Instead, aspects significant to one person register upon
another as both incoherence and an interpersonal distancing within
Beckett's own lived mirroring of Proust's literary apprehension.

From the beginning of his work with Bion, together with momentary relief, the experience of psychoanalysis as an authoritative,
controlling structure would present difficulty for the young Beckett.
His letters suggest that this difficulty would be acted out beyond the
boundaries of the consultation room, sometimes subtly, sometimes
dramatically. Within a month of beginning therapy, Beckett writes
flirtatiously, with a playfulness both engaging and distancing, to
Nuala Costello, an Irish woman from his Parisian circle with whom
the young man had hopes of a never-consummated sexual relationship (Knowlson, 1996, p. 178). One of only two letters to Nuala
Costello (cited as NC, with the date of the letter following) in Beckett's
correspondence, it is the first written document suggesting Beckett's
assimilation of psychotherapeutic rhythms in his writing. Beckett
writes of his inability to express himself directly, as if playing with
Nuala. This expression conforms with the backwards and forwards
disclosures within the therapeutic process. Yet, Beckett's control of his
writing is more precise than a patient's ramblings. His thoughts are
tight and return to a point. Unapologetically, he states, "one is not
what one is not", foreshadowing the future, "But there it is, either you
love or you don't" in the conclusion of *First Love* (Beckett, 1995, p. 45).
He tells Nuala,

> It's a great handicap to me in all my anabases and stases that I can't
> express myself in a straightforward manner, and that I cannot behave
> in a way that has the most tenuous propriety of relationship to circum-
> stance. I regret it very much, more than I can ever hope to be able to
> tell. But there it is. One is not what one is not. (NC, 27 February 1934)

Here, Beckett denies an ability for straightforward expression as he
simultaneously straightforwardly illustrates the way in which he
chooses to express himself. Not only does this suggest the literary
device of aporia, but it also demonstrates by literary example Ernest

Jones' observations of the neurotic's doing and undoing as desire is undercut unconsciously by its opposite. Beckett's deft, if regrettable, self-excusal from conventional behaviour similarly demonstrates the secondary gains of neurosis, also described by Jones. But for Jones as interpreter of Freud, neurotic behaviour is unrecognised. It operates from the dynamic unconscious (Jones, 1963). Beckett's correspondence reflects enlistment of an unconscious dynamic to conscious use as a literary device. Neurotic suffering itself is aggressively mobilised, from this position, as entitlement for unconventional behaviour. Further, the reader, Nuala Costello, is challenged to approach or flee with the threatening, "but there it is. One is not what one is not". Beckett, suggesting the attitude of his later narrators, demands that if the other wishes relationship, however unconventional, it will be on Beckett's terms.

His letter continues its pyrotechnics. Beckett twirls literary references, citing Virgil, Dante, Democritus, and Heraclitus. He pauses at the notion of "gress", as the property of abstract movement contained in such words as pro-gress and re-gress before moving on to the unspoken con-gress in a discussion of inflammations and lust. The letter is a triumph of manic bravado. In this density, it is similar to Beckett's writing in *More Pricks Than Kicks*, and challenges the reader to surmount peaks of literary reference in the hide and seek of finding the writer. However mindful or unmindful of it, Beckett's star turn is in the overall effect of the letter. It is a message to Nuala that he is hard work and can be nasty. Extending beyond the letter, the reader can imagine the same sort of wilful, insistent, ambiguous, and intellectualised presentation to his therapist.

Before concluding the letter, Beckett makes two related points about psychotherapy. Two months into the therapeutic process he had just recently extolled, Beckett links psychotherapy and the London Zoo through the device of their jointly shared bus stop. According to Knowlson, Beckett hated zoos and "was haunted by the inherent cruelty of nature itself and of man's unnecessary claustration of animals" (Knowlson, 1996, p. 158). Yet, somewhat archly, Beckett moves past the denizens of monkey hill and the small rodent house to describe patients as those "that sprawl in darkness and in shadow of resurrection". Beckett likens their destination to a different kind of claustration—within the consulting rooms of psychotherapy. However, the separate enclosures of Beckett's psychotherapies are highly nuanced and differentiated. Each practitioner has his own theory, just as monkeys have their monkey house, gnus their paddock, and goats their goat hills. Among them are Hugh Creighton Miller, the founder of the Tavistock Clinic, Karin Stephen, whose textbook on psycho-analysis was among Beckett's readings, and Melanie Klein, Jones' protégée, whose radical understanding of child development would later transform British psychoanalysis. Beckett's sardonic detail (and name-dropping) is telling. Only briefly engaged himself in psycho-therapy, he is positioning himself as a connoisseur of theory and technique, though, of course, to Nuala Costello, who probably has little idea of the differences suggested by Beckett's allusions.

With characteristic slyness, Beckett thus casts a judgemental and denigrating eye both on London psychiatry and its patients, explicitly extending his veiled complaint of a month before. In this sense, not only is Beckett's London psychotherapy a possible solution for a life-or-death problem, but it is also objectified by him, turned into a game played by many fellow sufferers as well as presenting a broad new array of neurotic positions for literary use.

He goes on to explain his potentially long absence from Dublin, writing that he has "no choice in the matter" because of his commit-ment to psychoanalysis. Of course, he will take his August vacation in Dublin and return yet again the following December, but, for the moment, burdened by therapy, Beckett complains of its length and role in forced separation, "God knows how long that will be, probably more than I like to contemplate".

Beckett then alludes abstractly to "the second state of man", which might refer to Proust's Second Nature—the habitual patterns about which Beckett had written, a few years earlier. Taken together, and knowable only to himself (rather than to Nuala, the letter's reader) through his Proustian construction of psychology, Beckett contrasts a falling back into habit's defensive patterns with the emergence, in therapy, of deeper instinctual feelings (Beckett, 1931, p. 12).

Yet, while the therapeutically hopeful context of this last musing is knowable to Beckett alone, the emotional tone of his letter to Cos-tello is ambivalent and possibly hostile in relation to therapy. What he conveys clearly is that he is suffering a lengthy, unknowably long process, in which he feels deprived, confined, and observed. Screwing up his courage, he resolves to benefit as much as he can rather than to end it. Again, as with his earlier letter, Beckett alludes to knowledge that is not possessed by the reader, which, hidden, suggests a very different message than that overtly communicated.

Several days later, writing again to Morris Sinclair, Beckett alludes to the coming of spring and likens it to his own victory over "darkness, nightmares, sweats, panic, and madness" (MS, 4 March 1934). However critically Beckett would view London's psychoanalytic establishment, he recognised that his own symptoms, including the lack of life's once-bearable promise, and fears of madness were kept at bay through the enterprise of psychotherapy. These two letters, one to Nuala and the other to Morris, written less than a week apart and only two months into Beckett's work with Bion, suggest a mobilisation of Beckett's defensive resistance to psychoanalysis in the knowledge of dreadful fears, both aroused and calmed, within the therapeutic relationship. At the same time, his letter to Nuala suggests his own intellectualised thought about different psychodynamic approaches as well as his linkage of information about neurosis within his writing.

In May 1934, four months into therapy, Beckett would write to his cousin that he has "no idea if God helps me or not" in alleviating his distress. He seems miserable, and is comforted, he says, by a single, "almost never-failing joy" in *Schadenfreude*. His is a perverse kind of envy, a reflection upon the "feast" of others' greater sorrow. Recalling the emotion of his story, "Dante and the lobster" (Beckett, 1995a), in contemplation of death and execution, he provides the example of a man facing death. Beckett arrives at the difference between the concreteness of fear and the uncertainties of anxiety and concludes, enviously, that the condemned man knows "exactly what is at stake", in contrast to Beckett's own unknowable and unbearable dread. He muses to Sinclair that "many sick people become criminals solely in order to limit their fear and gain that comfort". He terms such a psychological position a "refuge where there is no more danger, or rather one which is determined and which one can bring into focus" (MS, 5 May 1934). These concerns elaborate Beckett's musings in *Proust* about the defensive securities of habit and routine. Beckett is also explaining the self-protective action of what sixty years later will be called, within psychoanalysis, a "psychic retreat" (Steiner, 1993) in defending against unknowable anguish. For Beckett, limited reflective thought becomes possible, even when anxious, only when one's situation can becomes known and acknowledged to oneself.

This knowledge of what is "at stake" links Beckett's ongoing experiences of personal anxiety with the psychic dangers he'd written about from an intellectualised viewpoint in *Proust* (1931). A similar notion, to be presented a year and a half later by Jung, in his Tavistock lectures, would surely resonate with Beckett in consolidating his own base of self-knowing from which future productive work might proceed. In that third Tavistock lecture, Jung spoke of the importance not of lamenting one's symptom complexes, but of utilising them in productive activity (Jung, 1968).

Indeed, Beckett's letters reflect two major movements. The first is the linkage between his earlier psychological concerns in *Proust* about habit and security and his present condition, as reflected to Morris Sinclair in May 1934. The next development links the idea of self-knowledge and security with Beckett's articulation of his own psychological situation. This development would take another year, and be reflected in his letter to Thomas MacGreevy of 10 March 1935, where he clearly formulates his situation:

> For me the position is really a simple & straightforward one, or was until complicated by the analysis, obviously necessarily. For years I was unhappy, consciously & deliberately ever since I left school and went to T.C.D., so that I isolated myself more & more, undertook less & less & lent myself to a crescendo of disparagement of others & myself. But in all that there was nothing that struck me as morbid. The misery & solitude & apathy & the sneers were the elements of an index of superiority & guaranteed the feeling of arrogant "otherness", which seemed as right & natural & as little morbid as the ways in which it was not so much expressed as implied & reserved & kept available for a possible utterance in the future. It was not until that way of living, or rather negation of living, developed such terrifying symptoms that it could no longer be pursued, that I became aware of anything morbid in myself. In short, if the heart had not put the fear of death into me I would be still boozing & sneering & lounging around & feeling that I was too good for anything else. It was with a specific fear & a specific complaint that I went to Geoffrey, then to Bion, to learn that the "specific fear & complaint" was the least important symptom of a diseased condition that began in a time which I could not remember, in my "pre-history". (TM, 10 March 1935)

This summary of his treatment, approximately midway through his psychoanalytic psychotherapy, is a strong statement of Beckett's intellectual understanding of his own psychological situation; it suggests a consolidation of theory and self-knowledge, satisfying personally exactly the "what is at stake" referred to in his letter to Morris Sinclair a year earlier. Written to MacGreevy almost as a clinical formulation, this understanding would be Beckett's aetiological foundation upon which Jung's later comment about productive use of one's neurosis would flourish.

Beckett writes his second and final letter to Nuala Costello a few days later in May 1934. It is written again in a floridly dramatic manner, differing stylistically from his correspondence to family and friends. Mocking the American caricature of Irish life in the film, *Man of Aran*, he employs a phrase that portends the future Beckett. Extending his earlier contemplation of life as an ongoing process of death in the study of Proust, he characterises the Aran islanders' lives as "struggling to ensure our dying every second".

This letter also presents another similarity to the later Beckett. As in his earlier letter to Nuala, Beckett demonstrates exquisite control of his words, aiming clearly and straightforwardly for a particular effect, though attempting to disclaim it. The letter follows a form similar in style to Beckett's later writing: first a strong statement and then a falling back, undercutting what he has said. In this case, beneath the Joycean froth of his writing to Nuala, the thin-skinned Beckett writes viciously. Nuala, obviously, has interpreted his audacity in an unspecified context as "bloody cheek". How dare she!

Beckett is furious. He writes sarcastically that he seems "to have been most amusing" to her and that she is "so little equitable when I obviously suffer from the acutest paraesthesia to all that is said and written of me". The strength of his diatribe is surprising, after the tone of his previous letter. But then, Nuala is a woman friend, not a male cousin. His emotion is far from his discussion about fear and self-acceptance, just a few days earlier.

Beckett, here, writes white-hot. He has been hurt, and he marshals psychiatric jargon—his paraesthesia—to insist that whoever has contact with him must monitor their behaviour with his potential reaction in mind. In this, he re-emphasises the idea from his previous letter that Nuala's approach to him must be on his terms. Before changing the subject he insists, "So please never say anything to me that you *know* I couldn't care to hear". The letter's context suggests that the tongue-lashing meted out was far weightier than any crime, "an awful thing to have said to me, a positive dumdum" (NC, 10 May 1934).

The combination of these letters suggests Beckett's volatile psychological situation at this time, just months into therapy. On the one hand, he was relieved to be working toward resolution of his problems, including multiple symptoms that often caused him to despair that he was going mad. Beckett might well resonate with Ernest Jones' comments in *Treatment of the Neuroses* of "being torn by the conflicts warring in the recesses of his mind" in being "seized with the conviction that the worst is about to happen and that he is rapidly becoming insane – a consummation looked to with the utmost terror" (Jones, 1963, p. 2).

On the other hand, Beckett found the therapeutic process of three times weekly meetings itself tiresome and painful. In addition to the comforts of continuous study in the theory and technique of psychoanalysis, his emotional position suggests shame and self-pity protected by fierce attacks on others who approached him with anything other than profound consideration of his mental state. However hypersensitive to others' slings and arrows he might be, his own championship of his condition was strong and aggressive. He marshalled both humour and rage to attack both directly and indirectly. The letters are not the stuff of direct emotional contact, as between patient and therapist. Like any writing, no matter what they convey, they must be sufficiently interesting that the reader does not abandon the act of reading or corresponding. Nuala became disinterested. While she was to meet briefly with Beckett in September 1935, she was to remark of him, "You haven't a good word for anyone but the failures". Spurned by her, he ungenerously and derisively described her to MacGreevy as "an unclitoridian companion" (TM, 8 September 1935)

Beckett demonstrates in his letters to Nuala Costello a literary control similar to his later work in his novellas. After his harsh, if wordy, sentiment is conveyed, he changes the subject while remaining focused upon himself. Having condemned Nuala in words for her unfortunate choice of phrase, Beckett continues with a riotous dance through the fields of his own pathology, in arrogant certainty that the severely chastened correspondent is curious to follow! A passage written to Nuala continues, as I cannot give you the glittering account of my health that we all would wish, so I shall content myself with remarking, that the various eviscerations characteristic of my distemper are at the very top of their form. Can you imagine a quarry in ebullition. I have now ceased to wish to amuse you. Forgive me. Now whereas this interesting Neolithic effervescence had hitherto been so forgiving as to confine itself roughly to my center of inertia & environs, it has lately begun to embrace me without fear or favour from sinciput to planta. It take my mind off my corns, no small favour I assure you. No ordinary somersault will take place one of these days, something tells me in the late autumn, if such generosity of recul is any indication, and I am given to understand that is an index of the prime order. (NC, 10 May 1934)

Beckett, indeed, with Nuala, is at the top of his form. First he defines the world by a split between friend and foe. He begins with the disclaimer that his health is not what his supporters might wish. Rather, his symptoms are raging. He refers to violent, sudden stony outpourings radiating through his body from top to bottom; chuckling, he suggests the making light of his despair, saying that at least the new symptoms take his mind "off my corns". His complaint to Nuala is redolent of his later writing, refined later as

> I'll tell them to you some day nonetheless, if I think of it, if I can, my strange pains, in detail, distinguishing between the different kinds, for the sake of clarity, those of the mind, those of the heart or emotional conative, those of the soul (none prettier than these) and finally those of the frame proper, first the inner or latent, then those affecting the surface, beginning with the hair and scalp and moving methodically down, without haste, all the way down to the feet beloved of the corn, the cramp, the kibe, the bunion, the hammer toe, the nail ingrown, the fallen arch, the common blain, the club foot, duck foot, goose foot, pigeon foot, flat foot, trench foot and other curiosities. (Beckett, 1995a, p. 33)

Finally, suggesting that he actually knows something about the progress of therapy in such matters, he forecasts that therapy has another six months to run before he will be fine. Clearly, Beckett was editing his letter through his own omnipotence. Beneath the elegance of his prose, the suggestions of control in relationships, distancing of others through intellectual defences, verbal aggression, sarcasm, blame, together with the arrogance that others are enthralled by his ready discussion of revolting physical symptoms and the assertion that therapy has almost run its course, suggests a young man in considerable turmoil. The letter to Nuala Costello explodes with a patient's voice, but under the controlled pen of the letter-writer. Its direct address suggests his novellas, written ten years later, in its linguistic rhythm and contents: the self-protective claim to vulnerability with hideous attack on the other, disclaimed, and then, a statement evoking pity followed by an intellectualisation suggesting incorrectly that he knows his mind and has sharp clarity of awareness. Bion must have had his hands full!

By summer, Beckett is writing that he walks for hours, anaesthetising his pain with motion, but that his experimentation in writing continues with "making the most outlandish efforts to write what nobody wants to hear" (MS, after 13 July, but before 2 August 1934, p. 215). Returning to Dublin on holiday, he refers to his internal "basso profundo of privacy that never deserts one", while stating his acceptance that his panic is neurotic. Beyond the convention that panic is a neurotic symptom, it does appear that Beckett is touching an inner conviction. He is becoming aware of a deeply private aspect of schizoid self experience, a confining and claustrophobic mental state that continues throughout all other experience.

Back in London from Ireland, in September, he reports to Tom MacGreevy on his change of address. Mrs Frost, his new landlady, "is a kind of mother on draught", and a comfort. She is "a plaster for panic at all times" (TM, 8 September 1934). At the same time, he announces his return to therapy after the summer hiatus. Beckett refers to Bion as the "covey", suggesting MacGreevy's earlier familiarity with this term in relation to Bion. The term "covey" has two distinct meanings. According to Fehsenfeld and Overbeck (2009), it is a variant on the term "cove", or bloke, in English slang (p. 225, fn. 11). More conventionally, it refers to a small group or flock—as in partridges—and, at least for the purposes of examining Beckett's psychotherapy, would suggest Bion's joining with Beckett in the dyadic pair of psychotherapy. Beckett's use of the endearment suggests the emergence of a positive transference within therapy together with the patient's habit of discussing the ordinarily privileged therapeutic relationship more extensively with MacGreevy.

In the next sentence, Beckett states that having "got going again" in psychotherapy, he promptly missed the subsequent session. What was going on? According to Beckett, he had an appointment with an eye doctor; but having begun, having reset their relationship, Beckett's act was sure to send a signal to Bion that therapeutic treatment was insufficient to the patient's needs. However affectionately Beckett construed Bion, at this moment, Beckett was announcing loud and clear both to Bion and to MacGreevy as observer that something within the talking cure was insufficient.

And what might Beckett have needed, according to Beckett? His symptomatic focus was upon his eye, "which has been rather bad but which is all right to-day, more or less", with the help of eye drops and an eye-shade. Adapting Beckett's mission to the language of psycho-therapy, there was something Bion was not seeing, something that did not meet the eye. But having stated the problem to MacGreevy (we have no idea of what he said to Bion), Beckett veers off almost gleefully to report on another symptom, "one of the more endearing derivatives of impetigo on my lip, where there is quite a little colony of erectile tissue" (TM, 8 September 1934). Clearly, Beckett's focus on his symptoms was sacred to him. They were his continuing and amplifying fascination and cause for complaint, and, like some test of a knight-errant's efficacy, to rescue Beckett, Bion must be put to the test of conquering the ever-burgeoning symptoms.

Having suggested the inadequacy of psychotherapy in relation to his burgeoning symptoms, Beckett again writes, as he did with Nuala, that "I have hopes of analysis going a bit faster now", wishing for its completion within three months, by Christmas. Yet, the therapeutic situation he paints suggests an impasse, at best, an avoidance of the relational aspects of therapy, with attention to physical symptoms inadequately addressed by the talking cure, and increasing discomfort. What was the patient thinking? By his own description, his suffering had magnified and his chum, his covey, was unequal to the task!

Writing now under cover of art criticism, Beckett suggests his own sense of alienation:

> as the individual feels himself more and more hermetic & alone & his neighbor a coagulum as alien as a protoplast or God, incapable of loving or hating anyone but himself or of being loved or hated by anyone but himself. (TM, 8 September 1934)

Taken at his own word, Beckett was feeling alone, not simply from an absence of social engagements, but "hermetic", isolated and sealed-off, in his own inner world.

Beckett would soon find a suitable destination for flight from the hermetic sense of isolation, which, given his avoidance of his second session upon returning, he felt not only privately but also in relation to Bion. His solution would lie in the arrival of Geoffrey Thompson from Dublin in early 1935.

Beckett's next letter to MacGreevy, on 16 September 1934, is written in a very different register. It announces Geoffrey Thompson's arrival in London the following weekend. Thompson, who had referred Beckett to the Tavistock Clinic, would soon begin his psychiatric residency at Bethlem Hospital, where Beckett's visits would garner background material for the eventual writing of *Murphy*. Airily and without reference to isolation, Beckett writes to MacGreevy of his work with Bion that "I am alright, belting along with the covey with great freedom of indecency and conviction" (TM, 16 September 1934).

On 1 November, Beckett submitted four poems to *Poetry* magazine. Among them was Eneug, originally submitted to Dublin magazine in 1931, and containing images of a bleak open landscape, emptiness, galvanised under the experience of aloneness as the human condition. Beckett again returned to Dublin for Christmas and New Year, 1935. He complained both of his heart and of a "paralyzing" panic attack, "the worst ever". Yet, across the Irish Sea from the covey, Beckett wrote that "Bion is now a dream habitué" (TM, 1 January 1935). That is, Beckett's dreams now featured the person of his analyst. One year into the course of psychoanalytic psychotherapy, Beckett here suggests that he has internalised Bion as the object of transference.

Bion 's presence within Beckett's dreams reflects a difference in the interpretative sensibilities of cross-disciplinary researchers. Writing from the perspective of Beckett scholarship, Matthew Feldman understands Beckett's "dream habitué" reference as reflecting a "change of technique" on Bion's part (Feldman, 2006, p. 92). Yet, from the perspective of the practising psychoanalyst, no such technical change is suggested at all. Rather, the presence of one's psychoanalyst in a patient's dreams is business as usual within an engaged psychotherapy. Written from Dublin in the absence of Bion, Beckett is writing of his own experience alone.

Beckett's first year of psychotherapy with Wilfred Bion, as reflected in Beckett's own correspondence, appears to be a difficult process for both patient and therapist. The positive transferential relationship to Bion as "covey" is reflected in the presence of Bion in Beckett's dreams. Yet, at the same time, Beckett tells MacGreevy that with fierce symptoms experienced in Dublin, "I fear the analysis is going to turn out a failure" (TM, 1 January 1935). From the beginning of their work together, Beckett's letters had reflected his complaint and displeasure about the constraints of psychoanalysis, most notably the investment of time. The same dazzling feats of intellectualisation that Beckett brought to his correspondence were probably also directed at Bion, most probably heightened in the patient's condescension to his therapist's relative lack of knowledge. It is likely, too, that Bion experienced the same kind of fiercely protective attacks on Beckett's sense of shame and vulnerability that are reflected in the Nuala letters. Still, by New Year 1935, therapeutic progress had clearly been accomplished. Beckett was dreaming of Bion. Despite the probable difficulty of their work together, Bion's constancy had been internalised by Beckett. However, in retrospect, Beckett's avoidance of his second session back with Bion, following the summer vacation, to visit another doctor suggests a disruptive movement between patient and therapist that neither could clearly see.

CHAPTER FOUR

Year two: 1935

The first year of Beckett's psychotherapy with Bion concluded with the positive development of Bion's presence in Beckett's dreams balanced precipitously with Beckett's prediction of therapeutic failure because of the severity of his symptoms during his Dublin holiday. A therapeutic impasse, first suggested by Beckett's correspondence following his return to London after the summer of 1934, seemed to be growing.

Beckett's own letters suggest the forms of his resistance within psychotherapy. His extensive ongoing correspondence provided Beckett with an extra-therapeutic outlet for his growing complaints. We do not know if and when these were worked through in the therapeutic relationship. We do know that both Bion's Hadfieldian concentration on symptom remission with shallow attention to the dynamics of transference and Beckett's own symptomatic preoccupations might have served to constrain the breadth of their work together (Bléandonu, 1994, p. 43; Dicks, 1970, p. 67). Together with Beckett's continuing hope of an early conclusion to psychotherapy and his absorption in the intellectual project of psychodynamic study directed toward future literary production, Bion probably faced formidable headwinds with a patient whose letters reflect a range of difficult states of mind: a sometimes threatening "take it or leave it" attitude with relationship on Beckett's own exacting terms; a hyper-sensitivity to other's lack of understanding about his suffering, of which he was highly protective; the habitual pattern of displacing or splitting off certain contents, and locating them out of enquiry's reach; a fierce and sometimes attacking intellectualised defensiveness.

Despite Beckett's precipitous therapeutic balance, early in 1935, not only his scepticism about therapy, but also his retelling of recent history, seemed to change overnight. On 29 January 1935, he wrote to MacGreevy as if his recent, worst fears in Dublin had vanished, saying,

> I came back with Frank last Sunday week. He returned, & Geoffrey arrived, on the Tuesday morning. Geoffrey went back on the Wednesday night. He has secured a post at an asylum near Beckenham, & will be coming over at the end of this week to stay three months at least, for which I am grateful, as you can imagine. I have resumed with Bion and am feeling better, in spite of all the symptoms, which left me more or less alone during the holiday, having come flocking back. It is a kind of confirmation of the analysis.

The letter, brimming with comings and goings, reflects an exciting and singular new development: Geoffrey Thompson's arrival in London. It is almost as if the power of this event is sufficient to rewrite history, or, at least, for Beckett to attenuate his memory of recent symptomatic suffering, less than a month before. Beckett is thrilled. Thompson's arrival in England is for the purpose of studying psychiatry and psychoanalysis. He is to begin his own therapy with J. A. Hadfield, at Tavistock, Bion's own supervisor and therapist.

Announcing Thompson's arrival, in this single letter, Beckett revises his recent personal history. Perhaps his downgrading of exten-sive recent panics in Dublin passed unnoticed. It would take a close reader to track the vicissitudes of Beckett's symptomatic complaints and turns of mind, and there is no indication that Beckett himself was conscious of this change. Was this a manifestation of resistance? One would have to enquire closely. At least superficially, Beckett's newly robust endorsement of psychotherapy, folded into his exemplification of the ideal that symptoms vanish on holiday and return when ther-apy resumes, instead cast him into the role of successful patient. One wonders how Beckett presented himself to Bion during this period.

Clearly, something has gone missing. Beckett's attitude shifts from therapy as failure to therapy as success.

A week later, Beckett tells MacGreevy that Thompson has arrived and "is now sumptuously installed at the Bethlem Royal Hospital near Beckenham" (TM, 8 February 1935). Beckett has seen him once since his arrival, but sees Thompson's residency as a destination, "perhaps it will be somewhere to go in the Spring". In fact, Thompson would extend his service at Bethlem for one year, until January 1936.

With Beckett's probable unconscious distortion of facts concerning his panics, and his hopeful anticipation in the arrival of Thompson, a curious development occurs in Beckett's psychotherapy, discernible from fragmentary bits of information. Beckett fairly quickly consolidates an intellectually vague, if personally compelling, summary of his difficulties, expanded beyond the "specific fear & complaint" that were his reasons for beginning psychotherapy. He recognises his situation, leading to the "fatuous torments which I treasured as denoting the superior man", as deriving from a development in his "prehistory", rendering him "a composition that was invalid from the word 'go'" (TM, 10 March 1935). This letter to MacGreevy of 10 March 1935 reads like a textbook's retrospective summary of a successful psychotherapy.

It is as if Beckett has found a personally compelling solution for his sufferings, similar to his once-envied phantasy of having a death sentence of a certain date, disclosed a year earlier to his cousin. In this way, roughly a month after Thompson's arrival, Beckett seems to pause his therapeutic process, while continuing to attend sessions with Bion. Given the confluence of Beckett's symptomatic concerns and the emphasis within Bion's Hadfieldian training on symptom remission, it is likely that neither spoke about—or even noticed—this shift in their relationship. Instead, it is likely that Bion encouraged Beckett's continued associations towards resolution of his patient's "nuclear incidents", the important "turning points in the inner life of the child, as recollected on the couch" (Dicks, 1970, p. 67). Indeed, such incidents suggest the theoretically early "nuclear complexes", described by Freud as the mismatch between children's sexual theories and those of grown-ups, and a precursor to phantasies underlying the Oedipus complex (Freud, 1908c, p. 214).

At this time, Bion was relatively naïve about the workings of transference—and certainly of countertransference, which had not then been extensively theorised—and would have experienced this work as business as usual, but, no doubt, with an uneasy sense that something indefinable was amiss. Hadfield's rejection of the centrality of transference meant that his "reductive analysis" had already veered from the psychoanalytic mainstream. Only twelve years earlier, Ferenczi and Rank had described the task of psychoanalysis as "understanding and interpreting every expression of the patient above all as a reaction to the present analytical situation (defense against or recognition of the exposition of the analyst, emotional reactions to these, etc)" (Ferenczi & Rank, 1923, p. 25).

Failure to do so would expose the analyst to "the disastrous mistake of neglecting the actual task for the sake of abstract psychological interest". Yet, absent his own psychoanalytic experience, Bion was relatively immobilised within a treatment model focused only on symptom relief, supported by a supervisor he did not respect (Bléandonu, 1994, p. 42). Only later, together with other "Hadfieldians" at the Tavistock, including Thompson, would he elect formal psychoanalytic study at the Institute of Psychoanalysis (Dicks, 1970, p. 68), finally achieving membership in 1950 with the presentation of his paper, "The imaginary twin".

It is possible that Ferenczi and Rank were thinking of patients as complex as Beckett when they wrote,

One need not even think of the well known type of the obsessional neurotic who, after a lengthy analysis, has the whole analytic knowledge in his little finger, and can even surpass him in analyzing his own symptoms without having been in the least helped in regard to his suffering. No matter how much such a patient has learned from his analyst, and even understood, he has not yet experienced anything which has brought this "knowledge" home to him. (Ferenczi & Rank, 1923, p. 22)

Sixty-five years later, Reisenberg-Malcolm would refer again to this same type of patient, for whom

The analyst believes he is doing analysis with the aim of furthering therapeutic insight. The patient behaves as if this were true. But actually he is coming to analysis . . . to avoid any emotional learning. I think that in fact those people feel hopeless of ever being understood, and they need to maintain a relationship with an object, the analyst, who is not expected, or allowed, to function. What he is expected to do is (omnipotently) to declare them "well" and if possible make them into analysts or experts in analysis. Simultaneously, something called 'the analysis' is highly idealized and felt to be full of promise, and somehow expected to last for life. (Reisenberg-Malcolm, 1999, p. 126)

Indeed, Beckett was steeped in the psychoanalytic language provided by close readings of Karin Stephen and Ernest Jones. It was built upon a dynamic metapsychology he had mined from Proust. His original hints of discontent with the constraints of psychoanalysis, conveyed to Morris Sinclair a year previously, had deepened as difficult states of mind compounded his worries about continuing symptoms.

Beckett's letters that winter reflect two tracks. The one focuses on his discomfort, desire for relief, and resistance to psychotherapy; and the other showcases the compliant patient, claiming, "I am alright, belting along with the covey with great freedom of indecency and conviction". The consolidations noted above by Beckett in his March letter to MacGreevy, explaining the evolution of his difficulties and his sense of a condition broader than "specific goals and symptoms", was the triumph of compliance with a course of therapy, increasingly outside of the analyst's control.

While all this was going on, Beckett was integrating the neurotic condition as a literary trope. Its hatreds and loves, entitlements and contradictions, both described in current psychoanalytic literature and experienced in his own suffering, were achieving a place, reflected in his correspondence, among pre-existent layers of literary, philosophical, and metapsychological concerns. His correspondence reflects his splitting of issues, displacing the concerns of one sphere within another, as in his early correspondence with Morris Sinclair. It also reflects his assumption of neurosis as a right or prerogative to be insisted upon, of an aggressive entitlement to remain apart from societal norms, mirroring a dimension of neurosis made explicit by Ernest Jones. Most prominently, this conscious turn toward heralding the neurotic condition is demonstrated in Beckett's two letters to Nuala Costello. Given their shared linkage in Joyce's Parisian circle, Beckett's literary composition to Nuala also represents a transition from Joyce's literary style to a different mode, one which was more personal to Beckett. Neurotic entitlement, anchored in exquisite suffering, provides Beckett with a more contemporary, psychoanalytically informed correlate with the sufferings and joys of Dante's Belacqua, the muse of Beckett's earlier writing.

Dutifully, if grimly, Beckett slogs on through the winter of 1935. He reports to MacGreevy, "I see no prospect of the analysis coming to an end. I realize how lost I would be bereft of my incapacitation" (TM, 14 February 14, 1935). A week later he writes,

> I go on with Bion . . . histoire d'elan acquis [just a matter of momen-tum]. I see no reason why it should ever come to an end. The old heart pounces now & then, as though to console me for the intolerable symptoms of an improvement. Mother writes, she supposes I am brimming over with material for books . . . anything rather than desoeuvrement [having nothing to do, idleness]. (TM, 3 March 1935)

Increasingly, Beckett's interests external to psychotherapy turned towards both Geoffrey Thompson and the suffering of his psychotic patients. Very much in the tradition of psychological change described by Beckett in Proust, Ferenczi describes psychological adaptation as a progressive falling-apart, or splitting of older adaptations, under the pressure of the external environment. He noted that future psychological adaptation is preceded by a period of dissolving autonomy for "patients who fly from their own sufferings and have become hypersensitive to all kinds of extraneous suffering". Ferenczi wonders if, with earlier consolidations falling apart within psychoanalysis "whether these extreme, quasi-pulverized elements which have been reduced to mere psychic energies do not also contain tendencies for reconstruction of the ego" (Ferenczi, 1930, p. 220).

Ferenczi's question parallels Beckett's own fears in Proust. What happens to an individual in transit from moment 1 to moment 2, as he loses one context for another? For Beckett, the possibility that indifference, meaninglessness, was potential in every moment was frightening. This is the "desouevrement" in his letter to MacGreevy, a lack of interest, a state of anomie. Habit and ritual provide security, but too much habit results in stasis. Beckett's correspondence reflects that Bion's presence was becoming internalised, as reflected in Beckett's dreams, and that at the same time Beckett was beginning to experience a deep and frightening sense of aloneness. It is probable that Hadfieldian method had no way to contain this sense of fragmentation. In the meantime, Beckett was growing impatient and grumpy, hence, his first direct reference in correspondence to disillusionment with Bion: "The thought of venturing forth into the cold world in the evening is intolerable. I feel I must squabble with Bion, & so I do. On Monday I go for the 133d time" (TM, 8 February 1935).

As with Ferenczi's patients, Beckett would look outward to consolidate ego reconstruction. Stabilised by the security generated within his work with Bion, of an intellectualised rationale for his suffering (letter to MacGreevy, 10 March 1935), he would also attempt to understand the sufferings of others. This research, productively channelled, would eventuate in his first novel, *Murphy*. Notable in Beckett's correspondence to MacGreevy of 20 February 1935 is his mother's interest in Beckett's gathering information for writing. Together with the fact of May's economic support of Beckett's therapy, this is Beckett's first indication in his correspondence of her support for his hard-won self-definition as writer.

Initially, Beckett was disappointed in his excitement about Thompson's new availability. In contrast to Beckett's very open schedule, Thompson was very busy. Indeed, Beckett seemed jealous about Thompson's attention to his fiancée, Ursula Stenhouse. In mid-February, he told MacGreevy, "I have seen very little of Geoffrey. He has no time to spare, between the detainees at Bethlem, Hadfield, & Miss What is her name, and I have seen nothing of him" (TM, 14 February 1935). However, a week later, bored in his museum wanderings and with the slow slog of therapy, Beckett brightens at the hope of visiting Thompson at Bethlem the following Sunday (TM, 20 February 1935). Two weeks later, he reports glowingly on Thompson's progress:

> I spent an evening with Geoffrey and to-day I am going down to Eden Park to spend afternoon & evening. He is in excellent form and is now attached to the outpatients psychological department at Bart's, so that he can proceed to little analyses on his own! (TM, 10 March 1935)

Gradually, Beckett reconciles himself to Thompson's engagement, writing understandingly to MacGreevy on 5 May that Thompson has not contacted him because he is in love, "c'est l'amour".

There is no record of further correspondence either about Bion or Thompson until 22 September 1935, but in this period, two events of major significance to Beckett occur. During the last week of July, he travelled, alone with his mother, throughout England, with stops at Porlock Weir, Stratford, Wells, Lynmouth, Winchester, Bath, Gloucester, and Rugby. Throughout, Beckett remained asymptomatic. It is almost as if the twenty-nine-year-old has devised a way to test or examine the efficacy of his work with Bion. Asymptomatic survival during extended contact with May Beckett might have suggested itself to Beckett as a sign that therapy had successfully accomplished its task. Remarkably, he, or they, passed!

Then, in late summer, Beckett visited Thompson on the wards at Bethlem. He writes to MacGreevy, "I was down at Bedlam this day week & went round the wards for the first time, with scarcely any sense of horror, though I saw everything from mild depression to profound dementia" (TM, 22 September 1935)

The trip, congruent with his mother's encouragement earlier that year, was devoted to information gathering for a book he had begun, which would become *Murphy*. So far, he was having the same creative pains familiar from his composition of *Proust*: "I have been forcing myself to keep at the book, & it crawls forward. I have done about 9000 words. It is poor stuff & I have no interest in it" (TM, 22 September 1935).

Additionally, Beckett tells MacGreevy that he has been asked to witness the register office recording of Geoffrey Thompson's 2nd November marriage in Dorset. The letter suggests that Beckett's life is full of productive activity. Although we have no record of what was going on in psychotherapy, it seems likely that Beckett's reports to Bion were similarly positive. Only a few breezy lines suggest that something unusual might be occurring in the consulting room. Referring back to his symptoms, Beckett writes,

> The intestinal pains are worse than they have been so far. Bion is not interested. Geoffrey checks a smile. I feel absolutely certain that I will get no further with analysis than I have done, that from now on it is money thrown away. Yet I have not the courage to call it off. I also feel certain that there is something wrong with my guts, yet I have not the courage to consult a doctor on my own. Where one is as devoid of courage as I am there seems to be nothing more to be said or done. (TM, 22 September 1935)

Quietly, and only to MacGreevy, Beckett drops the hint of a bomb. Something has changed in his relations to Bion and Thompson. Each receives similar authoritative credit for attending to his ills. It is as if his transference has become divided between his long-time friend and his analyst, each related through their institutional and personal affiliations at the Tavistock. We have no record of whether Beckett discussed this issue with them—probably not. Certainly, in his 1976 RTE interview reminiscing about his relationship with Beckett, Thompson gives no indication that his renewed friendship with Beckett, while he was in psychiatric training, was in any sense unusual (Thompson, 1976). It is probably that neither Thompson nor Bion recognised the effect of this new relationship on Beckett's psychotherapy.

Indeed, Thompson provides interesting biographical information, missing from other Beckett scholarship. Three points are of particular relevance in consideration of Beckett's psychotherapy. The first concerns Beckett's ward visits at Bethlem. Beckett, according to Thompson, visited patients on the wards at Bethlem not once, but numerous times. While Beckett, late in life, remembers the patient upon whom he modelled Mr Endon, in Murphy (Knowlson & Knowlson, 2006, p. 69), Thompson remembers someone else in whom Beckett took particular interest. Thompson suggests that the patient, a young psychotic man, profoundly attached to his mother, reminded Beckett of his own struggles. The young man, legs extended and balanced on his boot heels, waited for a mother who would never come. She had given her son new boots with the paradoxical injunction not to wear them out by walking. And so the dutiful boy sat, clothed in a long great-coat, with heavy boots, prepared for a walk finally allowed by his mother. Thompson describes his condition as "absolutely fixed, and could move no further".

Listening to Thompson's radio interview and aware that Beckett's own mother had just recently approved her son's literary vocation, one can imagine Beckett's relief at his own release. Identifying with the young man, he must have recognised that despite the pain of his own condition, the inaccessible profundity of the psychotic's pain was at the level of permanent paralysis. Not so his own. He could go on. And so he must, just as that night seventeen years ago, when his father raised him up from collapse on the Foxrock road (Knowlson, 1996, p. 51).

If, as Beckett had affirmed in March, he was "invalid from the word go", then, viewing that young man with Thompson at Bethlem, he knew for certain his could and must be a productive invalidity. The young man waited for a mother who would never come; his situation was different. Not only had Sam's mother finally given her assent, but there was always someone, somehow—whether his father Bill, MacGreevy, Bion, or Thompson—who extended a supportive hand with the possibility of forward movement. Inside, there would always be another who

> Hand in hand with equal plod they go. In the free hands – no, Free empty hands. Backs turned both bowed with equal plod they go. The child hand raised to reach the holding hand. Hold and be held. Plod on and never recede ... Black greatcoats to heels. Dim black. Bootheels. Now the two right, Now the two left ... (Beckett, 1996, pp. 93–99)

Beckett, with the non-critical and containing support of Geoffrey Thompson, recognised his own obsessional and schizoid features as simply human (letter to Mary Manning Howe, 14 November 1936). If permanent, they were not immobilising, as were the ailments of the young man in greatcoat and boots at Bethlem. It would be Beckett's work "to turn this dereliction, profoundly felt, into literature" (Knowlson, 1996, p. 235).

Rather casually in the RTE interview, Thompson also remarks, "we used to go to lectures and things together," citing two lectures in particular. One was a lecture by the founder of British psychoanalysis, Ernest Jones. Beckett must have revelled in this meeting. He was deeply interested in Jones' guidebook to physicians, *The Treatment of the Neuroses* (Feldman, 2006). Indeed, this book alone might be read as a primer to the understanding of future Beckett characters. Jones vividly portrays the internal derangement of the neurotic mind, torn in conflict. Jones' neurotic sufferer yearns for a moment of peace, apart from the incessant presence of incomprehensible internal forces. The neurotic is always poised on the edge of the unknown, terrified of the possibility of a new and hideous internal visitation, either of old symptoms or something different.

Interpersonally, Jones' neurotic battles with society. However oblivious of his behaviour, neurosis remains his preciously defended amulet, and, through it, the neurotic has warrant to provoke distress in those nearest and closest to him (Jones, 1963, pp. 7–8). Intra-psychically, Jones details the dynamics of internalisation, the way that the neurotic takes in the external world according to his own lights, and projects his internal world, riven with hatred, upon others as transference.

The modern reader can imagine the young writer Beckett's resonance in his discovery of Jones. Certainly, while providing a window of intellectual understanding about Beckett's own condition, Jones would be interesting enough. But far more important is Jones' vivid portrayal of the psychoneurotic as a character in the modern world. Jones provides a generalised, coherent model, in his "hysteric", of a psychoneurotic world view, a recognisable preconception of Beckett's future characters.

Beckett's gratitude to Jones emerges in *The Unnamable*. It is anchored in the context of the narrator's finding his own voice, distinct from the interpretative intrusions of his psychoanalytic auditor, Mahood, or Basil. It is perhaps the most profound moment in the "trilogy" from the psychoanalytic perspective of working through resistance. The narrator plays joyfully with his analyst—a demonstration from Beckett's pen of what future analysts, following Winnnicott, will term the "transitional space" of psychoanalytic action. The narrator keeps changing the analyst's name until finally he hits upon "Jones". He reverses himself, giddily asking the addressed auditor to make him stop associating. The intended wink hearkens back to British psychoanalytic politics of the 1930s, with disagreements between Bion's Tavistock and Jones' British Psychoanalytical Society. Clearly, moving from Bion to Basil to Mahood to Worm can be thought of as falling within the scope of play, but proceeding to Jones seems to be pushing the envelope. Little did Beckett know that his own Bion would become a member of the British Psychoanalytical Society at roughly the same time as the publication of the "trilogy", hence joining Jones!

Following Beckett's attendance at a Jones lecture, Thompson's next invitation to Beckett was to hear Carl Gustave Jung. Thinking back during his 1976 interview, Thompson remembered the tone of Jung's voice and recalled Jung's now-famous comments about a young girl who died, never having been psychologically born. He remembered how Beckett was moved by this comment, speaking often about it.

Thompson's comments add to biographical understanding of Beckett during this period. While his psychological notebooks were largely filled with detail from Ernest Jones' papers, there is no biographical indication of Beckett's having attended a Jones lecture. It is probable, too, especially given the playful aside in the "trilogy", that Beckett was aware of institutional differences, and discussed the lecture in therapy with Bion. By this time in therapy, with what must have seemed a consolidation of the patient's self-awareness of his own condition, together with the addition of his broadening psychiatric interests aimed at composing a new novel, Bion was probably very approving of Beckett's attendance.

In the context of this series of events and relationships, Beckett's otherwise enigmatic reference to Bion's singular social invitation to dinner and Jung's lecture begins to become intelligible. Beckett mentions the event in a letter to MacGreevy on 8 October 1935, where he discusses the event just as he later discusses his landlady's row "which never stops" with his upstairs neighbours. What is so remarkable is that there seems to be nothing unusual in this event, which would certainly change the nature of the psychoanalytic transference in therapy. But what if Bion, following Hadfieldian technique, was only loosely attending to transference? And what if, in any case, Beckett's "use" of Thompson was widening his field of therapeutic transference objects, anyway?

The intestinal pain Beckett refers to above, in connection with a gutless resolve to conclude his psychotherapy, is, after all, though formally addressed to MacGreevy, more fundamentally addressed to both Thompson and Bion. Beckett writes, "Bion is not interested. Geoffrey checks a smile", as if Bion and Thompson have adjoining chairs in the consulting room. If the therapy was drawing to a close, it was largely because Bion was tolerant of Beckett's rather extravagant enlargement of transference. A more experienced therapist than Bion was at that moment might have interpreted the incorporation of Thompson and allowed the therapy to continue.

Beckett's attendance at the Jung lecture is cited in passing, within his correspondence. Because there seems to be no anticipation, it must not have surfaced as a significant event in psychoanalytic psychotherapy. Thanks to Geoffrey Thompson's radio interview, a possible course of events related to what, today, would be a major "boundary crossing" (Gutheil & Gabbard, 1993) in psychotherapy becomes more intelligible. Because Thompson does not mention Bion's attendance at the event, it is possible that Thompson invited Beckett first—just as he had taken Beckett to the Jones lecture.

After all, Beckett was a close friend, deeply interested in psycho-analysis, and there seemed, from their extra-therapeutic relationship, to be no censure either from Hadfield to Thompson or from Bion to Beckett about their deepening friendship.

Bion's prominent attendance at the earlier two Jung lectures is discussed in Chapter Five, and it might be assumed that, knowing of Beckett's interest in going, the probability of his going with Thompson, and the wish to showcase his own institution in relation to the British Psychoanalytical Society, Bion wished to fold this extra-curricular outing back into the therapy. Certainly, this is what Beckett reports to MacGreevy when he writes apprehensively, "I hope he [Bion] hasn't done us both a disservice by inviting me to meet him in that way" (TM, 8 October 1935). Given Beckett's comprehensive read-ing in psychoanalysis, it might be that he was more concerned than Bion about the unusual nature of this technical breach.

Attendance at the Jung lecture was an interpersonal event bring-ing together both the institutional social system at the Tavistock and Beckett's two significant auditors, Bion and Thompson and their supe-riors. Beckett not only saw Jung, but also the great Hadfield, whose training was at that time significant both to Bion and Thompson. Not only was Jung's anecdote about the little girl meaningful to Beckett, but also, fitting a capstone upon the work of his psychotherapy, was another Jungian comment.

To that date, Beckett had recognised with Bion that the early roots of his distress must be lived with, even if not fully mastered. During their work together, endorsed through financing by Beckett's mother, May, Beckett's mother had also endorsed her son's vocation as a writer. Also, visiting with Thompson, the man who had initially referred Beckett to psychotherapy, Beckett was able to differentiate his own ability to create from the frozen, immobilised plight of the psychotic. Even if panic had caused him to feel crazy, he was not. Finally, Jung's comments would endorse his creative use of himself:

> Complexes are autonomous groups of associations that have a tendency to move by themselves, to live their own life apart from our intentions . . . the poet has the capacity to dramatize and personify his mental contents. When he creates a character on stage, or in his poem or drama or novel, he thinks it is merely a product of his imagination; but that character in a certain secret way has made itself. Any novel-ist or writer will deny that these characters have a psychological

meaning, but as a matter of fact you know as well as I do that they have one. Therefore you can read a writer's mind when you study the characters he creates. (Jung, 1968, p. 81)

Associations themselves, the very stuff of Beckett's psychoanalysis with Bion, might be understood as giving expression to discrete characters. It would be several years until Beckett would experiment with this concept, affirming it in *The Unnamable*:

> All these Murphys, Molloys and Malones do not fool me. They have made me waste my time, suffer for nothing, speak of them when, in order to stop speaking, I should have spoken of me and of me alone. But I just said I have spoken of me, am speaking of me . . . They never suffered my pains, their pains are nothing, compared to mine, a mere tittle of mine, the tittle I thought I could put from me, in order to witness it. (Beckett, 2006b, p. 297)

The rest of the year was anticlimactic. Beckett attended the Thompsons' wedding. Psychotherapeutic termination was scheduled for the end of December. Bion would send his last bill to May, in Dublin, in early January. By then, Beckett, whose own claustrophobic state of mind, which his friend Thompson referred to as "shut in a small space" (Thompson, 1976) had begun to relapse, as is common with such individuals who have prematurely exited therapy, but this recognition within psychoanalysis would develop only after the contributions, many years later, of the mature Bion (Meltzer, 1992). In that moment, early in 1936, Beckett, in Dublin, was again symptomatic and angry with Bion. He wrote to MacGreevy that

> Bion in his last acknowledgement of the filthy "trusted I had by now taken up with my work with pleasure and satisfaction", as he was sure I must, "even though not entirely freed from neuroses"! Mother's whole idea of course is to get me committed to life here. And my travel-courage is so gone that the collapse is more than likely. I find myself more than ever frightened by the prospect of effort, initiative, & even the little self-assertion of getting about from one place to another. Solitude here, more sober than before, seems the upshot of the London Torture. Indeed I do not see what difference the analysis has made. (TM, 16 January 1936)

Reading Beckett's correspondence, the word torture stands out in relation to his work with Bion. During this period, Beckett only alludes to torture one other time in his correspondence, and it is in direct relation to his articulation of his mother's "savage loving", almost two years after the completion of psychotherapy (TM, 6 October 1937). Beckett himself becomes aware of the potentially crippling consequences of continued residence with May, hastening his final departure from Dublin to Paris. Might the two "tortures" be related? Might the "torture" of London, with Bion, itself refer to a negative, maternal transference, never fully articulated? Certainly, it was buttressed, and possibly muted, by his supportive, positive use of another transference object, Geoffrey Thompson.

During the next nine months in Dublin, Beckett finished *Murphy*, conducted a sexual affair, and left Ireland and his mother, as he had often in the past when Peggy and the Sinclairs lived there, for Germany and, finally, Paris.

Beckett would continue to keep tabs on Bion through his contacts with Thompson. Writing from Berlin in December 1936, Beckett tells MacGreevy that he has sent Bion a Christmas card. He also comments on the relationship between Bion and Thompson who

> is well dug in in Harley Street, with more patients than he can manage. Bion is his "supervisor" in the clinic, does me the honour to remember me, deprecates my untimely departure, just when I was all set to become the uomo universal, & looks forward to getting his hooks into me again. Quien sabe! (TM, 22 December 1936)

This is a remarkable letter in that it brings together Beckett's two psychoanalytic mentors, Thompson and Bion, in their later professional relationship. Beckett also represents Thompson as conveying Bion's message of hope that psychotherapy might continue again!

Still later—in the summer of 1938, Beckett writes to MacGreevy about Bion and Thompson, reporting that, on a trip to London, Beckett "had lunch with Geoffrey & Ursula on the way through. He is working from 8AM to 10PM, with short intervals to snatch food and complains of poverty. He & Bion take piano lessons" (TM, 4 August 1938).

Thompson would function as Beckett's link to Bion for at least three years following psychotherapy. Somehow, during his second year of psychoanalysis, Beckett, probably without the awareness of either Bion or Thompson, expanded his therapeutic field from a dyad to a triad.

CHAPTER FIVE

Broadening the context of this psychotherapy

Today's reader of the Bion–Beckett psychotherapeutic relationship encounters Bion's direct voice only twice, each time during the discussion period following Jung's first and second Tavistock lecture (Jung, 1968). Bion is first heard in a follow-up question to Jung, related to Dr Henry Dicks' earlier question about affects and feelings. Jung describes an experiment participated in by Jung and a former professor at the Clinic. Knowing his colleague well, Jung enquired about a case he believed to be "hellishly disagreeable" to his chief. The immediate response was a "deluge of emotion", disturbing what had, moments before, been his chief's calm management of feeling. Following two questions by Dr Eric Howe, Wilfred Bion asks,

> Do you think there is any significance in the fact that he knew you knew of the unpleasant experience in the second experiment and that this had some bearing on the difference of emotional reaction which he showed . . .? (Jung, 1968, p. 30)

The second time we hear Bion's voice is during the discussion session following Jung's second lecture. Here, the context is somewhat different. Jung himself is on edge, and participations by Drs Eric

Howe, Eric Strauss, and Ian Suttie further provoke his defensiveness. Throughout the lectures, there is tension in the air as Jung contrasts Freud's technique unfavourably with his own. Just the evening before, Jung's earlier lecture had concluded with reference to a *pechvogel*, a German synonym for the Yiddish *schlemiel*, the unknowing fool (Jung, 1968, p. 23), and also a prominent character in Freud's *Jokes and their Relation to the Unconscious* (Freud, 1905c). That the *pechvogel* cannot help himself as he bumbles through the world might well have been demonstrated by Jung himself. Addressing an audience of British physicians, most employed by the Tavistock, an institution founded in the study of post-trauma stress following the First World War, Jung's reference might well have sounded like sabre rattling, just days after the passage in Germany of the Reich's only two laws, the anti-Semitic Nuremberg laws in September 1935.

Bion then rather artfully intervenes in the increasingly tetchy discussion with a question linking Jung with the esteemed *British Medical Journal*, a manoeuvre that subtly reminds one and all of the invited guest's status and claims on their respect. The intervention allows Jung to regroup and to proceed to his conclusion (Jung, 1968, p.72).

Each of Bion's comments reflects not only his sensitivity to the relation between individuals, both dyadically and in a group setting, but, more profoundly, to his understanding of the strength of unspoken communication, never explicitly articulated. Bion's question about the heightened response of an individual to another who knows of his difficulty is directly applicable to the relation between patient and therapist invested together in therapy. Here, the heightening of the patient's emotional response beyond the placid indication of neutral feeling is a function of implicit knowledge and trust in the therapist's knowing the patient. The second intervention reflects both a profound sensitivity to maintaining the "work group" and decorum of the meeting, as well as Bion's keen capacity to signal his intentions powerfully, if laconically.

Following Bion's second comment, Jung moves towards a conclusion by citing the example of his friend and analysand, William McDougall, the American psychiatrist. What Jung does not need to say at the Tavistock is that McDougall was also the mentor of J. A. Hadfield, who had both organised the Jung lectures and who had functioned as training director and mentor to Tavistock's

"Hadfieldians", like Bion. Yet, Jung's somewhat mystifying vignette might also be taken as a compliment to the subtle artistry in his recent rescue by Bion. Jung says,

> People may say: What a fool to say causality is only relative! But look at modern physics! The East bases its thinking and its evaluation of facts on another principle. We have not even a word for that principle. The East naturally has a word for it, but we do not understand it. The Eastern word is Tao. My friend McDougall has a Chinese student, and he asked him: "What exactly do you mean by Tao?" Typically Western! The Chinese explained what Tao is and he replied: 'I do not understand yet'. The Chinese went out to the balcony and said: 'What do you see?' 'I see a street and houses and people walking and tramcars passing.' 'What more?' 'There is a hill.' 'What more?" The wind is blowing.' The Chinese threw up his arms and said: 'That is Tao'. (Jung, 1968, p. 76)

Jung links Tao to his concept of synchronicity, as "being together and coming together at the right moment". Yet, for that moment, in that second Tavistock lecture, Jung's reference was not abstract, but concrete praise for Bion, who had rescued the evening. Bion's intervention had restored the balance and rightness of the moment without drawing attention to itself.

It is possible that Bion's recognition of this moment of great political capital within the psychiatric training hierarchy at the Tavistock was instrumental in his decision to invite his patient, Samuel Beckett, to Jung's next lecture the following night. Despite the irregularity of inviting a patient to a social event, especially in regard to the transference as a technical dimension of psychotherapy, it is probable that this would not have caused a stir. First, Bion's institutional stature in relation to Hadfield was strengthened after his strong intervention following lecture two. Second, Hadfield himself had rejected the significance of transference. Henry Dicks writes that Hadfield's "more discerning" trainees themselves—including Dicks, Bion, and Geoffrey Thompson—had criticised Hadfield's

> deliberate and reasoned rejection of the significance of the transference. Not that he failed to observe it; but he did not evaluate it in the same way as the psychoanalysts. To him it was a transient phenomenon in the uncovering of infantile behavior and material. (Dicks, 1970, p. 67)

Dicks continues, writing that Hadfield's own transference technique, in practice, was "to push it as soon as possible away from himself". Because of his continuous attempt to escape transference, Hadfield's "reductive analysis" technique corresponded to a repetitive procedure of what Dicks calls "forced fantasy", centring upon singular incidents in the patient's life and lending " a certain unreality and artificiality to the procedure". Numerous Hadfieldians, including Dicks, Bion, and Geoffrey Thompson, formed a "rebel" group that would go on to formal training at the Institute of Psychoanalysis (Dicks, 1970, p. 68). Bion would later train with John Rickman, whose own analytic experiences had been with Freud, Ferenczi, and Klein, before Bion initiated a second analysis with Klein, herself.

Bion's two recorded comments at the Jung lectures suggest his own exquisite sensitivity to what is said and unsaid but communicated between people, as well as the centrality of such process within psychotherapy. As a member of Tavistock's rebellious Hadfieldians, Bion's interest in the dynamics of transference were probably in alignment with the psychoanalytic *zeitgeist* in London, recognising an increasing centrality of transference within the psychoanalytic relationship. Some months before the initiation of Bion's work with Beckett, in June 1933, James Strachey had delivered a lecture to the British Psychoanalytical Society that was published in 1934 under the title, "The nature of the therapeutic action of psychoanalysis". Tracing the history of psychoanalytic technique from Freud's "'Technical' papers" and the 27th–28th chapters of his *Introductory Lectures on Psycho-analysis* to Freud's recently published *New Introductory Lectures*, which were also studied by Bion's patient, Beckett, Strachey's paper announced a watershed moment in psychoanalysis impossible for an engaged practitioner to miss. On one side of this theoretical divide was an earlier version of psychoanalysis with which Hadfieldian reductive analysis might coexist. Here, symptom remission followed a post-hypnotic form pioneered by Freud, with the authority of the analyst's interpretative suggestion to the patient understood as the motor of change. On the other side was a deepened understanding of the patient's transference, with direct experience in the present relationship between patient and analyst, the fulcrum of change.

Minimally, Strachey's argument would signal the centrality within psychoanalysis of how thinking works: how the individual's construction of reality and fantasy operates in the therapeutic relationship and how it becomes modified in the process of this dynamic engagement. Bion's participations at the Tavistock, especially his question following Jung's first lecture, suggest that such considerations might be in his thoughts, or, if not within his thoughts, then not far off.

Strachey's treatment of psychoanalysis's technical challenges provides today's reader with a contemporary anchorage, *ca.* 1933–1934, in the thinking of mainstream British psychoanalysis. For Bion, Strachey's endorsement of transference as the pivotal tool in clinical psychoanalysis probably reinforced his resistance to Hadfield's method as misguided. Yet, given the contemporary absence of conclusive thinking about analytic technique described by Strachey, it is likely that Bion shared "occasional feelings of utter disorientation which few analysts are fortunate to escape" (Strachey, 1934).

Still, despite the uncertainties of the therapeutic process, it is probable that Bion's own personal experiences of the inability to think, sustained during traumatic combat experience in the First World War, paralleled Beckett's own experience of incoherence when gripped by panic (Souter, 2009). Bion's own capacity for identification and empathy with his patient, as well as his own historical acquaintance with such moments of incoherence, later discussed in "Making the best of a bad job" (Bion, 1987), might have grounded Bion's amelioration of Strachey's "utter disorientation". Bion writes,

> I can recall an experience in which a patient was anxious to arouse powerful emotions in me so that I would feel angry, frustrated, disappointed, so that I would not be able to think clearly. I therefore had to choose between 'appearing' to remain calm and clear-thinking. But acting a part is incompatible with being sincere. In such a situation the analyst is attempting to bring to bear a state of mind, and indeed, an inspiration, of a kind that would in his opinion be beneficial and an improvement on the patient's existing state of mind. That interference can be resented by the patient whose retort can be to arouse powerful feelings in the analyst and to make it difficult for the analyst to think clearly.

Bion continues,

> In war the enemy's object is so to terrify you that you cannot think clearly, while your object is to continue to think clearly no matter how adverse or frightening the situation. The underlying idea is that

thinking clearly is more conducive to being aware of 'reality', to assessing properly what is real. But being aware of reality may involve being aware of the unpleasant because reality is not necessarily pleasing or welcome. (Bion, 1987, p. 323)

Bion's mature "opinion" was that clear thought and its modelling, despite the terrors of ongoing reality, was an improvement upon the aversive and frightening. It is likely that such internal fortitude allowed him to weather the difficulties of his engagements within the emotional storms of psychotherapy.

Perhaps Bion's own experiences also underlay his first question to Jung about two individuals' reciprocal knowledge, echoing awareness of his own resonance with another's anxiety.

Some of the uncertainty in then-contemporary treatment was due to a radical transformation both in the clinical presentation of patients and in the widening scope of psychoanalysis, as it expanded both to the treatment of children and to addressing distress beyond the original "neurotic" range of Freud's original hypnotic treatment—including psychotic presentations and to those of character disorder (A. Freud, 1936; Gray, 1994; Reich, 1928). In time, this would also apply to thinking about diagnosis. Both Bion's own therapy with Hadfield and Beckett's work with Bion, for example, while probably approached as the "neurotic" presentation of anxiety disorder by Hadfield and Bion, would, because of their narcissistic and schizoid attributes, later be characterised as character disorders, alerting the therapist to a more challenging clinical presentation than that contemplated by Strachey. From within the context of late twentieth-century psychoanalysis, the question of "therapeutic action" itself widens according to the psychology of the patient, as well as that of the analyst. Gray writes that "The therapeutic action in the analytic treatment of this spectrum of patients varies not only with the particular methodology applied, but also with the psychological nature of the analysand" (Gray, 1994, p. 89).

However, as he was not yet conversant in a language of potential therapeutic roadmaps, including the participatory actions and thoughts of both patient and analyst, Strachey's original contribution would have seemed a welcome beacon in the psychoanalytic darkness. As Kris later describes a discrete patient's insight, the same applies to the development of psychoanalytic theory, "much or most of analytic therapy is carried out in darkness, with here and there a flash of insight to lighten the path" (Kris, 1956, p. 452).

Refracted through the mature Bion's interests in linked thoughts, Strachey's paper must have presented a fascinating authorisation for analysts to think about thinking. At its core is the difference between a patient's acceptance or non-acceptance of the therapist's suggestion—meant to resolve symptomatic presentation—and the patient's resolution of symptomatic distress through the facilitation of his self-examination in relation to the analyst. Additionally, as Strachey points out, even given the patient's intellectual acceptance of the analyst's suggestions, under this technique, derived from Freud's original post-hypnotic treatments, there was no assurance of symptom remission.

Bion, through his own experience in Hadfield's suggestive treatment, knew the problem first hand, as well as the resistance that a patient might present to an analyst's intrusive enquiry. Indeed, to the end of his life, Bion would ridicule J. A. Hadfield's analytic technique as "Mr Feel It in the Past". This reflected Hadfield's somewhat clumsy attempt to have his patient resonate with the past origins of contemporary distress in the analyst's presence (Bléandonu, 1994, p. 41; Dicks, 1970, pp. 67–68). That this symptom-focused orientation of reductive analysis resulted in the heightening of Bion's resistance to the analyst was, therefore, a conscious experiential memory for Bion during his analysis of Beckett. Derived from Bion's first therapeutic experience, though nowhere stated or even formulated, Bion's question to Jung seems to ask, how does one person employ language and action in the presence of another that attempts to communicate knowledge of both the pain and the richness embedded in the other's thought and feeling?

Despite the technical inefficiency of this early model, it reflected a conceptual and easily understandable clarity, consonant with Freud's theory about both dream formation and jokes. The symptom was understood to function both in protection of the personality from an unacceptable trend in thought and, at the same time, partially gratifying that trend. Just as in the construction of dreams and jokes, the symptom represents a compromise that both allows and disallows the repressed thought into consciousness.

The benefit of this compromise for psychotherapy, as Strachey notes, is that both the unconscious trend and the personality's defensive operation against the trend operate within reach of consciousness.

Rather than functioning structurally within an inaccessible deep unconscious, these operations occur within the sphere of the ego, where emergence into consciousness is possible. Given this situation, the analyst's technical task is to make the patient aware of the unconscious trend.

Given his dissatisfaction with Hadfield's reductive analysis and the technique of locating symptomatic roots in past feeling, experienced in session, Bion must have wondered how to facilitate the linkage of these two thought-related fragments when solution was defended against by the very psychological process that enforced the separation. Strachey certainly wondered about this problem, and located a partial answer within the transference relationship as a vehicle of psychoanalytic success.

The outside observer of psychoanalysis might miss Strachey's radical innovation. The action, after all, appears from the outside to be the same: the patient's symptom, representing both gratification and defence against an unconscious trend, is addressed by the analyst through suggestion or interpretation. Strachey notes the general observation that, with the development of transference love, symptoms deflate within the therapeutic relationship as psychic conflict underlying the symptom—the unconscious trend and its defence—takes form in the interpersonal engagement of patient and analyst. What shifts is the model of how all this works. While Freud emphasises the importance of transference love in transforming the field of patient distress from the symptom experienced extra-therapeutically to a new manifestation shaped within the treatment relationship, Freud's notion remained that the analyst must intuit the unconscious trend; even doing this effectively risks failure when despite intellectual appreciation of the situation, the patient's situation does not change. The result, as in reductive analysis, was hit or miss.

Under Strachey's new understanding, the dynamics of the transference relationship are based in the patient's internalisation of the therapist as an auxiliary superego. Based in Freud's development of thinking between his technical writing and the early 1930s, especially with relation to *Group Psychology and the Analysis of the Ego* (1921c), Strachey integrates Freud's developing thought about the superego with Klein's thinking about the continuous developmental progression of introjection and projection as the personality engages with the internal world in the shaping of it.

Understanding the continuous shifting of the patient's transference presentations from archaic, idealised images of both good and bad external objects, Strachey posits the patient's incremental acceptance (and internalisation) of the analyst's benign, or at least non-punitive, participation. Beckett hints at this kind of internalisation in his own case when he writes to MacGreevy that Bion has become a "dream habitué". It suggests the analyst's functional presence as a discrete object in the thinking of the patient.

With his integration of Klein's thinking, Strachey also expands the idea of transference love to transference hate, putting the full range of affective relations to the other within the range of therapeutic enquiry. With this expansion of Freudian thinking, Strachey moved mainstream psychoanalysis closer to Hadfield's triadic model of instincts in which Bion had trained, a broader understanding than Freud's. Here, Strachey's redefinition of therapeutic action must have resonated positively for Bion. According to Dicks,

> Hadfield had stressed that there was at least a triad of instincts—namely the sexual libido, aggression or self-assertion, and dependence, with its need for attachment behavior, which he regarded as the source of tenderness and infantile self-preservation. (Dicks, 1970, p. 67)

Bion was already aware not only of love and aggression, but also of the dependent attachment, which would one day be reflected in his own "basic assumption" groups, modelled after Hadfield's triadic understanding of instincts (Bion, 1961). For Bion, Strachey's redefinition might suggest that the wide variety of transference manifestations in the moment-to-moment unfolding of psychoanalysis would conform conceptually to Hadfield's expanded model of instincts.

Each of these attitudes, conceptually, would emerge from within the patient–therapist relationship in the context of the patient's expressions and the analyst's suggestive interpretations. This back and forth conforms, roughly, to the frontier of psychoanalysis described by Strachey. However, for Strachey, it is the analyst's skill in understanding the "mutative interpretation", that titration of patient-related material that the patient is able to internalise in disconfirmation of a distorted view of the therapist, conforming to an archaic model of relationship. The action of the therapist's mutative interpretation is to cause the patient to question himself—to wonder whether his own certain convictions about the other are correct. With the patient's focus on his own thinking, facilitated by the therapist, Strachey shifts psychoanalytic change from the hit-or-miss of a patient's willingness to accept the therapist's interpretative authority to the patient's own independent work of thinking, aided by the other.

Given Strachey's radical theoretical transformation and Bion's continuing work at the Tavistock under Hadfield, it is unlikely that he practised "mutative interpretation" with Beckett. Still, the shift described by Strachey was from the therapist's insistence to the patient, which potentially heightened the resistance, to the therapist's acceptance that central to the work was the patient's self-generated thinking in relation to the therapist. Analytic change begins in two movements. The first is the patient's questioning of his own certainty. This leads to the next advance, the recognition that his own preconceptions are inaccurate. Certainly, Beckett's transference to Bion was volatile. At times, he viewed Bion in the image of an archaic persecutor, as in his likening of therapy to the observation of confined zoo creatures, both immediately after the beginning of therapy and after its conclusion (NC, 27 February 1934; TM, 16 January 1936). Alternatively, Beckett would sometimes see Bion as a more benign presence, his "covey", in real time.

Strachey's therapeutic action paper aligned psychoanalytic theory with the conceptual metapsychology generated by Beckett in *Proust*. Therapeutic change is emergent in the breaking of habit relative to one's experience of another. Yet, habit is strong; it reasserts itself continuously, challenging the individual to continuous self-enquiry. Strachey's reorientation helped shift the patient's role in psychoanalytic practice from compliant acceptance of analytic authority to exploration of the give and take between analyst and patient.

The problem of invitation and its resolution

The problem in Bion's invitation to Beckett was twofold. Certainly, it would be welcomed within the momentary institutional politics of the Tavistock, given Bion's heroic intervention during Jung's second lecture. Second, what might now appear as a transference "boundary crossing" within mainstream psychoanalysis, and certainly within

Strachey's revision, would not have ruffled Hadfield at all. His own conception of transference was limited to exploration of discrete symptoms rather than to the patient's evolving, dynamic relationship with the therapist. Although unusual, Tavistock psychoanalysis arguably managed to skirt the boundaries of wild psychoanalysis in that it was directed to (1) the expansion of patient self-awareness through psychoanalytic experience, and (2) the prevention of heightened patient resistance to psychoanalytic technique (Freud, 1910). Yet, Bion, with one foot out of Hadfield's camp *en route* to the British Psychoanalytical Society, was certainly aware of the irregularity of the invitation in muddying the transferential field. Given his intellectual grounding in psychoanalytic theory, it is probable that Beckett, as patient, was also aware of this irregularity.

The invitation begins to make sense only in the context of a therapeutic endgame, two months before Beckett's unilateral termination of three times weekly treatment in December 1935.

Increasingly, during 1935, Beckett's psychological interests focused on the profoundly disturbed patients under Geoffrey Thompson's care. It is likely that, as with Beckett's readings in psychoanalytic subjects, Bion endorsed this fieldwork. Bion, soon *en route* himself to formal psychoanalytic training, was in a curious theoretical bind. His treatment of Beckett was combative—perhaps too difficult for its conduct under Hadfieldian "reductive analysis". While its primary action was centred in the transferential field between Beckett and Bion, it is likely that the conventional life and death battle of libido and destruction in the reductive transference was insufficient. In his letters, Beckett claimed the benefits of self-knowledge through the work, but his resistance was heightened as well, in his announcement of a Christmas termination, with its odd echo of the familiar triumphal declaration at the beginning of the First World War.

Thompson, himself beginning his Tavistock training, had already invited his friend, Beckett, to lectures of both Ernest Jones and Jung (Thompson, 1976). Given his own participations during Jung's prior lectures, one and two, Bion must surely have "heard" a theoretical perspective from Jung resonating deeply with the physical and emotional distress of his patient. It seems likely that because of Jung's discussion already functioning as a "third" for Bion, an external referent allowing him new observational clarity, the therapist was able to think more clearly about his patient.

Given Beckett's probable attendance at Jung's 2 October 1935 lecture together with Thompson, it is likely that Bion recognised an opportunity for deepening the transference relationship by extending to Beckett his own invitation, possibly even sweetening the deal with an invitation to a fish dinner at a traditional French bistro, the Etoile Restaurant on Charlotte Street.

Historical claims that the Bion–Beckett therapeutic relationship was "unusually friendly" mistake the magnitude of this event (Knowlson 1996, p. 170), and also misread the nature of the socialising. While socially mundane, this invitation was, in psychotherapeutic terms, an acting-out by an inexperienced psychotherapist attempting to counteract the difficulties, in treatment, of a challenging and awesomely gifted patient. In terms of Bion's later ideas about thinking, it might be seen as a last-ditch attempt to acknowledge the patient's feelings—to respond to them and damn the consequences.

Bion's invitation to his patient addressed two imperatives. It was virtually costless and, perhaps, an advantage, in terms of his standing within the Tavistock and his relationship with Hadfield, whom Bion had rescued from potential embarrassment during the question and answer period following Jung's lecture. While departing from psychoanalytic convention, the invitation to the patient might be argued to address the formation of a more dependent transference, in line with Hadfieldian doctrine. If successful, it would further reflect positively upon Bion's creativity within the Tavistock, where innovative differentiation from convention was encouraged (Dicks, 1970).

It also addressed Beckett, the patient. In this, the invitation was perhaps a replay of the former Major Bion's most heroic gamble, taking up another's weapons when his own were exhausted and continuing to fight, as he had done in the action for which he was recommended for the Victoria Cross (Bion, 1985). Within the field of transference, the invitation was potentially a violation of psychoanalytic boundary, surely having a later impact on the patient. Would it save the therapy, deepening it? At the very least, the patient would receive more informed thoughts about psychoanalysis—the thoughts of a great theorist as coda to a difficult treatment. At best, it might resonate with the patient in unpredictable ways.

The experiment seemed to work. We do not know what Bion and Beckett subjectively heard, discussed, or saw together at the lecture, but there are some indications. Beckett's own fragment of record, emerging twenty years later in the radio play *All That Fall*, comes in a moment of reflection when a character recalls a long distant psychologist's remarks about a child who died before ever having been born (Beckett, 2006c). This fictional recollection corresponds exactly to Jung's third lecture description of a ten-year-old with a vivid and extraordinary awareness, in dream-life, of deep, mythological archetypes. Jung had said, "she had never been born entirely" (Jung, 1968).

This formulation, of a child never completely born, was Beckett's own description of his own psychological condition (Bair, 1978). Although Beckett was characteristically contemptuous of Jung the evening after the lecture ("I can't imagine his curing a fly of neurosis"), and was left thinking that Jung's analytic psychology was " less than the dirt under Freud's nails" (TM, 8 October 1935), the experience of Jung's words left an impression still powerful twenty years later. While the same partial motif occurs earlier, in *Malone Dies*, its elaboration in *All That Fall* along the same lines as the Jung lecture suggests that the experience remained hauntingly "present" to Beckett for all that time. The same experience is further referenced later in Beckett's life, within the short play *Not I*, structuring the emergence of the unspoken but unconsciously registered as an ongoing, vital, living experience. Indeed, the motif of the barely born child can be seen as a sort of intermittent bass-line throughout his work, perhaps most startlingly rendered in *Waiting for Godot*: "They give birth astride a grave, the light gleams an instant, then it's night once more" (Beckett, 2006c, p. 82).

Bion's own presentation to the British Psychoanalytical Society, fifteen years later, of a patient much like Beckett but fifteen years older as he underwent psychoanalysis after a failed initial psychotherapy, mirrored the quality of Beckett's comments in their oscillation between contempt and favour. For Bion, this rhythmic dimension of the therapeutic experience as perceived by the therapist, reflected the patient's desire for interpersonal approach. Despite the patient's genuine disappointment at the therapist's incapacity to understand, "go on; it's your turn" also suggests a kind of gratitude in the relief of another's potential for understanding (Bion, 1967). This oscillation between disappointment and relief prefigures the movement between the paranoid–schizoid and depressive positions posited by Bion some thirty years later.

Bion's clinical case composite relates patient and therapist as "imaginary twins", and it is this twinship that is claimed by later psychoanalytic scholars to be the emotional–intellectual relation between Beckett and Bion (Anzieu, 1989; Simon, 1988). While capturing the rhythmic, non-verbal linkage between participants in deep relationship, the therapist's fantasy of the patient's phantasy of imaginary twinship mystifies the many simple and human interactions that formed the cornerstone of the Bion–Beckett relationship, culminating with a modification of therapeutic technique in October 1935.

The twinship itself emerges in the analyst's imagination and conforms to the shape of an internal object, very much at the cutting edge of theory building by Bion's analyst, Melanie Klein. Thinking back fifteen years to Beckett's own treatment focus upon multiple symptoms (of eyes, teeth, chest), the memory of Beckett's case conforms, too, to Klein's 1935 view of symptoms as internal objects. She writes,

> the patient complained about different physical troubles and then went on to say what medicines he had taken—enumerating what he had done for his chest, his throat, his nose, his ears, his intestines, etc. It sounded rather as if he were nursing these parts of his body and his organs. He went on to speak about his concern for some young people under his care (he is a teacher) and then about the worry he was feeling for some members of his family. It became quite clear that the different organs he was trying to cure were identified with his internalized brothers and sisters. (Klein, 1935, p. 159)

One of the purported twins, Samuel Beckett, opined caustically about mysticism itself. Of Jung, following the 2 October lecture, he wrote,

> He protests so vehemently that he is not a mystic that he must be one of the very most nebulous kind. Certainly he cannot keep the terminology out of his speech, but I suppose that is a difficulty for everyone. (TM, 8 October 8)

But, if the Bion–Beckett relationship was not mystical, what was it? Bion's "On arrogance" (1958), as well as "Attacks on linking" (1959), if related at all to Beckett (whether wholly or in part), suggest that, for Bion, it was hard work. Beckett's letters, sent to many of his friends during the course of his work with Bion, suggest the same thing. For example, Beckett's letter to his friend Thomas MacGreevy on 8 February 1935 finds him tired of his 133 sessions. He relates, "The thought of venturing forth into the cold world in the evening is intolerable. I feel I must squabble with Bion, & so I do".

Certainly, such therapeutic comments reflect a familiar set of patient transferences within psychotherapy as the patient struggles with both the intimacy of engagement and resistance to being known by another. Together with Beckett's capacity (reflected above in his comments about Jung) to vent his sharp opinion, this oscillation between intimacy and withdrawal might be paired with Bion's desire as a trainee therapist to understand, however inadequate that understanding might have felt in the patient's harsh judgement, and perhaps to be a loved therapist.

Their psychotherapeutic engagement linked Beckett, the Jungian unborn child, with Bion, the wounded warrior who had lost a sense of self in brutal combat, many years before their meeting (Souter, 2009). While Beckett's condition seems to have been more obstinately psychological and constitutional, growing directly out of infantile experience, Bion's is more clearly linked to life circumstances in later childhood, adolescence, and early manhood. Together with the circumstances under which Bion chose the profession of psychiatry, Bion's earlier experiences, perhaps more than his fledgling, pre-psychoanalytic steps in studying psychoanalysis, facilitated his ability to "lead" within his psychotherapy with Beckett, having earlier faced debilitating trauma and survived.

Bion's own creativity, therefore, was directed to the delicate balance in psychotherapy between the analyst's psychology and the patient's. His patient, benefiting from this creativity, was free to develop his own aesthetic creativity. It is possible that such freedom provided Bion with a jumping-off place for his own envy of Beckett's creativity. Late in life, Bion was to echo Beckett's theme of the "unborn baby" (Bion, 1990, p. 120), but for Bion, this referred to the realm of unrealised ideas. He would also attempt to write his final memoirs in a fashion suggestive of the late Joyce, whose *Finnegan's Wake* had served as an early apprenticeship for Beckett.

Bion's invitation to Beckett can be understood as a critical dynamic moment in their work together, unknowable theoretically but suggested through the contributions of Bion many years later. Systemically within the Tavistock, Bion's invitation served both to solidify his complicated relationship with his supervisor, mentor, and therapist, Hadfield, and to consolidate his own institutional position. Although departing from the rigorous treatment requirements of psycho-analysis, Bion's rebellion could be read as an innovative deviation from Hadfield's reduced understanding of transference, and, thus, justifiable theoretically, as the fostering of a "dependency" relationship—one of the three basic assumptions of group behaviour later developed by Bion. Within the therapy, Bion's introduction of Jung to Beckett provided each participant with a single point of reference upon which to focus in their mutual understanding of one another. Conceptually, to follow the later Bion, this enactment provided each with sufficient diminution of envious aggression and sexuality to appreciate their mutual contributions to one another: to "think", as Bion was later to put it. Indeed, to be heard fully, to be known, at least in one moment, was a successful takeaway for the patient, who wrote, several years later in the mufti of *Watt*, a loving coda of the best in therapy. Beckett, as writer, portrays this perfect attentional fantasy of one for the other near the conclusion of his novel, *Watt*, as Watt says goodbye to his partner, Sam. Watt wants Sam to know everything, to feel everything that goes on in his mind, and, in a singular and tender moment of impossibility, their parting, the object of everything is the putting on of a shoe. The narrator is Sam.

> But he could not bear that we should part, never to meet again (in this world) and I in ignorance of how Mr Knott put on his boots, or his shoes, or his slippers, or his boot and shoe, or his boot and slipper, or his shoe and slipper, when he did so, when he did not merely put on a boot, or a shoe, or a slipper. So, taking his hands from my shoulders, and laying them on my wrists, he told how Mr Knott, when he felt the time had come, taking on a cunning air would begin to sidle up to the boots, up to the shoes, up to the boot and shoe, up to the boot and slipper, up to the shoe and slipper, sidle sidle little by little with an artless air little by little nearer and nearer to where they lay, in the rack, till he was near enough, pouncing, to secure them. And then, while he put on the one, the black boot, the brown shoe, the black slipper, the brown boot, the black shoe, the brown slipper, on the one foot, he held the other tight, lest it should escape, or put it in his pocket, or put his foot upon it, or put in a drawer, or put it in his mouth, till he might put it on, on the other foot. (Beckett, 2006a, p. 343).

The passage is a tribute to the confidence of the patient in the reliability of what Bion was later to characterise as the container–contained relationship (Bion, 1963), even focusing at length upon the shoe and foot in perfect harmony.

Bion's heroic boundary violation served its purpose. Addressing an impasse, a bipersonal construction created by the unrecognised contributions both of therapist and patient, Bion's experiment facilitated the therapeutic couple's "joint ability to confront or make thinkable what is before them" (Ferro, 1993). In this sense, Bion's invitation might be understood as an activity attempting to continue psychotherapy in the face of Bion's inability to articulate as yet unformulated experience and Beckett's increasing desire for termination.

The therapist, at this stage of psychoanalytic history, lacked the conceptual tools to work with his erratic and gifted patient. Arguably, these would not be developed for some 30–50 years, with Donald Meltzer's work on the claustrum (Meltzer, 1992). Nevertheless, the patient is clearly left with a sense that the therapist is not afraid, will stay with him, and, above all, with a profound sense of what real mutuality might feel like.

CHAPTER SIX

Beckett's Bion and Bion's Bion

Who was Beckett's Bion? References in his correspondence range from the benign chumship of the "covey" to the perpetrator of the "London Torture". In time, aspects of Beckett's construction emerge in literary clarification from Basil's burning stare to the brotherly camaraderie of gunner (Beckett, 1995a, p. 112; 2006b, p. 292). Indeed, the oscillations of Beckett's expressive feeling in relation to both Bion and the psychoanalytic experience itself are highly reflective of different moments of transference.

Our reading of this particular therapeutic pairing suggests a powerful generative influence both for patient and therapist, although emergent at different moments of their long careers and in contexts far removed from the interpersonal intimacy of the consulting room. The full development for each exceeded a decade. Beckett's seemed to have been a continuous wrangling with transference, concluding in his postwar productions. Bion's gestation was longer, and is first artic-ulated in a Kleinian depiction of the therapist's meaningful engage-ment with a difficult patient, documented in his own membership presentation to the British Psycho-analytical Society some fifteen years after the conclusion of his work with Beckett. The sensitivity of Bion's presentation approaches the lyrical tenor of the intimacy described years earlier by Beckett, in *Watt*, in the depiction of Knott's bootlaces by Watt to Sam.

But behind Beckett's Bion and the Bion elaborated through his mature psychoanalytic writings, penned half-a-century and more into his life, there existed another Bion; the Bion who encountered the young writer Samuel Beckett, on referral from one of J. A. Hadfield's patients, Geoffrey Thompson. Who was he, behind an exterior of therapeutic "neutrality"? At the time Samuel Beckett first consulted Bion, the newly minted psychiatrist was nearing middle age, and had a very full and traumatic life behind him. Despite that, he seems to be in some ways barely starting out: just beginning a real career, unmarried, short of money, apparently still an apprentice.

Bion was born in India in 1897. He was one of the last generations of Anglo-Indian children who carried the memory of an early childhood in a hot, exotic landscape and culture back to a miserable English schooling during later childhood and adolescence. This peculiarly Edwardian experience has been represented in children's fiction, notably in Frances Hodgson Burnett's *The Secret Garden* (1910), and also via aspects of the life and work of Rudyard Kipling (Shengold, 1975). Bion's experience came a full generation after Kipling's abandonment in 1871, and was in significant ways less catastrophic than Kipling's. However, although Kipling's life experience was a generation earlier, the literary explorations and representations of childhood loss were exactly contemporaneous with Bion's experience: Kipling's *Jungle Stories* were published in 1894, just before Bion's birth, and he won the Nobel prize for literature while Bion was in the earlier years of his school exile; *The Secret Garden* was published a few years later.

Bion's Indian childhood came in the latter days of the Raj. It is difficult to get an objective take on what the experience might have been, overlaid as it is in his autobiographical writings by subsequent trauma and suffering. On the face of it, the childhood reads like an exotic version of the opening of Joyce's *Portrait of the Artist as a Young Man* (2003), and, indeed, seems to owe certain features to it: the memories of warmth and cold, the bewildering adult stories. He seems to have had a strong primary attachment to his *ayah* and a puzzled, irritated, but wary attitude to his parents. While Bion does not provide many details, it appears that he has had the typical experience of the Anglo-Indian child, who by the age of three or four ... had already picked up several languages—e.g., speaking to parents in English, to ayahs in Bengali, to servants in Hindustani, and to garden-coolies in Santali, in sharp contrast to their parents who had minimally succeeded in acquiring a sufficient grasp of Hindustani to be able to impart simple orders to house-servants. (Díaz de Chumaceiro, 2003)

Bion's descriptions of his infantile sexuality also seem to owe a little to the ayah's care: Chaudhuri (1988) describes how anxious Victorian mothers were made by their children picking up "Hindoo customs", and Bion provides fleeting glimpses of Indian child sexuality in the early pages of his memoir. All this came to an end when, at the age of eight, his mother made the long trip back to England with him, and left him in the cold and unfamiliar world of the British boarding school. His sufferings were severe, and like Rudyard Kipling before him, he seems to have adapted by developing a contempt for the people around him, who did not understand where he had come from. Much of his misery would have been the result of the loss of his family and his ayah, but some of his discomfort seems to have been what we might now call cross-cultural sexual confusion. His semi-public "wiggling", as he called his infantile masturbation, has him plunged in a cold bath by his parents in India, and threatens to have him expelled from school: he gives several examples of adult kindness in their disapproving responses, but it is clear that the extreme sexual furtiveness required by the English was not what he had learnt in India. Looking backwards, the account of himself as an unpleasant child seems to have been shaped by what came later: the loneliness at boarding school, the English dislike of his colonial indecencies, and his general inability to grasp the situation, what was happening, where the beautiful landscapes and weather had gone, why his parents had abandoned him (Bion, 1982). In retrospect, the idyllic and indulged Indian childhood is almost obliterated, no doubt also because it would have been so painful to remember from the chilly world of school. In its place is a cowardly, deceitful, stupid boy, who has to strive mightily to seem halfway normal: just the sort of boy, of course, whose parents would have abandoned him. When he did see his mother again, after three long years, almost half a lifetime for him at the time, he briefly failed to recognise her (F. Bion, 1995).

The memories of India, the jackals, tigers, monsoons, street sweepers, seem not unlike some of Kipling's accounts, but the grey damp of

English school life is represented as a flattened negativity, entirely without the charm of Burnett's Yorkshire landscapes: no dust, no hot sun, no monsoon rain,

> just a dirty . . . well *not* rain. Rain! Now *that* was something like—if only it *would* rain—like when you heard it coming, roaring and hiss- ing and moaning and sighing over the trees and the grass in the distance till suddenly—there it was! *That* was rain! *That* was sun! (Bion, 1982, p. 411)

The uncharacteristic numbers of italics in this passage enact the solidity of the lost India, and the "not" quality of England in the boy's imagination. Kipling describes his imaginative obliterations of the English foster-parents ("Kutch-nay, a Nothing-at-all", Shengold, 1989, p. 248); Bion describes most of the people who torture him as fright- ening, but it seems to be the landscape he represents as "Nothing-at- all". Perhaps overlaid by what came later, the grey dirty landscape of his first days in England seems to prefigure no-man's-land, chillingly. When he gets to spend Christmas at a friend's home, the landscape comes briefly to life, with ice, holly, mistletoe, as does the food, hot cocoa, freshly made bread and cake, porridge and cream, until return- ing to the featureless tea and toast of school.

Bion describes himself as eventually coming to terms with his new world, scarred and diminished, and with a newly stiffened upper lip. He did quite well at school, particularly by excelling at sport, but, as luck would have it, graduated just in time for service in the First World War. In an uncanny repetition of Rudyard Kipling's experience once more, Bion's father was horrified that his boy might not be accepted into the service, and pulled strings to ensure that he would be. The similarity is mercifully limited: Rudyard Kipling's seventeen- year-old son died horribly, devastating his parents with guilt and remorse (the boy's death seems never to have occurred to them as a possibility), but Bion survived. In fact, in narrative terms, the senior Bions "die", obliterated from the subsequent autobiographies. Bion's mother is last seen as the reason he is anxious to get back to the Front; the fast-forward to her death just before the next war. After serial betrayals, what forgiveness?

The years of abandoned endurance leave the boy relatively unresponsive, and the description of meeting up with his parents

immediately after leaving school is suffocatingly difficult to read, as
past and present swirl through the mind of the autobiographer:

> There breaks a yet more glorious day. And this—dark, sodden,
> sulphurous Liverpool Street—was *it*. Surely it *must* be a pool whose
> stench-borne waters close over one for ever. So like the shell-hole—no,
> no; not yet. That was later; or long ago; take your choice. (Bion, 1985,
> p. 104)

Although the sequence of events is hard to follow, the despair that
envelops him is extremely clear. The outbreak of war has drained the
last year of his schoolboy accomplishments of significance, and he
feels like a failure at the time of graduation. The journey back to meet
his parents in Russell Square becomes a deathly ordeal, "the roar of
traffic in the streets below 'bore all its sons away'", echoing the Isaac
Watts' hymn about mortality. Bringing their son up as a proper
Anglo-Indian middle-class boy means that the parents have been
painted out of their son's life. His parents are left with a "chitinous
semblance of a boy from whom the person had escaped". The writing
confuses the causes: the "precocious departure for the war", the loss
of school, the loss of India, the loss of an intimate bond with his
parents. He feels that the tenuous bonds with his parents both keep
him sane and threaten his sanity. But the main outcome of the visit is
belief in his father's irritation with his oafishness and his failure to be
accepted for the army. His attempt to rejoin his family is represented
as sexual paralysis, with an inability to walk very similar to that experienced years later by his patient, Samuel Beckett, after his own
father's death. For Bion it was "paralysis from the pelvis down. I felt
that anyone could see I was not walking but shuffling. I hauled
myself, iron rail by iron rail, to the Russell Square hotel lunch and
Russell Square paternal moral nurture" (1985, p. 108).

This is a striking image of the war experience that is, at this stage,
yet to come. In *The War Memoirs*, Bion describes how men follow the
tank "with hands thrust deep into the pockets and slouching tread. It
was curious to watch the little ribs of the tank track-plates continually
climbing up and up the back of the tank" (p. 159). The iron rails of
Russell Square combine in memory with the treads of the caterpillar
tracks circling endlessly, the slowed-down sense of doom. Bion's
"entanked" quality is written here as predating his actual experience

with tanks, a "chininous" exoself protecting the abandoned child which will find perfect expression in becoming a tank commander.

The conventional uprooting and institutionalising of a small child at boarding school had left Bion with a characteristically damaged sense of self-worth and an undeveloped sense of relationships, family, and self (Hunneybell, 2009). His time in the army seems to have compounded his sense of the fragility of relationships and the meaninglessness of personal qualities. In Bion's own frame of reference, his family is made up of split off, inarticulate, and, as he later says, "mad" (Bion, 1997) fragments, coughing, barking, or laughing ferociously as did the tigress, the jackal with its "'fiaow' call" (Bion, 1982, p. 13) and the men in India. This mysteriously aggressive, eroticised "coughing" and its relationship to the parents is horribly revisited in the apocalyptic telling and retelling of the death of Corporal Sweeting. This episode is described many times across Bion's life (Souter, 2009), with different emphases at each telling, but essentially the narrative describes a young man whose lung is ripped out by a shell fragment and who, trapped in a hole with Bion, drives him mad by repeatedly asking piteously why he is unable to cough, and whether Bion will write to his mother. The first time Bion describes this incident he does so writing to his own mother. The images are dense, but if coughing represents the noises made by angry frustrated lovers (a child's memory of the noises of lovemaking in the Indian night?), war literally knocks it out of you. "Clouds of steam" billow from Sweeting's side (Bion, 1985), the enormous cavity in his chest a gruesome image of castration raised by an order of magnitude. The image has the qualities of a screen memory: it represents a series of crises in Bion's early war service and clinical experience. The little boy frightened by parental eroticism, represented by the angry tigress and the jackels who make the "Arf Arfer" noise, the barking laugh which echoes "our Father" and characterises the men in India, the schoolboy who developed the "talent for splitting" (Duffell, 2000, p. 176) said to be typical of boarding school survivors, and, crucially for the relationship with Beckett, the inexperienced psychotherapist faced with a huge wound that dwarfs his pathetic field dressing. More shocking is the image of his own and now recently abandoned exploded tank, with incinerated bodies hanging out of it like the intestines of a huge animal (Bion, 1985): what happens to a person's "innards" when under attack?

All these fragments, then, made up the man who was demobbed. A traumatic removal from an encapsulated childhood idyll, heroic under fire, as evidenced by a DSO and a recommendation for a VC, but with a typical "boarding school survivor's belief that he does 'not believe that he matters, that anyone would want him' . . ." (Hunneybell, 2009) and in addition a terror where the insides of bodies are concerned. Above all is a "contempt . . . for that boy [as he had been in childhood]; as if to acknowledge him is to acknowledge weakness, failure, need, and vulnerability—heavens forbid" (Hunneybell, 2009). In the face of this self-directed contempt, Bion used his military experience to gain acceptance to Oxford, and took a now-celebrated path through a BA with a major in Philosophy, language study in France, schoolteaching, where he was accused of paedophilia and was too frozen to defend himself, and finally medical training.

When Bion began psychiatric training in 1930, he inevitably brought these experiences in a diabolical mix. His sexuality was frozen in a combination of classic boarding school abandonment, suffering, ignorance, and confused shame (Duffell, 2000, p. 173). He describes what Hunneybell notes is the classic reliance on the sole private space at boarding school, "bed-space", to recreate the maternal, but, for Bion, this was experienced as developing his powers of emotional deception so that they matched his mother's. In addition, his experience at the Front compounded his alienation from his family, his anxieties about bodily integrity, and his survivor guilt. The experience of studying for an Oxford BA seems to have had a comforting maternal quality (*All My Sins*), but did not take him forward into life. In terms of the relationship with Beckett, the year at Poitiers University (Bléandonu, 1994, p. 36) improving his spoken French is significant.

It seems clear, however, that his life to that point had led him into difficulties that were inevitable for the peculiar combination of sexual immaturity and physical toughness he presented: Bléandonu tactfully renders this as "deep dissatisfaction". His relationships with girls seem virtually non-existent: the only girl he describes with deep feeling in *The Long Week-End* is a fourteen-year-old, the pregnant child he describes (Bion, 1982, p. 281) as haunting his dreams for years. His first ventures into psychotherapy, with a therapist whom he contemptuously names "Mr Feel-it-in-the-past" or "Mr FiP", seem to have been precipitated by having been jilted by a Miss Hall (Bléandonu, 1994, p. 39), and the description of his fantasies of revenge by kneecapping are startlingly adolescent (Bion, 1985, p. 30). The clinical techniques employed by Mr FiP might have been clunky, but, on the evidence in the autobiographies, he was on to something. Bion's agonised mixture of romantic passion, schoolboy aggression, and collapse when abandoned were very early feelings; he was, indeed, "feeling it in the past".

That Bion, at thirty, could not tolerate any further emotional rejection is not surprising, having lost everything already: beloved home and country, ayah, mother, school, comrades, a sense of his own courage and kindness. That said, the crudity of Mr FiP's approach could not help Bion's incipient intellect. With what can only be thought of as a dogged survival instinct, he attached himself to the three most eminent psychoanalysts he could find, one after the other: first, J. A. Hadfield, second, John Rickman, and third, Melanie Klein. He was still in therapy with Hadfield when he took Samuel Beckett into treatment. The treatment was not sophisticated: Hadfield minimised transference, and a number of his students were critical of this, and "went on to complete their training at the Institute of Psycho-Analysis" (Bléandonu, 1994, p. 43).

Then, as always, Bion was beset by money worries: he was of the class that, having received a minor public school education, knew exactly how he was meant to dress, behave, and live, but might not have had the resources to do so. He had a very small number of patients, an unsatisfactory psychotherapy, and had been effectively abandoned by both parents. He had had little sexual experience, and had little confidence in his talents. He was wracked with survivor guilt from the war and, perhaps, also from boarding school. There was just enough shared with Beckett to excite Bion's envy. Beckett's solid middle-class background, loving father, literary status, and close relationship with James Joyce himself, was calculated to arouse Bion's envy. In addition, Beckett was a challenging patient: he provoked his inexperienced therapist by wide reading and mastery of psychoanalytic writing, including Freud, Ernest Jones, and Karin Stephen. Additionally, his already published *Proust* was a work of literary metapsychology. Beckett, by this time, was a young man of great *avant-garde* culture, and had compiled enormous notebooks on psychoanalytic theory. Bion was out of his depth with this young man, intellectually, socially, and clinically: the tools to deal with this patient did not then exist, and were not to do so for perhaps fifty years, growing out of responses to Bion's own late works. What was to be done?

In this case, all that Bion had to offer was what he had shown at school and on the battlefield, courage under fire. Able to think about being stuck within the inability to think or act, Bion was able to respond authentically in a clinical emergency. With a distressed patient acting out and about to prematurely end the therapy, and with no clinical tools to help him respond, Bion offered a fish supper and a cutting edge lecture: a lifeline, a way out, a view of the "real" therapist in the scary Tavistock world of "tooth and yank", and a proof of his esteem. With these few tools he effectively wished Beckett well, and allowed him to go on his way. It was a therapeutic version of the pathetically inadequate field dressing which was all he had to offer the eviscerated Sweeting on the battlefield. Beckett, however, was able to respond, and to make use of these therapeutic tokens for the rest of his life.

PART II

AN INTERPRETATIVE
CONSTRUCTION OF BECKETT'S
LITERARY DEVELOPMENT AND
BION'S LATER CLINICAL THEORIES

CHAPTER SEVEN

Free association: Beckett's private theatre

Strong biographical documentation portrays Samuel Beckett's intellectual development leading to his post-war "trilogy" (Bair, 1978; Feldman, 2006; Knowlson, 1996). Existing in plain historical sight as a parallel realm, split off from the critical determinants of this developmental line, are two significant and interrelated psychological developments. The first is Beckett's struggle in consolidating his adult sense of identity as a writer. The second is Beckett's deep emotional acquaintance with the disruptive visitations of panic, immediately fragmenting the individual's sense of cohesion and coherence.

Each is documented critically within Beckett's biographical material and lead directly to his two-year course of psychoanalytic psychotherapy in London during 1933–1934. Yet, little is made either of their convergence in psychoanalytic psychotherapy or of that therapeutic influence upon Beckett's later work. Critically, within Beckett Studies, three intellectual aspects of this period are biographically highlighted: Beckett's wide reading and note-taking of psychoanalytic texts, his visits to Geoffrey Thompson at Bethlem Hospital, supplying much background for *Murphy*, and the importance to Beckett of a comment made by Jung at a lecture he attended in 1935, which would later emerge in his 1954 radio play, *All That Fall*.

Correctly, from the vantage point of psychoanalysis, scholars have recognised a kinship between the mature writings of Bion and Beckett. These would develop, independent of mutual contact, over a period of twenty years. The wish to locate this asynchronous development within the therapeutic pairing of Beckett and Bion is understandable, but psychoanalytic attempts to understand it have been inconclusive. For example, *The Imaginary Twin*, presented in 1950 by Bion for membership of the British Psychoanalytical Society, seems to correspond with a schizoid patient much like a Beckett character. But, as Bion writes in his introduction to *Second Thoughts*, the "case" is a narrative composite, its presented memories "not to be treated as more than a pictorialized communication of an emotional experience" (Bion, 1967, p. 2).

Certainly, the "imaginary twin" pictorialises Bion's experiences as psychotherapist, possibly with Beckett. Although their work together preceded Bion's psychoanalytic training, the narrative begins with a description of the patient's earlier years of a failed psychotherapy, concluding with the therapist's dismissive recommendation of psychosurgery as the patient's best hope. Here, perhaps, in relation to his later psychoanalytic identity, is Bion's creative dismissal as failure of his earlier Hadfieldian orientation. Were the "imaginary twin", at least in part, the Samuel Beckett of Bion's imagination, then the life-affirming second therapy, a Kleinian psychoanalysis, would gratify Bion's earlier invitation for Beckett to re-engage with him in psychotherapy (TM, 22 December 1936). Where earlier psychotherapy was thought by Bion to have failed, Bion's fantasy prescribed that psychoanalysis might fail harder.

The patient of that paper, at forty-three, is Beckett's age at the time of Bion's writing, and Bion's own recognition of the rhythmic give and take of "association–interpretation–association", as well as his supportive, therapeutic relaxation in "a jocular evasion of my complaints", suggest that long-past Jungian boundary crossing which similarly must have "softened" Bion's sense of the patient's "resentment" during the final three months of Beckett's therapy. Indeed, Beckett's own symptomatic preoccupations must have suggested themselves to Bion, in consideration of his earlier patient's alignment with the clinical descriptions of Bion's analyst, Melanie Klein, who wrote,

> the patient complained about different physical troubles and then
> went on to say what medicines he had taken—enumerating what he

had done for his chest, his throat, his nose, his ears, his intestines, etc. It sounded rather as if he were nursing these parts of his body and his organs. He went on to speak about his concern for some young people under his care (he is a teacher) and then about the worry he was feeling for some members of his family. It became quite clear that the different organs he was trying to cure were identified with his internalized brothers and sisters. (Klein, 1935, p. 158)

The "Imaginary twin" paper greatly succeeds in conveying the Kleinian case for the internal object and projective identification as "verbal formulations of sensory images constructed to communicate in one form what is probably communicated in another" (Bion, 1967, p. 2). Its images are composite. Some are fictionalised, some might correspond to patients and even to Bion himself—as in the patient's question as to whether "it was worthwhile going on". Bion himself had asked the same question of Rickman (Conci, 2011). However, what shines through clinically, and also resonates with Beckett's later reflections, is the therapist's subjective recognition of the patient's invitation "as if he were saying, 'Go on; its your turn'" (Bion, 1967, p. 5). The reader immediately remembers the chess game portrayed by Beckett in his first novel, *Murphy*, published in 1938.

Beckett's ongoing and extensive correspondence with Thomas MacGreevy during the period of the "London Torture", while not an accurate record of psychoanalytic psychotherapy, reflects his own fluctuating emotional relation to Bion. We know the importance to Beckett of Bion's focused attention; and how outraged Beckett would become if he interpreted Bion as misunderstanding or lacking in attention. After the termination of treatment in December 1935, Beckett harboured unpleasant memories of Bion which, by December 1936, had shifted to his affectionate sending of a Christmas card. At least through 1938, Beckett remained mindful of Bion through correspondence with Geoffrey Thompson.

But the Second World War intervened; and their paths diverged finally. Each had undergone significant experience of the other; and together with this, each had committed himself to uniquely personalised meanings of psychoanalysis. For Bion, the route was formal psychoanalytic training, including analyses with Rickman and Klein. For Beckett, with personal experience of psychotherapy and psychiatric hospital fieldwork, as well as comprehensive notes on the fundamentals of psychoanalysis, the route was literary. Built upon a solid metapsychology developed from Proust, Beckett would detail the individual's authentic inner voice—advancing beyond his critique of Joyce's teleological portrayals. Populating the internal world of his "puppets", the Murphys, Malones, and Molloys in different contexts and times, Beckett mirrors the complex narrative threads of ongoing intensive psychotherapy. Beckett's is a ramifying literary record of states of mind, not unlike Proust, but from within the relational dynamics of the psychotherapeutic encounter.

Two particularly moving moments in Beckett's *Watt* illustrate. These concern the mutual bridge building of Watt and Sam, culminating in a touching of foreheads and Watt's later desire that Sam understand fully the meaning to him, of the experience of buttoning Mr Knott's boot (Beckett, 2006a, p. 343). This latter reference is particularly poignant, given Beckett's own acquaintance with Proust's attention to a buttoned boot (Beckett, 1931, p. 27). However, while significant meaning is self-derived within Proust, with memory vitalising the human condition, in *Watt*, the other's recognition is critical to the generation of emotional meaning.

Beckett's changeable emotional perspectives on Bion, together with the sensitively portrayed possibility of one individual's capability of knowing the mind of another, hearken back from the 1930s to an earlier watershed moment in psychotherapeutic history. The Bion–Beckett psychotherapy took place at the end of a psychotherapeutic era in which the patient's ego was seen as the passive vehicle for transmission of unconscious content (A. Freud, 1936). Indeed, during the course of the Bion–Beckett psychotherapy, James Strachey was to deliver his classic paper, "The nature of therapeutic action of psychoanalysis", re-presenting therapy as the dynamic engagement of two actively striving individuals (Strachey, 1934).

Still, at the historical moment of Beckett's psychotherapy, neither patient nor analyst had the words or conceptual language to express the growing relatedness of patient and analyst. Bion was further constrained by his training in "reductive analysis", a variation of psychoanalysis emphasising symptom remission through the resolution of multiple, discontinuous transferences. This psychoanalytic variant was developed by J. A. Hadfield, who was both Bion's therapist and Tavistock supervisor during this period of pre-psychoanalytic practice.

Beckett's therapy would have proceeded via the method of free association, developed during the pre-analytic hypnotic period and alternatively called "chimney sweeping", and the "talking cure" by Bertha Pappenheim, the first psychoanalytic patient in her guise as Anna O. She also called the continuing action of her underlying thought her "private theatre". Exploring the individual's ongoing private theatre, with its frustratingly partial apprehensions of one's internal world, would become Beckett's central literary pursuit.

While hypnosis allowed both therapist and patient the fiction that the patient's ego was passive, a fiction maintained through the 1930s, the report in *Studies on Hysteria* shows a strong-tempered, sometimes domineering woman—even under hypnosis (Freud (with Breuer), 1895d, pp. 21–47). Focused on the dynamics of the unconscious, it would be years before Freud developed the concepts of transference and countertransference, underpinning the reciprocal projections of patient and analyst.

Even with the discovery of transference, the aesthetic quality of active relationship between patient and analyst might go unspoken. This would have been the case during Beckett's period of analysis, when the patient's free association would be met by the analyst's evenly hovering attention from which interpretation might be returned, like a tennis ball, to the patient. Still, even in the absence of an explanatory theory, Beckett, like his psychoanalytic precursor, Anna O, would know implicitly both his effect upon the analyst and Bion's upon him. He would know from Bion's responses that more or less cohesive narrative associations produce different response in the analyst than incoherent rambling, and that free association itself might become the vehicle of defensive resistance. Long before Bion's work with Beckett, analysts were well aware of "abuse of free association", including patients' wilfully senseless associations in compliance with the letter, if not the spirit, of free association, long silences, together with the claim that "absolutely nothing occurs" to the patient, and the claim that "too much occurs to him at once and he does not know what to relate first of all" (Ferenczi, 1919, pp. 177–180)—similar to the idea reflected in the introduction to *Molloy* that, "I don't know how to work anymore. That doesn't matter apparently" (Beckett, 2006b, p. 7).

Panic provided Beckett with the experiential prototype of personal dissolution. The sudden onset of its symptoms included palpitations, chills and hot flushes, accelerated heart rate, sweating, trembling, shortened breath, sensations of smothering and choking, chest pain, nausea, dizziness, derealisation and depersonalisation, as well as the fears of losing control, going crazy, and dying. Beckett's own study of Proust, while admiring of involuntary memory's power, would return again and again to the possibility that in developing from one moment to another, the individual might cease to care about what he had valued yesterday. What was meaningful might suddenly vanish—just as panic effaced the calm immediately before.

Free association, unchecked by response, mimics the relentless generation of ongoing thought. Directed by the analyst to avoid self-judgement, the patient's associative chain is meant to allow uncon-scious derivatives to emerge, but could just as well reflect the lack of cohesion in one's cognitive process. The succession of thought, all by itself, might disrupt comprehension either by self or by another. Unprepared to receive chaotic communication, the effect upon the naïve listener might induce a state as disruptive as Beckett's panic. Bion's mature work would focus both on this linking of thought and on the disruptive effect of "beta elements" upon therapeutic compre-hension, both within the individual and between the patient and analyst, as a core dimension of psychotherapy (Bion, 1967).

While experiences of panic, coupled with the difficulties of resolv-ing adult identity, were precursors to Beckett's psychotherapy, the very experience of psychoanalytic psychotherapy would provide Beckett with a tool of direct address to another, useful to an author palpating the boundaries of narrative structure. Beckett's substitution, in writing, of free association for narrative sense-making in direct address would both destabilise the reader's understanding of a char-acter while demanding the reader's rapt attention. Through imple-mentation in writing of psychoanalysis's "fundamental rule", but without the psychoanalyst's trained and focused listening , Beckett might approximate the replication of panic or catastrophe in the unprepared reader. This discovery would invert the author's tradi-tional role in relation to the reader as careful guide, both laying down and elaborating a cohesive narrative. Beckett's own warrant for this demand upon the reader is reflected in his 1931 monograph on Proust, which, together with his later experience of psychoanalytic psychotherapy, provide both blueprint and resources for his literary project.

Beginning Molloy

The psychoanalytic practice of free association is founded on a paradox of bounded freedom. While the uncensored productions of the patient are formally free to range across any and all contents, they are ultimately tethered through associative linkage with the dynamic unconscious. What appears to the naïve listener as verbal freedom is linked through multiple over-determination to the speaker's unconscious motivations. Seemingly free verbal production is not really free at all. Rather, it is the mouthpiece of unconscious activity.

The second dimension of this bounded freedom is that free association is a rarified state, existent only within the context of the psychoanalytic relationship. There, the patient's associations meet the considered reflections of the analyst's "evenly suspended attention" (Freud, 1912e). From within this integration, association forms a meaningful concept within the analyst's mind, emergent in its offering to the patient as interpretation. How the patient receives the interpretation expands the acts of free association and analytic listening. The working through of resistance to transference would become the centre of the patient's psychoanalytic activity (Freud, 1914g). Beckett's own depiction of an individual's hesitance to accept another's interpretation, experienced as an intrusive incursion upon the privacy of personal thought, is expressed in relation to the character Mahood, a Bion-like auditor: "It is his voice which has often, always, mingled with mine, and sometimes drowned it completely" (Beckett, 2006b, p. 303).

To be therapeutically meaningful, free association requires the action of two participants. Without the containing, contextualising presence of the analyst's targeted receptivity, the speaker's association might be reduced to babel. While possibly meaningful to the speaker himself, its receptivity by others parallels the mutter and rant of the psychotic, externalising what the better socialised choose to contain silently. Even within the process of psychoanalysis, as the mature Bion would later explore, an individual's "attacks on linking" might act to fragment meaning, both internally and in external communication.

Beckett's acquaintance with psychotic patients, gained through visits to Geoffrey Thompson, then a psychiatric resident at Bethlem Hospital, is broadly reflected in his novel, *Murphy*. Beckett's Bethlem visits highlighted his recognition of an important differentiation at the border of psychosis. On one side of the border, the pre-psychotic side, there were individuals like his protagonist, Murphy. No matter how conflicted in his own internal and external relations, Murphy needed others—as Beckett illustrates in Murphy's relation with Mr Endon. Yet, across that border, in the realm of the psychotic, no such need existed. Mr Endon's internal world was self-contained, requiring no external validation from Murphy.

Beckett's lifelong friend, Geoffrey Thompson, comments on Beckett's special interest in a young hospitalised patient, approximately Beckett's own age and with a deep, symbiotic relation to his own mother, also similar to Beckett's. Thompson describes the young man as dressed for the outdoors in a long greatcoat and boots, similar to many later Beckett characters. The patient sits at the door to the hospital, legs extended before him, balancing on the edges of his heels. He waits for a mother who will never come. She has provided her son with stout boots for walking, and, in a fine contradiction, has instructed her son not to wear the boots out by walking. He waits for release: if not from mother, than at least from the double bind of being both encouraged and discouraged from walking (Thompson, 1976).

Beckett might well have resonated with the predicament. It recalls the moment when, straining under a weighty load, he collapsed on the road home to Foxrock at age twelve, only to be raised up by a concerned and encouraging father, despite his mother's punitive and self-concerned worry (Knowlson, 1996, p. 51). Beckett's signature learning was that despite incapability in going on, one must go on. The significant other might stop you, befuddle you, confuse you, but one continued on, often through the help of another, as with Geoffrey Thompson after Dawson Street or his father on the Foxrock road.

During the period of his psychiatric hospital visits, Beckett, though struggling, relied on the continuing presence of his analyst, Wilfred Bion. But the young man at Bethlem waited solitary, sealed off from the relief of another. The contrast between them described a divide between psychological struggle and psychological collapse. The decisive factor was openness to dependency upon the other.

Beckett had returned regularly to Ireland throughout the period of his therapy with Bion, almost as if to calibrate the degree of symptomatic discomfort he would experience at home with his widowed mother. Yet, that summer, Beckett had decided upon an unusual project. It was especially unusual for a young man struggling to consolidate an adult identity differentiated from his family of origin. That summer, Beckett and his mother would spend a week together, vacationing on the coast of England. Retrospectively, it appears that Beckett might have attempted this enterprise as a capstone event, proving the worth of psychotherapy in symptom remission. And, by this standard, the vacation succeeded. Beckett had remained symptom-free. Unlike the young man at Bethlem, he seemed, through the agency of psychotherapy, to heal in relation to his mother. For Beckett in that moment, during the summer of 1935, clear difference emerged between different levels of psychological struggle. His own situation, allowing him a conflict-free weeklong holiday with his mother, contrasted greatly with the young man's sealed off position against people and must have seemed monumental.

His attention, during the early months of 1935, was to the composition of *Murphy*. Vigorous intellectual activity had always served Beckett as a retreat from psychological pain. And in the intervening years between *Murphy* and the "trilogy", with Beckett's Europe in the throes of the Second World War, the painful contrast between the momentary vicissitudes of personal thought and fear for life and survival amid murderous external carnage could not have been stronger. The life of the mind offered familiar refuge.

Both *Murphy* and *Watt*, composed by Beckett during the Second World War, utilise the convention of third person narration. With *Molloy* in the post-war "trilogy", Beckett moves to the use of direct address. Thematically, Beckett had moved to the more deeply internal from *Murphy*'s overtly psychiatric frame to *Watt*'s ongoing thinking in his transit along Dublin's Harcourt Street Railway, between its two ends—one a circle, one a square (O'Brien, 1986). At the same time, extraordinarily local in its transit through Foxrock and the foothills of the Wicklow Mountains, *Watt* also contemplates the relentless press of internal thought. Written in wartime exile, Watt's own scuffling vagrancy recalls the humorous and resilient tramps of J. M. Synge. Knowing Beckett's own plight as refugee, the reader chuckles at the fantasy of Beckett's ironic contemplation, stumbling on the roads of France, of Synge's words from *The Vagrants of Wicklow*:

> In the middle classes, the gifted son of a family is always the poorest—usually a writer or artist with no sense for speculation—and in a family of peasants, where the average comfort is just over penury, the gifted son sinks also, and is soon a tramp on the roadside. (p. 202)

Molloy moves from the psychiatric framework of Bethlem through the conflicted processes of internal thought, to his own learnt experience in the emotionally fraught talking cure, his own private theatre. In this turn, Beckett continues to probe his character's internal world while significantly shifting his authorial relation to the reader.

From Beckett's earliest writing, his work had presented challenge to its readers. Often demanding the understanding of obscure references and multiple languages, like Joyce before him, he seemed to revel in the multiplication of complexities. The reader was challenged, if sufficiently interested, to scale the constructed literary mountain. Free association was a game changer. While the authorial task requires narrative control in order that the reader builds a sense of both coherence and cohesion while assimilating new plot development, Beckett's use of free association would destabilise both. The reader would continue to absorb new contents, but without benefit of a solid, meaningful foundation. While in psychoanalysis, such confusion within the analyst might be clarified by a question to the patient, because the dyadic process moves in two directions. Freud, for example, must momentarily abandon his practice of free association in relation to the "Rat Man" in order to clarify a confusing and incoherent narrative (Freud, 1909d, p. 212). The patient has successfully confused him, temporarily paralysing Freud's ability to construe coherently.

Writing is even more challenging. Its direction is one way only: from author, via character and plot, to the reader. The result of ongoing confusion within the reader is destabilisation. The first pages of *Molloy* provide a good example. Formally, the work begins with its first word, but in its narrative, as direct address, the character not yet introduced as Molloy announces a "beginning" only on the second page, following a long preamble. What occurs before the "beginning" establishes the relationship between text and reader; what continues from that beginning elaborates this relationship.

Establishing the reader's relation to the character is problematic. It begins with the attempt to locate the narrative's setting. Molloy begins in associative reverie: "I am in my mother's room, it's I who live there now. I don't know how I got there. Perhaps in an ambulance, certainly a vehicle of some kind. I was helped. I'd never have got there alone". What appears to be a retrospective description of events from his mother's house is confusing. Is mother's house metaphorical? Does it suggest, rather, a kind of psychological regression? The ambulance and need of help suggests hospitalisation. These are clues but there are no answers.

The character continues his monologue: "There's this man who comes every week. Perhaps I got here thanks to him. He says not. He gives me money and takes away the pages. So many pages, so much money".

Immediately, we recognise a weekly visit from another person. And because we are aware that at least one question—the question about arrival at the location—has been asked and answered, we recognise that the narrator is in some sort of communicative relationship with the man. It is a relationship bound in production: the narrator produces and receives monetary payment. Just as a patient beginning psychotherapy typically claims an ignorance of how work should proceed, Molloy's narrator says that he does not know how to work. Not knowing how to work is commonly expressed by psychoanalytic patients, often in terms of not knowing what to say in free association (Ferenczi, 1919). Just as in psychotherapy, the associative work continues in *Molloy*, regardless of this difficulty, so here, too, the narrator says, "That doesn't matter apparently."

Within the work of psychotherapy, the patient freely associates and receives the therapist's reciprocal response. Often, while listening to the patient, much of what is said is left without comment. This is also the case with the narrator's writing. Some pages are taken away and others are returned for comment, "marked with signs I don't understand". The narrator appears passive. He might not understand. He might not, as Freud writes, "find the courage to direct his attention to the phenomena of his illness" (Freud, 1914g, p. 152). Perhaps the narrator, however willing to write, is unwilling to know his situation. Perhaps, as reflected in the reader's experience, the narrator finds the situation unknowable.

He says, "I don't work for money. For what then? I don't know." The narrator uses an association to this ignorance to ruminate upon his mother, a possible son, a love that might have been true, and then deflects thought, pushing it away, by claiming "I've forgotten it again."

Moving again to the "queer" man who comes to see him weekly, he says he is thirsty. For drink? For knowledge? For associations or history? The reader is left only with mounting questions in the face of rambling monologue, returning to his relation with the man and writing. He says, " It was he told me I'd begun all wrong, that I should have begun differently". Is he referring to the beginning of his tale, in a formal sense? Is he referring to his beginnings of life in a psychological sense? Freud comments that in initiation of treatment

> it can happen that he (the patient) does not properly know under what conditions his phobia breaks out or does not listen to the precise wording of his obsessional ideas or does not grasp the actual purpose of his obsessional impulse. (Freud, 1914g, p. 152)

And here, calling himself "an old ballocks" for beginning at his own beginning when he should have begun somewhere else, according to someone else, he comments on the act of being externally judged. Is he ashamed? Perhaps he is; perhaps the situation is more complicated. He writes,

> It was he told me I'd begun all wrong, that I should have begun differently. He must be right, I began at the beginning, like an old ballocks, can you imagine that? Here's my beginning. Because they're keeping it apparently.

With this seemingly simple set of associations, Beckett actively befuddles. Employing the tool of free association, he extends the "game" played upon the reader from his earlier work, "talking to him, teasing him, even taunting" in his "dismantling" of a novel's conventional form (Knowlson, 1996, p. 145). Minimally, doubt is cast upon the singularity of a word's meaning. Is the beginning that he "should have begun differently" the "beginning" that is kept, so valued by the unspecified others? The reader does not know.

Beckett's own correspondence to Thomas MacGreevy, during the course of his psychotherapy, suggests the meanings of the term "beginning" are very different. In this sense, the original "beginning" is the patient's first formulation, his presenting problem. The "beginning" that is ultimately accepted, "kept", is a formulation between patient and analyst, about the origins of patient distress. Writing to Thomas MacGreevy, Beckett himself says it well:

> It was with a specific fear & a specific complaint that I went to Geoffrey, then to Bion, to learn that the "specific fear & complaint" was the least important symptom of a diseased condition that began

in a time which I could not remember, in my "pre-history", a bubble on the puddle. (TM, 10 March 1935)

Yet, for the reader uninitiated in Beckett's own experiential "puddle", including the direct experience of psychoanalysis, the undifferentiated confusions of even a simple term, "beginning", must confuse. Confused, the reader is acted upon in an unexpected way by the writer. The reader is submerged in the narrator's private theatre. But for the context in writing rather than in psychoanalysis before its evolution from Anna O's talking cure to a treatment spanning neurotic, pre-psychotic, and psychotic disorders (the expanded psychoanalytic field of the mature Bion), the effect is panic or disorientation.

Beckett, as a keenly observing patient, would have been aware of his own power to "lose" or even alienate his therapist through silence or confusing verbal production. This is what the narrator in *Molloy* does to the reader by the end of page one. His winking reference to being an "old ballocks" is hardly jocular. It either refers to his own ignorance at not knowing at the start of a therapy what he might learn by the end, or it attempts collusion with the reader (possibly in opposition to the "queer man")—as if a humorous self-denigrating aside might make him seem a bumbling fool rather than an artist in pursuit of the reader's confusion.

Before launching into what is meant to be the beginning of the narrative's story, whichever or whatever that might be, Beckett's character cannily undercuts his direct address yet again. Saying that his beginning must have meaning, that it "must mean something" because it has been paid for and accepted by the queer man and the others, he denies that it has explicit meaning for him.

The trick is that he is offering it to the reader. This suggests that something is desired from the reader. After all, we know already that this character produces his writing in expectation of some kind of reciprocity. And, while he cunningly leaves it up to the reader to judge the worth of his production, he presents, nevertheless, a production that he tells us already has a track record of acceptability by others. So what does he want?

Minimally, attention is demanded. Hidden in his explicit attribution of worth to others, with an implicit repudiation of his own assessment of its personal worth, he believes none the less that what he is about to say is meaningful because it will secure the reader's continuing attention. Words have, therefore, demonstrable interpersonal effect. A complex ambivalence is displayed: while formally denigrating the worth of what he shall say, he also desires the other's attention, which he attempts to secure through reference to a third party. Perhaps the reader is foolish to continue under such circumstances. Perhaps the reader is curious to deepen an understanding of what is presented before him.

The free associative technique utilised by Beckett in *Molloy* launches the reader into a realm of uncertainty. Following Bion's later formulation, its effect in the absence of a responsive other, both asking and receiving reciprocal clarification, is to attack linkages on meaning while, at the same time, it conveys to the reader a disowned desire from the speaker for an attention which might easily be disavowed. The use of free association in the absence of a responsive other places the reader in the role of interpreting narrative disorder as it increases in density, without a guarantee of authorial clarification. By so doing, Beckett radically changes the relation between author and reader from careful stewardship in the creation of coherence to immersion in often incoherent facts and feelings, seemingly lacking cohesion. In this way, Beckett places the reader in the role of the overwhelmed psychotherapist—as in the psychoanalytic era before this kind of interpersonal engagement was well understood.

Molloy presents a complex example which, together with the rest of the "trilogy", stretches Beckett's free associational experiment to the limit of the reader's endurance, and, as within its original action in psychotherapy, Beckett's experiment results in a radical change of the narrator's point of view. Chapter Ten will continue discussion of *Molloy* and beyond. The next chapter returns to the origins of Beckett's incorporation of free association within literature, with his four novellas. Exploration of the novellas deepens our understanding of Beckett's relation to both character and reader, and reflects a literary developmental step in appreciation of the "trilogy" and *Waiting for Godot*.

CHAPTER EIGHT

The novellas: Part One

T hirty-one years after the conclusion of his analytic work with
Samuel Beckett, Wilfred Bion suggested that the analyst's attitude toward the patient's narrative should be free of constrain-
ing memory and desire. He wrote,

> Do not remember past sessions. The greater the impulse to remember
> what has been said or done, the more the need to resist it. This impulse
> can present itself as a wish to remember something that has happened
> because it appears to have precipitated an emotional crisis: no crisis
> should be allowed to breach this rule. The supposed events must not
> be allowed to occupy the mind. Otherwise the evolution of the session
> will not be observed at the only time when it can be observed—while
> it is taking place. (1988, p. 16)

Rather, for Bion, "the only point of importance in any session is the
unknown". Bion's observation, of course, relates to formal psychoanalytic technique. Bion himself would remember the past in integrating his earlier therapeutic experience with subsequent psychoanalytic
training. The memory, so critically required to be absent during
sessions, would be harnessed to link experience and theory as clinical
explanation of sensuous, therapeutic engagement (Bion, 1967, p. 2).

His former patient's interest in literary uses of psychiatry had been profoundly affected by his experiences in London. The Murphy project had functioned for Beckett as a psychic retreat, to which the mind flees from the anxieties of other fields—notably, in this instance, the therapeutic transference relationship. In this way, it also functioned as therapeutic resistance leading to probable impasse. It had had also functioned as a transitional space, a container of activity integrating Beckett's consolidation of identity as a writer, his productive use of Geoffrey Thompson, his exit from the stressful demands of psychotherapy, and his symptomatically disastrous return to Dublin. With *Murphy's* completion, Beckett felt freedom enough to mourn the deaths of his father and Peggy Sinclair, to recognise the toxicity of the "savage loving" binding him to his mother, and to act on the imperative of physical separation from his mother's home. Yet, Beckett's therapeutic relationship to Bion remained unresolved.

The richness of Beckett's London experience was foundational for both *Murphy* and *Watt*, especially in relation to Beckett's thinking about the cloistered psychological processes of dependent individuals living within the confines of highly structured, closed environments. His four novellas shift from the formal institutional settings of psychiatric institutions, to the therapeutic action of psychoanalysis, known to Beckett from his own experience. They are stories told by individuals to the reader, one to one. They reveal Bion's session-by-session unknown, working not only through the slow accumulation of contents, scenes, and images, but also via the slow recognition that the author is acting demandingly upon the reader through the medium of his characters.

While Beckett's earlier works describe both settings and characters' states of mind from a narrative third person position, the novellas shift to the first person. This shift allows the direct address of one individual to the other, and the address of the narrator finds its target within the receptive experience of the reader. The sea change wrought by Beckett incorporates the intimate back and forth of the psychoanalytic dialogue reduced to monologue within the one-way trajectory of character to reader. Yet, just as free association may be used as a defence against revelation, its narrative surprises concealing as they reveal, just as the psychoanalyst's receptive experience of what might sound coherent might reflect the speaker's genuine incoherence, so, too, does Beckett's use of free association act upon the reader's states of mind. The novellas induce states of mind in the reader that reflect their narrators' unacknowledged states of mind. While the ostensible "story" unfolds, the more fundamental unfolding is in the reader's inchoate knowledge, acted upon by the author through the narrator's projection of words and images. The result is a deepening of the reader's affective "apprehension", an experiential understanding of literature addressed by Beckett in *Proust*.

Unlike the dyadic working of psychoanalysis, the novellas require the reader to become the singular container of the narrators' affects. The narrator fades when the story ends. The reader endures. Narrative action is one-way. Implied within this literary form, there can be no psychoanalytic recognition of the narrator's unknown, reflected back for the benefit of the narrator. Rather, the Beckett character rids himself of emotions, depositing them in the reader, whose function to the author becomes confusing. Is the reader meant to be a rubbish dump, the graveyard of uncertain and unpleasant affects? Or, in keeping with Beckett's earlier thinking about literature, is the technique meant to ensure that the reader remains interested until the conclusion, effectively averting the Beckett nightmare of emotional disinterest—the horror he had uncovered in his study of Proust. Indeed, there is some warrant for this in the novellas themselves, preoccupied as they are with disinterested turnings from dependency and security, echoed in the imagined "fuck off" of a mother's cruel address (Beckett, 1995a, p. 81). Inflected from this defensive posture, perhaps authorial intent is less to extrude unpleasant aspects than to hold the patient's attention by and through them—possibly until the reader infers his own interpretive meaning.

Quietly, in first person address, Beckett's narrators act decisively upon the reader as other. A decade after Murphy and separated by the traumatic divide of the Second World War, the novellas achieve what neither Beckett's little child outside Connolly's Store with his mother nor Murphy in relation to Mr Endon could: they impress themselves firmly within the mind of the other—the reader—whose attention, however fleeting *must* hold them. Beckett ensures, at the risk of his narrators being scorned or hated, that the reader is not indifferent. Indeed, as difficult as it might be for the reader to resist the Beckett narrator's affective imposition, the creative act of reader as recipient is to construe, according to his personal lights. This is, similarly, the task of the individual object of projective identification. Ogden writes, the recipient experiences himself in part as he is pictured in the projective fantasy. In reality, however, the recipient's experience is a new set of feelings, experienced by a person different from the projector. They may approximate those of the projector, but they are not identical: the recipient is the author of his own feelings. Albeit feelings elicited under a very specific kind of pressure from the projector, they are the product of a different personality system. (Ogden, 1982, p. 17)

Just as Anna O, the famous precursor of all psychoanalytic patients, was to recognise in Breuer's hypnotic treatment the liberation of her "private theatre", so Beckett employs the reader as audience to his narrators' psychological states. The reader of Beckett assumes, without knowing it, the position of psychoanalyst, but a psychoanalyst outside the consulting room, passive and without tools. It is the psychoanalyst transformed into an open, receptive target of any and all of the other's slings and arrows. Despite their characters' quirky charms, reading the novellas can feel unnerving.

The author's traditional role in relation to the reader was in establishing a literary framework through which the reader might not only gather elements of character and plot, but also reflect upon past action in a manner consolidating the forward movement of the work's coherence and cohesion in the reader's mind. Famously in English literature, Laurence Sterne's 1759 novel, *Tristram Shandy*, pioneered the digressive narrative approach. He writes, for example,

there is a master-stroke of digressive skill, the merit of which has all along, I fear, been overlooked by my reader,—not for want of penetration in him,—but because 'tis an excellence seldom looked for, or expected indeed, in a digression;- and it is this: That tho' my digressions are all fair, as you observe,—and that I fly off from what I am about, as far, and as often as any writer in Great Britain; yet I constantly take care to order affairs so that my main business does not stand still in my absence . . . the machinery of my work is of species by itself; two contrary motions are introduced into it, and reconciled, which were thought to be at variance with each other. In a word, my work is digressive, and it is progressive too,- and at the same time. (Sterne, 1962, pp. 55–56)

While anticipating the reader's surprise, Sterne's direct address is always consciously mindful of cultivating the reader's attentional labours. Beckett's digressions differ from Sterne's, as do his arrows of plot progressions. Beckett's digressions have the qualities either of elaborating foregoing statements or of linkage to emergent statements. In this, they resemble nothing so much as Freud's ideas of condensation and displacement, ultimately powering the narrative to conclusion in subtle revelation of the narrator to the reader. Revelation is never direct, but through the reader's intuition actively provoked by Beckett's depiction of the narrator's state of mind upon the reader. In this, Beckett employs what Sterne might term the "machinery" of psychoanalytic free association in literature.

Beckett's attitude of the narrator assumes the reader's interest as an entitlement or precondition. And the novellas begin as if mid-episode: musing in a cemetery, recovering from a fall, describing the actions of anonymous others. They meander loosely to junctures that seem central only in retrospect. Just as in Bion's conception of psychoanalytic listening, their first person associations face the unknown, and are all characterised by an evocation within the reader of shifting emotional relatedness to the narrator. Rather like the mature Bion's advice to psychoanalysts on the conduct of the analytic session, "progress" in Beckett is measured in its registration upon the reader of an "increased number and variety of moods, ideas, and attitudes seen in any given session" (Bion, 1967). Each Novella itself functions as a session, a snapshot in time, of a series of mental states related to the narrator's psychological situation, and presented to an auditor presumed to be fully attuned.

Fittingly, there is biographical confusion about the writing of the novellas. Knowlson dates *The End* first, begun in English on 17 February 1946 and completed in French by the end of May. The other three novellas were originally written in French and translated: *The Expelled* in October; *First Love* in October–November; and *The Calmative* in December (Knowlson, 1996, pp. 325, 328). Ackerley and Gontarski approach structurally, along the lines of the novellas' formal presentation: *First Love*; *The Expelled*; *The Calmative*; and *The End* (Ackerley & Gontarski, 2004; Beckett, 1995a).

Does it matter? Beginning with *First Love* and concluding with *The End* imposes an external narrative coherence even before the reader begins. This ordering begins with a "first" and concludes with an "end". Its ordinal structure aggressively denies, but cannot suppress, the underlying incoherence of four tales, highly related, but presented outside of a conventional narrative frame. First might begin first, but that is not how Beckett wrote them. Therefore, the present reading of the novellas, as the literary incorporation of free associative narrative presented to the reader's mind, follows a different path. Following the path of the author's production, we shall examine the four novellas. The first two novellas, *The End* and *The Expelled*, will be considered in detail, *The End* in this chapter and *The Expelled* in the next, together with consideration of all four in relation to both their unique psychological contents and the reader's experience.

The End

The End, the first of four Beckett novellas written within one year, begins by eliciting the reader's concern. The reader is introduced to the narrator through a long series of carefully described actions concerning his discharge, as patient, from a charitable facility, upon which he had been dependent for many years. He is given finite resources and an assurance "they didn't say in so many words that I was as well as I would ever be, but that was the implication" (p. 79). Despite the narrator's extreme dependency upon the institutional "they", his reasoning strikes the reader as clear. His use of the word "implication" signals that he is a man of intelligence, capable of reflection. His anger at the news of eviction seems understandable. He kicks the bed that attendants dismantle. He jokes bitterly that the paper he is asked to sign is a "safe conduct" pass into the outer world.

He has no option other than to proceed, himself and alone, into what he takes to be enemy territory, the outside. He recognises that even the provision of his final kit is not really meant to sustain him; but rather to preserve against damage to institutional "reputation in the long run", lest they be perceived as uncaring. Fondly, he looks to his "companions of so many bearable hours" (p. 79), the inanimate objects he will never see again. Yet, unlike the child's movement away from the security provided by his "transitional object", with a diffusion of personal interest and capability across larger dimensions of the external world, Beckett's narrator is unprepared. He reverberates with the loss of multiple, transient securities.

On parting, he is told mockingly that "no one understands a tenth of what you say" (p. 80). It is a cruel judgement. If true within the context of the story, it means not only that the narrator is unprepared to fend for himself in the external world, but also that this unpreparedness is known by another and acted upon sadistically. It also conveys to the reader that the narrator is meant to be psychiatrically impaired, and the story told as if from the emotional position of such a person—but with the addition of a limited capacity for coherent reflection, or, at least, storytelling.

This characterisation of psychotic-like organisation, but with the additional non-psychotic benefit of rational and reflective cognition, will become a Beckett signature. It is, for example, extended by him years later, in *Texts For Nothing*, where the narrator slips into physical deterioration and death while retaining what appears to be a reflective voice. However, in this latter work, what appears earlier to be reflection is, rather, presented as the unrelenting commentary of partial self-objects, active in the unconscious. It is Beckett's narrated action of personal fragmentation, a falling into atomised bits of which parts of the self remain aware.

Both the reflective voice within psychotic organisation and the unceasing unconscious commentary of later works appear to be conscious or unconscious manifestations of Jung's urging, heard by Beckett at the third Tavistock lecture in October 1935:

> Complexes are autonomous groups of associations that have a tendency to move by themselves, to live their own life apart from their intentions. I hold that the personal unconscious, as well as the collective unconscious, consists of an indefinite, because unknown, number of complexes or fragmentary personalities. (Jung, 1968, p. 81)

Either the apparently rational reflection of a psychologically impaired individual, or the unrelenting unconscious voices of an individual whose own physical apparatus has seriously deteriorated, represent such fragmentary personalities. Beckett's narrator, both a singular personality as his own object of storytelling and as a composite of multiple voices, registers these divergently communicated bits directly upon the reader in the freely associational narration employed by Beckett in his novellas.

The narrator of *The End*, without apparent emotional punctuation, alludes to the historical roots of his distress, very literally, in an act of transition. Having been told that he must not loiter in his exit from the institution, he passes through the garden. With a knowing and perhaps cruel grin at Proust, Beckett links the "strange light which follows a day of persistent rain" to the sighing of the earth and, with it, the narrator's associative memory: "a small boy, stretching out his hands and looking up at the blue sky asked his mother how such a thing was possible. Fuck off, she said" (Beckett, 1995a, p. 81).

Here, then, unremarked, is the narrator's incised experience of human activity undermining the basis of trust and faith in compassion. The narrator, without an eye-blink, casually links the childhood memory of maternal cruelty to the current deprivations of both eviction and his own current lack of sustenance. It is the perfect psychodynamic association, and extraordinarily compressed—from Proust to Freud in five sentences.

Without narrative embellishment, potentially lost within the stream of words emergent in the narrator's direct address to the reader, this specific historical memory of trauma is the referent for the unfolding present trauma, to which the reader is now witness.

The narrator wishes that he could turn back. He wants to see his last institutional mentor again. But he does not. Superstitiously, he prefers to believe that the possibility for a future reconciliation might exist if he is not confronted directly with the finality of his expulsion. Defensively, he attempts to preserve the possibility of the impossibly broken human connection. For the reader, the effect is heart-breaking. The narrator is shaken, unsteady, just as one imagines the small child to be, having been so dismissively addressed by the mother of his memory. Defensively, he states a categorical truth, as if decision were under his own control instead of his injured passive dependency, "and anyway I never turned back on such occasions" (p. 81).

And then, immediately, the reader learns that the character is literally "lost". He writes, "I had not set foot in this part of the city for a long time and it seemed greatly changed". His stoical resolve in straightforward storytelling begins to fragment. For the reader, as for the narrator, the storytelling reaches an inflexion point in disorientation.

Yet, despite the narrator's disorientation, he holds the reader's attention firmly. The reader's experience does not fragment or become incoherent. In fact, the narrative takes on a dreamlike quality as he notes

whole buildings had disappeared, the palings had changed position, and on all sides I saw, in great letters, the names of tradesmen I had never seen before and would have been at a loss to pronounce. There were streets where I remembered none, some I did remember had vanished and others had completely changed their names. The general impression was the same as before. (p. 81)

The narrator doubts himself. Defensively he says, "It is true I did not know the city well. Perhaps it was a different one". But the defensive feint is undone by his admission of purposelessness, and loss, "I did not know where I was supposed to be going" (p. 81).

The narrator's earlier anger and disappointment at the failed illusion of ongoing comfort and dependency in the charitable institution has evolved into the trauma of loss and, worse, a panic of disorientation. Indeed, it is this disorientation that undermines, for the narrator, even the foundational pilings of the city's buildings. His own foundations, already weakened from dashed trust and hope in others' generosity, have been shaken. Throughout, the reader is helpless. Even the most compassionate reading is never to be felt by the narrator. Narration is a one-way street, and the narrator is on his own, forever unaffected by the reader's empathic response. This relationship is complex. It is not, somehow, that the narrator speaks expecting no hearing, as if for himself alone. Rather, he speaks to be heard despite the unspoken conviction that there will never be a reciprocating answer or voice.

Suddenly, there is a turning in self-awareness from disorientation, as the narrator comments harshly upon his own appearance, as if he were making a joke. Yet, it is not funny, neither for him nor for the reader. He writes, "my appearance still made people laugh, with that hearty jovial laugh so good for the health" (p. 81).

His humiliation is complete. Defensively, he accepts that he is the object of derision and shame, and, commenting as if he were supporting that common practice of mocking the unfortunate, he mocks back at the attitude of the more fortunate as a "hearty jovial laugh so good for the health". Is this a dig at the reader? Is the reader laughing too, or still on his side?

He recovers. Although he finds an old familiar seat near the river, he believes that the river is flowing backwards. Or so he says. He stops this line of thought with, "that's all a pack of lies I feel" (p. 82). It appears as if his internal voices are competing within him, as if the voices of depersonalisation and disorientation momentarily are fighting it out with reality. "That's a pack of lies" is a statement of feeling, his sense of awareness that his registration of perceptions deceive him.

He stabilises himself with a glance at an unmovable object, his bench. This facilitates avoidance of what seemed menacing a moment before, the clashing of internal voices.

We are told, rather, in descriptive imagery about charitable acts toward horses, that he seems envious that animals' care is ongoing whereas his own has been ended. He "longed to be under cover again, in an empty place, close and warm, with artificial light, an oil lamp for choice, with a pink shade for preference" (p. 82). Those were the days! He reminisces longingly that in the past "from time to time someone would come to make sure I was all right and needed nothing". The effect, even of this regressive and womb-like longing, he reports was "horrible" (p. 82).

The reader has been absorbing a well-wrought, reflective discourse, purporting to be of a psychotic man, disoriented on ejection from a long-term care facility. It is a narrative of internally felt terror. Led moment by moment through his narrative, the reader has only empathy for the situation. There is nothing else to be done but to read. The reader can only witness.

Then comes relief. Our narrator, describing an arcane and vaudevillean process of doffing his hat, is finally able to secure lodging, food, and chamber pot. The reader inwardly sighs. For long months, the narrator is able to replicate his formerly cloistered existence, safe in its limitations. Then, he is again evicted. This time, because his landlord has absconded with his money and vanished. The little he had to give has been stolen, its value as barter for personal security misrepresented. He writes, "I felt weak" (p. 86). Stumbling into the stark light of day, he takes a bus into the country. He has been expelled once more.

And the story yet again turns. The narrator becomes dishevelled, sleeping in, and now smelling of, dung. He begs for food. He takes steps to recover his lost money but fails. He wanders, losing track of time, and again, both the city and the country seem changed for him. Again, he becomes disorientated, but, somehow, the disorientation is deeper. He grumbles a belief that he has seen his son in the street. This comment only becomes contextualised through the reading of another Beckett novella, *First Love*, with the narrator's belief in a son he has never known. Yet, without context, the observation seems random and incoherent.

Minimally, such an association would invite a reader's desire to ask for elaboration. Yet, in the context of Beckett's one-way free association, it becomes just another fact in a stream of consciousness directed to the reader. Beckett's genius is to challenge the reader's ability for linkage, to draw together two disparate meanings in an act of synthesis.

This action is demonstrated within psychoanalytic psychotherapy by the analyst—and also functions as a model for the patient's deepening of linked thought. Yet, within the aesthetic conveyed by Beckett, it also provides the reader with an opportunity to "meet" the projected contents of the narrator(s) with the reader's anticipation of meaningful, coherent thought. Within the psychoanalytic language of D. W. Winnicott, this corresponds to a "good enough" maternal function, the meaningful seeking out of what the infant/child/narrator has hidden. For Beckett as artist, this drawing together of meanings for the reader is the successful accomplishment of the literary task. Lecturing undergraduates at Trinity he said

> At what point in [the] self-consciousness does [the] play come to an end? When [the] mind faces facts, when [the] mind has an integral awareness of [the] facts . . .when there's [a] unification of awareness . . . the conversations between [the characters and their] confidents [only offer a] fragmentary awareness. [Their] function [is] to express [the] division in [the] mind of [the] antagonists. (LeJuez, 2008, p. 58)

The story continues with the narrator's meeting of a tramp he knew from long ago, who now scratches out a mean existence, living in a cave with his ass. Despite the narrator's sorry state, the other man extends an invitation to him. The reader, yet again, is heartened. Despite the more enduring disorientation, the reader wonders, perhaps there will be hope?

The story seems to change with the emergence of a new quality in the narrator's direct address. Mockingly, he plays with the meaning of words in a small act of cruelty directed at the other man. On the surface of his monologue, he states, "I reminded him that I wasn't in the habit of spending more than two or three minutes with anyone and the sea did not agree with me" (p. 88). This effectively distances our narrator from his potential benefactor on two scores—his general distance from others, and his dislike of the cave's location. But know-ing that the man's donkey also sleeps in the cave, he asks, "what's wrong with your ass" in response to the man's invitation for him "to go home with him and spend the night" (p. 88). The other man, rather naïvely, responds, "Don't mind him . . . he doesn't know you". Slapstick humour diffuses this moment, but underneath the question are two possible accusations, each ugly. The first is a simple rejection of the other's hospitality, with a throwing-back upon the other, in hostility, the mean circumstances of his life. The other, in alignment with the sexual connotation of ass and cohabitation, is that the cave-dweller is not generous at all, but desirous of homosexual contact. The sharp rebuke, in this sense, is a paranoid and defensive warding off of our narrator's own sexual projections upon the other. Nowhere is he safe.

Still, he agrees to cave-dwelling, and loses track of the time he stayed while paying attention to his own suffering—"treating my crablice with salt water and seaweed" as well as pain of the skull and itching extremities (p. 89). At this point, he discovers a "phial" in his pocket gone undiscovered in the final confiscation of property at the hospital. We are to learn that phial is a calmative, or tranquillising drug.

The narrator refuses his host's offer to prepare a single cave for his benefit, but accepts the offer both of the key to his mountain "cabin", a rude wooden shed, and a knife. Our protagonist proceeds to the mountains for a short interlude. There, he finds a place, "strewn with excrements, both human and animal, with condoms and vomit"; and notes that "in a cowpad, a heart had been traced, pierced by an arrow" (p. 90). Love is relegated to ordure, and filth presides. Indeed, at least in the recounting, the other man's generosity has also been deni-grated—as if affirming the narrator's evolving resolve to distance others.

In a bizarre scene, the narrator says that a cow "saved" him, presumably by providing him with some milk, but this is a stretch. The narrator does not explain how or what he means. Rather, he des-cribes an odd tale, suggesting a conflation of cow and human women. He writes,

> Goaded by the icy mist she came in search of shelter. It was probably not the first time. She can't have seen me. I tried to suck her, without

much success. Her udder was covered with dung, I took off my hat and, summoning all my energy, began to milk her into it. The milk fell on the ground and was lost, but I said to myself, No matter, it's free. She dragged me across the floor, stopping from time to time only to kick me. I didn't know our cows could be so inhuman. She must have recently been milked. Clutching the dug with one hand I kept my hat under it with the other. But in the end she prevailed. For she dragged me across the threshold and out into the giant streaming ferns, where I was forced to let go. (p. 90)

He continues that, drinking the milk, he reproached himself, "I could no longer count on this cow and she would warn the others".

Overwhelmed by the cow, he fears she will tell others: here, the cow suggests a sexual threat from women, just as the narrator has registered a sexual threat from men with the cave-dweller. Is the cow a cow at all, or a "symbolic equation", a concretisation of woman as bovine? Sexuality is on his mind, but perversely crammed into a tight, festering corner, like a dung valentine.

No sooner than this scene is described, our narrator is again on the road. Coming along for the ride, the reader is still puzzled about the confusing incoherence of what has just been described. The reader is in a position far from his earlier empathy. He has witnessed the narrator reject another human's sympathetic generosity and seems to locate sexual trespass, marked as filthy, everywhere, all the while clutching a tranquillising phial. The reader continues to listen as the narrator describes his own decompensation, of both mind and body: his

face notably seemed to have attained its climacteric. The humble, ingenious smile would no longer come, nor the expression of candid misery, showing the stars and the distaff. I summoned them, but they would not come. A mask of dirty old hairy leather, with two holes and a slit, it was too far gone for the old trick of please your honour and God reward you and pity upon me. It was disastrous. What would I crawl with in future? (p. 91)

Still describing a nightmare existence, the narrator persists in his reflective capacity to observe his own state. He continues in self-referential, psychoanalytic mode as he contemplates a life "beyond the stupid hope of rest or less pain" (p. 91).

The story grows increasingly less coherent. Our narrator begs "at a sunny corner", wearing an old pair of dark glasses. He mentions that they had been the property of a former tutor, thus reminding the reader that he was once a man of learning. But the reflection on his tutor, like the incident of the cow, rings oddly.

> He had given me the *Ethics* of Geulincx. They were a man's glasses, I was a child. They found him dead, crumpled up in the water closet, his clothes in awful disorder, struck down by an infarctus. Ah what peace. (p. 91)

Again, as with his discovery of the phial, he realises that not all of his possessions have been confiscated. Yet, as monologue becomes increasingly self-referential, the reader has no clue any longer as to meaning. What does emerge clearly from the narration on begging, is the narrator's contempt for those that give charity. His dependent rage at the other, the generalised other who has thrown him out of the charity hospital, who has stolen his money, who has since childhood, told him to "fuck off", achieves a transferential voice. Describing his begging-box, he writes,

> So I got a tin and hung it from a button of my greatcoat, what's the matter with me, of my coat, at pubis level. It did not hang plumb, it leaned respectfully towards the passerby, he had only to drop his mite. But that obliged him to come up close to me, he was in danger of touching me. In the end I got a bigger tin, a kind of big tin box, and I placed it on the sidewalk at my feet. But people who give alms don't much care to toss them, there's something contemptuous about this gesture which is repugnant to sensitive natures. To say nothing of their having to aim. They are prepared to give, but not for their gift to go rolling under the passing wheels, to be picked up perhaps by some undeserving person. So they don't give. There are those, to be sure, who stoop, but generally speaking people who give alms don't much care to stoop. What they like above all is to sight the wretch from afar, get ready their penny, drop it in their stride and hear the God bless you dying away in the distance. (p. 92)

The moments of trauma, registered only pages before by the reader, have shifted into focused and sardonic commentary. And what of the reader's charity? What is in the act of reading, for the reader? What is this extension of concern, of empathy anyway? Perhaps, then, the reader himself is also just another of the "sensitive souls" dropping their attentional penny in stride, just to hear the narrative equivalent of "God bless you dying away in the distance"?

Certainly, the narrator will not let this construction of the reader pass easily, but acts aggressively to scandalise the reader, to assault his sensibilities. There is no mistaking the violent shift of tone as he describes his physical attentions to scratching, earlier less aggressively described in terms of seaweed and crablice. With a vengeance, he returns to writing,

> one can masturbate up to the age of 70, and even beyond, but in the end it becomes a mere habit. Whereas to scratch myself properly, I would have needed a dozen hands. I itched all over, on the privates, in the bush up the navel, under the arms, in the arse , and then patches of eczema and psoriasis I could set raging just by thinking of them. It was in the arse I had the most pleasure. I stuck my forefinger up to the knuckle. Later if I had to shit, the pain was atrocious. (p. 93)

The narrative pretence of civility orientated to securing a compassionate, empathic hearing has now fully shifted. In short order, our narrator describes his location of a riverside shed, alive with water rats. There, expressing " a certain pleasure" only for the second time—now in rudimentary carpentry as the first had been in anal masturbation—he constructs a coffin-like box of an old boat and boards. He writes, "I don't know how long I stayed there. I was very snug in my box, I must say. It seemed to me I had grown much more independent of recent years" (p. 97).

Independent or regressed? He describes the dwindling of social and physical needs, even the dwindling of his words, within his box. His achievement? "To contrive a kingdom in the midst of the universal muck, then shit on it, ah that was me all over" (p. 98).

And then come hallucinatory visions. Here, Beckett returns, via his character, to the soft reassurance of paternal care, and an echo of the Dublin Mountains out to the Irish Sea:

> I saw the beacons, four in all, including a lightship. I knew them well, even as a child I had known them well. It was evening, I was with my father on a height, he held my hand. I would have liked him to draw me close with a gesture of protective love but his mind was on other things. (p. 99)

And here, our narrator parts company with the reader. Through the boat's open hole, pried open with the knife given him by the man in the cave, the water flows. He takes his calmative.

But however softly the passing, Beckett's narrator has held the reader's attention through the ultimate act of self-destruction. The reader, perhaps as disturbing to the narrator as a father who might have drawn him "close with a gesture of protective love", has passively monitored the story's telling in a one-way outpouring of multiple transference and passion. And without the benefit of calmative, the reader sits, contemplating what Beckett has done through the person of the narrator: a final hostility has been visited upon the reader in the forcible witnessing of another's suicide.

The next chapter discusses *The Expelled*, together with discussion of all four stories in relation both to their unique psychological contents and the reader's experience.

CHAPTER NINE

The novellas: Part Two

The present chapter continues discussion of the novellas within the context of Beckett's literary use of free association. It begins with consideration of *The Expelled* and continues in discussion of all four stories' unique psychological contents as well as the reader's experience.

The Expelled

The Expelled begins with an obsessional act of recollection, familiar to most adults. It is the mental act of remembering the number of steps in a staircase, once counted a "thousand times" and now lost to memory. More concretely, the reader recognises the difficulties in accurately recollecting life's numerous familiar daily details, after having changed the circumstances of one's life.

Yet, the reader's initial identification shifts as the narrator's own thinking is interrupted by another thought—even more finely grained than the first. The second thought concerns the method by which one counts off space with one's foot. Other obsessional reflections follow, becoming more difficult to understand until finally, like the narrator, the reader is somewhat confused. To call his situation a "dilemma", says the narrator, is "not too strong" a word. Certainly, this is now the case for the reader.

Beckett's narrator presents the reader with the dilemma of disorientation. The reader believes he is following and understanding a text until he is thrown off by what appears to be convoluted reverie:

> And when I say that the figure has gone from my mind, I mean that none of the three figures is with me any more, in my mind. It is true that if I were to find, in my mind, where it is certainly to be found, one of these figures, I would find it and it alone, without being able to deduce from it the other two. I would not know the third. No, I would have to find all three, in my mind, in order to know all three. (Beckett, 1995a, p. 46)

Without pause, and with the reader relying only on what might be the story's original imagery of imagining long-vanished steps, the narrator continues,

> Memories are killing. So you must not think of certain things, of those that are dear to you, or rather you must think of them, for if you don't there is the danger of finding them, in your mind, little by little. That is to say, you must think of them for a while, a good while, every day several times a day, until they sink forever in the mud. That's an order. (pp. 45–46)

The reader cringes. What is this? Given the number of times the narrator has said, "in my mind", it appears to be a statement of obsessional method for maintaining the presence and disappearance, in memory, of significant people and places. But the numerous references to "in my mind" suggest, too, an inside joke—perhaps hostile— as to another who has sought that the narrator, in fact, locate thoughts in his mind. This is certainly a phrase near and dear to psychotherapists, and particularly perhaps to group psychotherapists working in the Bion–Tavistock tradition; in this instance it remains the reader's association, without answer from the narrator.

What we do know is that the narrator says first one thing, and then undoes it, reversing himself. Attempting to distance himself from this quick reversal, he pretends certainty with a message, "That's an order", seemingly only to himself, as he seems not to have noticed that his direct address is to the reader.

Were the reader to stop, to close the book, he would scratch his head at the incoherence of this address. It has no context. It does not, therefore, occur in a psychoanalyst's office, or on the street, or in a café. Yet, the intensity of address supposes an intimacy between narrator and reader, of an interest in the narrator by the reader. Perhaps the reader is believed to be in the narrator's mind. Perhaps the assumption is that the narrator is contained or held within the reader's mind. It might be the presumption of this intimacy alone that propels the reader's continued interest in going on.

With the next paragraph, the reader is returned to solid ground. The narrator returns to his earlier focus on his originally imagined steps, and seemingly now calm, says, "After all it is not the number of steps that matter. The important thing to remember is that there were not many, and that I have remembered" (p. 47).

However straightforward this statement may be, the memory endures for the reader of the earlier incoherence, and it continues to gnaw underneath the relentless accumulation of facts and images presented by the narrator.

The narrator has fallen down a small number of steps. This has happened before, as the non-specific others with whom he lives have cruelly beaten and humiliated him. This time it is different. Eviction is final. The reader's only clue is that having lived in the same place from childhood, the narrator has now "overgrown into" maturity. It is not a child who is being turned out, but the overgrown child who is a man.

The narrative now becomes simpler, almost clear. The fall has not been serious and the narrator rests in the street, striking a somewhat cavalier pose with head resting upon the palm of his hand, his elbow supporting it all, propping himself up from the gutter. In a vaudevil-lean turn, a hat sails by, his possession returned to him by the others. And with this, the narrator says, "the spell was broken" (p. 47).

For the reader, this is the perfect moment to pause for reflection, because reflection is surely necessary, only two pages into this novella, to help clarify the creeping sense of disorientation. What begins in obsessive doubt and intellectualised defence, presumably to regain some sense of equanimity, leads to a moment of calm and then to the narrator's reflection "on my situation, notwithstanding its familiarity" (p. 47).

We are presented with a behavioural sample in a linear fashion, in the narrator's direct address, which moves from obsessional panic addressed with an equally obsessional defence, to a moment of relative calm, and onward to the use of somewhat different, certainly more literary language, "notwithstanding its familiarity". Within moments, the narrator's mental states change radically. All mental states, however, are focused on the recollection of memory. As for most of us, the smallest details are vague, but the broad strokes remain. No, as the narrator finally tells us, memory is not the problem. He remembers well enough. Then what is the dilemma? A good guess, given the degree of anxiety the narrator generates in the fear of memory loss, is his elective pain in maintaining the integrity of very painful memories. For the reader, it is a hypothesis grounded in the induced emotional experience of the narrator's own incoherence, and organised around the centrality in the narrator's thoughts of humiliation by others, in childhood and beyond. That this discourse mimics psychoanalysis is suggested by the narrator's several references to locating objects in the mind. This reminds the reader of Freud's analogy of free association as a window to the mind's passing thought.

The timeline is also disjointed. The narration occurs in an unspecified present. It is in that present that the obsessional panic arises. The movement, first to relative calm and, later, to reflection, suggests that same present, although the focus throughout remains past events of childhood and early adulthood. It is also probable that the narrator's picaresque "spell" of bemused reflection after eviction is historically incorrect, and a bit of defensive grandstanding for the reader after his initial disorientation. It is meant to reassure that the narrator is a reliable informant, "notwithstanding" what has already unfolded: multiple memories looking backward to different moments of the past.

Just as the numbering of steps linked to the narrator's expulsion, his memory of the sailing hat links to earlier history. He recalls that his father purchased the hat for him, and remains unsure about the father's hostile intent. The hat was the object of the narrator's humiliation from other boys. Did the father not know that his son was someone already "whose soul writhed from morning to night, in the mere quest of itself" (p. 48)?

Yet, he retained the hat even when his father died. However painfully, it tied him to the act of paternal giving. Would he ever be rid of it? "Some other time, some other time", the reader is told (p. 48). Having little, and that painful, the narrator holds on tightly.

The narrator returns to the moment of his eviction. He recalls that he was "in the prime of life, what I believe is called the full possession of one's faculties" adding facetiously, "Ah yes, them I possessed all right" (p. 48). Poignantly, he turned to look at the house, remarking to the reader, "I who never turned back when leaving".

This is a direct narrative link to the first novella, *The End*. It intimates to the reader that the stories are told by the same narrator. Whether they tell of different actual evictions, or elaborate the internal memory of a more primal eviction, the stories' images are substantially the same. In *The End*, if not in the prime of the narrator's life, as in *The Expelled*, the authorities found him substantially in possession of his faculties. There, too, the narrator remarks that he never turned back when leaving. What the narrator suggests is stoical virtue is an act anchored in denial of reality. It suggests a desire not to foreclose the fantasy of return with definitive rejection.

Looking up again at the house from his fallen position at the bottom of the stairs, the narrator sees his window "outrageously open". He observes that, "A thorough cleansing was in full swing. In a few hours they would close the window, draw the curtains, and spray the whole place with disinfectant. I knew them" (p. 49).

His expectation was to have lived in that house forever. He says,

> I wasn't afraid to look, for I knew they were not spying on me from behind the curtains, as they could have done if they had wished. But I knew them. They had all gone back into their dens and resumed their occupations. And yet I had done them no harm. (p. 49)

Looking forward to Beckett's third novella, *First Love*, the central act of expulsion is similarly celebrated by antagonists in the narrator's memory through the physical purging of the narrator's former room. As in *The Expelled* and *The End*, in *First Love*, the narrator depicts himself as harmless. However, he erects an elaborate defence around his hurt. He rationalises that were he the recipient of his late father's inheritance, he would treat his relatives differently, and recognises their cruelty in disobedience to his father's wishes rather than in direct relation to himself as victim.

Employing the same images in multiple stories, each narrated by an anonymous narrator, Beckett presents overlapping narratives, emphasising different internal states of mind and aspects of a single character, as in a series of psychoanalytic sessions. This repetition of similar scenes across multiple stories not only suggests continuity in the re-workings of traumatic memory, but also the centrality to the narrator of ongoing rumination of specific, underlying issues. This is a claustrophobic world of the mind—stuck "in the mind" indeed—circling around the hurts that shape narrational interpretations of internal and external experience.

Following the novellas in the order of their historical writing, therefore, facilitates the reader's contextualisation of the work beyond the constraints of narrative and what narrative evokes. In fact, this aspect of reading—exactly contrary to Bion's ideal analytic attitude in that it requires, in fact demands, memory and desire—provides the reader with a delicious additional motivation to continue reading. This is in the creative linkage of hide and seek, a meeting of reader's understanding with the narrator's telling, and in the following of Beckett's stylised associational format, it corresponds to what Christopher Bollas terms "perceptive identification", not so much an identification with the narrator as an appreciation of the narrator's unique identity. Working hand in glove with the action of projective identification, Bollas writes,

> If projective identification gets inside the other, perceptive identification stands outside to perceive the other. The term "identification" means quite different things for each concept. In projective identification it means identifying with the object; in perceptive identification it means perceiving the identity of the object. Both forms of knowing need to work in tandem with one another in a creative oscillation between appreciating the integrity of the object and perceiving its identity and then projecting parts of the self into the object, a form of imagination. (Bollas, 2006, p. 716)

In the novellas, therefore, the reader works towards the solution of a puzzle, striving to understand what is truly going on within these narrative tellings that is only disclosed through appreciation of the whole, rather than through any of its singular, constituent parts. At its best, the reader is able to achieve a consolidation, just as the narrator's projection locates his internal conflicts externally, within the reader.

The psychoanalytic pacing of the novellas as sessions is an "aha" moment, making more tolerable the periodic confusion and incoherence induced in the reader by Beckett's narrator(s). This potential coherence is made more difficult by the formal ordering of the novellas from *First Love* through to *The End*. While suggesting a developmental progression for the reader, the appearance of sequence undermines the historical points of linkage as each story follows the other, gathering for the reader in intensity. Nevertheless, having recognised the psychoanalytic session in the rhythm of the novellas, whether read singly or in any order, their context becomes unmistakable.

Again, as in *The End*, the narrator enters an unfamiliar town. This time, he writes, that it was the "scene of my birth and of my first steps in this world", but that he had gone out little, preferring the claustrophobic familiarity of his small room. Now he was disorientated, "lost before the confusion of innumerable prospects". His first act was religious. Echoing the Psalmist, he "raised my eyes to the sky, whence cometh our help" (p. 49).

Musing now, to the reader, ahistorically, he talks about a German trip, to the Luneberg Heath (p. 50). Unmistakably, this reference, together with the narrator's mention of his father's death, eviction, and the reality or fantasy of others' joy in his departure, strongly links *The Expelled* to the next novella, *First Love*, which begins in the cemetery where the narrator's father is buried and linked, then, to a German cemetery. In this way, through repetitive images cast both in similar and somewhat modified form across all four novellas, the reader constructs a more coherent sense of wholeness than from simple registration of seemingly disparate facts.

Within *The Expelled*, the reference to the Lundberg Heath is loosely connected to the narrator's description of claustrophobic existence. Suggesting reactive flight from this life within a room to life in the outdoors, he tells the reader that "I thought life would be good in the middle of a plain". The good life, beyond the bedroom, therefore, is one lived out of doors, but lived in great separation from other people, surrounded only by empty expanse. But this solution both disappoints and relieves the narrator, who says, "Yes, I don't know why, but I have never been disappointed, and I often was in the early days, without feeling at the same time, or a moment later, an undeniable relief" (p. 50).

The reader notes that the direct address is reflective of the narrator's multiple states of mind. It is no longer anxious, no longer defended. The narrator is settling in, after a difficult start, to his digressive associations.

The narrator now tells of his setting off, describing a lurching bizarre gait including: "extraordinary splaying of the feet to right and left of the line of march" and torso, "flabby as an old ragbag, tossing wildly to the unpredictable jolts of the pelvis" (p. 50). The reader immediately recognises this strange gait as Watt's own! In *Watt, en route* to Mr Knott's house, Beckett describes a similar, peculiar stride:

> Watt's way of advancing due east, for example, was to turn his bust as far as possible towards the north and at the same time to fling out his right leg as far as possible towards the south, and then to turn his bust as far as possible towards the south and at the same time to fling out his left leg as far as possible towards the north, and then again to turn his bust as far as possible towards the south, and then again to turn his bust as far as possible towards the south and to fling out his left leg as far as possible towards the north, and so on, over and over again, many many times, until he reached his destination, and could sit down. (Beckett, 2006a, p. 191)

The narrator appears to be attempting to engage the reader in the pseudo-comic, but this is not funny at all. Is he baiting the reader? In *The End*, he poked fun at himself, only to mock others: at relatively the same point in his monologue he refers to his "oddities" and says, "my appearance still made people laugh, with that hearty jovial laugh so good for the health" (pp. 81–82). Here, too, might he be using physical deformity as a comic defence against psychological vulnerability?

The narrator thinks back to childhood origins for his peculiar stride and summarises, "Poor juvenile solutions, explaining nothing . No need then for caution, we may reason on to our heart's content, the fog won't lift" (p. 51).

Perhaps this is true enough for the narrator; but what is the situation for the writer? Beckett wrote an eloquent case description of his own difficulties while in treatment with Bion (TM, 10 March 1935), but, at the same time, was working with a therapist who was both unconvinced in the efficacy of a "Mr-Feel-it-In-the-Past" psychotherapeutic orientation, yet still sought its deep, childhood roots in congruence with the method of "reductive analysis". Perhaps Beckett, like his former therapist, was unconvinced that psychological determinants could emerge with such crystalline clarity.

The narrator continues his tale. He comments ironically on a policeman's punitive, superegoic warning, "like a bit of Old Testament", before a disturbing vignette about a small child. The reader remembers the "fuck off" of mother to child in *The End* as the narrator, perhaps that little boy, grown older and now visiting his aggression upon others, says,

> I had to fling myself to the ground to avoid crushing a child. He was wearing a little harness, I remember, with little bells, he must have taken himself for a pony, or a Clydesdale, why not. I would have crushed him gladly. I loathe children, and it would have been doing him a service, but I was afraid of reprisals. (p. 51)

He lunges ahead, fulminating about the nastiness of children, until

> I fell then, and brought down with me an old lady covered with spangles and lace, who must have weighed about sixteen stone. Her screams soon drew a crowd. I had high hopes she had broken her femur, old ladies break their femurs easily, but not enough, not enough. (p. 52)

As if in confederacy with the reader, now probably shocked at the narrator's apparent enjoyment in recounting his sadism, he says that he "Took advantage of the confusion to make off, muttering unintelligible oaths, as if I were the victim, and I was, but I couldn't have proved it" (p. 52).

Rationalising his violence, he winks to the reader at his own clever sociopathy in mimicking his own psychiatric disturbance as a ploy.

Not finished yet with impressing his world view upon the reader, he builds to a crescendo:

> They never lynch children, babies, no matter what they do they are whitewashed in advance. I personally would lynch them with the utmost pleasure, I don't say I'd lend a hand, no, I am not a violent man, but I'd encourage the others and stand them drinks when it was done. (p. 52)

Here, for the reader, is an almost perfect recitation of the psychoanalytic, "identification with the aggressor". Carrying the scars of his own mistreatment, the narrator sees himself not only as victim but as victimiser, and visits cruelty upon others (A. Freud, 1936, pp. 109–121).

On the one hand, the effect upon the reader is hideous. The reader becomes the repository of another's ugly phantasy. The narrator, himself a fictional construction by Beckett, portrays a fictional situation which the reader is to internalise—whether marked by him as potentially true, given character development, or the fictional character's own probable fiction. As if by magic, and in literary form, Beckett achieves with the reader what the psychoanalytic subject desires from the analyst and the infant from the mother: the use of the other as a containment or holding environment for the projection of the subject's bad objects—his intolerable internal phantasies.

Within both psychoanalysis and within "good enough" parenting (Winnicott, 1953), the two-way relation between the individual and the containing object allows for, first, non-punitive neutralisation of hostile projections, and, second, their more benign return to the subject for constructive integration within his expanding reality sense.

Not so with the reader, however. Beckett's one-way projection induces the same fantasies within the reader, who is stuck with them. It is the interpersonal equivalent of Kafka's torture machine in "In the penal colony". Built to inscribe an enlightening message in the flesh of the damned, so that each knows the specific cause of their punishment, the machine goes awry and, instead, crucifies. Certainly, when it works, "It's a wonderful piece of apparatus "(Kafka, 1948, p. 185). So, too, is the interpersonal action of projection into the other, who acts in the role of maternal containment for unbearable internal objects.

Beckett's own psychoanalysis unfolded before the development of this theory. But the action of the patient's layering emotional experience, possibly overwhelming experience, upon the other, was, nevertheless, present. It is possible that Beckett's own late splitting of his transference to Bion, through the agency of Thompson, was meant to defend against the patient's fear of the analyst's potential retribution. Beckett himself hints at fear of his analyst's retribution to MacGreevy, following attendance with Bion and Thompson at Jung's Tavistock lecture, when he writes that Bion might have "done us both a disservice by inviting me to meet him in that way", immediately followed by a literal escape clause, "I don't think I shall go on with the analysis after Xmas" (TM, 8 October 1935).

It matters little that it would take decades, counted in the development of Bion's professional psychoanalytic life, for him to recognise the idea of analyst as container to contain toxic psychic elements jetti-soned by the patient. Beckett's own self-observation—coincidentally with an earlier edition of Bion—allowed him to feel, if not clearly to articulate, the powerful and unspoken effect of the patient, through the vagaries of free association, upon the analyst. Beckett's literary achievement, through the novellas, is in replicating this implicit inter-personal action in the person of the reader relative to the narrator.

The Expelled continues, apparently in a linear fashion, but it is not, in fact, quite linear. The narrator tricks the reader, skipping from one historical period of his life to another. Almost as an aside, he mentions that the money inherited from his father might have been stolen, throwing him into a penniless period. But then, mysteriously, the narrator becomes the benefactor of an inheritance, possibly of someone

> who dandled me on her knees while I was still in swaddling clothes and there had been some lovey-dovey. Sometimes that suffices. I repeat, in swaddling clothes, for any later it would have been too late, for lovey-dovey. (p. 55)

And what is "lovey-dovey"? It seems to be some version of maternal care, now satirised. Beckett's early short story, "One case in a thou-sand", based on a clinical vignette described to him by Geoffrey Thompson (Thompson, 1976), relates the protagonist to his old nanny "whom as baby and small boy he had adored" and who holds the secret to a childhood trauma, "so trivial and intimate that it need not be enlarged on here" (Beckett, 1995a, pp. 20–24) but linked to his childhood desire to grow up in order to marry her. Certainly, this would be consistent with the psychoanalytic idea of childhood sexu-ality.

But this small bequest, at a distinctively different time than that described as occurring on the day of the narrator's expulsion, facili-tates the actions that bring the narrative to a close. What appears to link these two very different time periods is the presence in the narra-tor's memory of a funeral. We do not learn the significance of the funeral to the narrator in *The Expelled*. Perhaps it is somehow related to the father's death, which later begins the narrative of *First Love*, but that can only be a guess. The information is not available.

Instead, the reader is led away from the funeral's significance by the continuing narrative. This is exactly the defensive operation observable in psychoanalysis, when a clue to an issue of significance is casually dropped in the context of quite another set of issues. It will take time and multiple iterations for the analyst to connect, in his containment of the narratives, any significance.

For now, the reader is taken on an engaging series of interchanges with the driver of a horse-drawn cab which points, as homage, in two literary directions. That the link between this story element and the ongoing narrative is via a funeral, and that the cab is booked later in the day for a funeral, immediately suggest the horse-drawn funeral cab in the opening chapters of Joyce's *Ulysses*. That the narrator leads the taxi-driver on—with the cabbie's belief in his passenger's sexual interests, culminating with the introduction of the narrator to the driver's wife—suggests another famous cab-ride, that of Emma Bovary through the streets of Rouen. The psychoanalyst Sodré points to Flaubert's "clear differentiation between the creative use of imagination which enriches life and its perversion into addictive daydreaming used to replace awareness of life, and destroy real meaning" (Sodré, 1999, p. 49).

Here, the party to the narrator's historical composite is the reader, led unwittingly through the allusive compression of Joyce and Flaubert, as channelled by the narrator. Indeed, Beckett had been influenced by each, and praised Flaubert's capacity for presenting an "irreducible" confusion in an "inner precision" conveying incoherence (LeJuez, 2008, p. 29).

Like Emma Bovary, Beckett's narrator takes the reader for a ride, telling a fantasy which, while maintaining his passive passenger role, puts him actively in the driver's seat, thus determining both the cab-driver's day's agenda and the reader's receptive attention. Here, as with Sodré's description of Emma Bovary, the narrator's lifeless fantasy "needs to be compulsively enacted in external reality" under his own control as he trades on the other's erroneous understanding of the narrator's interests until, after spending the night in the driver's stable with the horse, the narrator bolts.

Similarly, the narrator bolts in his narrative. Of course, just as in *The End*, he has found a temporary and claustrophobic stopping-place in the stable as he had in the Greek woman's house and in his friend's cave. But even the presence of the horse—as well as the man and woman upstairs—causes him to flee. Loving—whether human relatedness to the horse or to the sexuality implied by the cab-driver and his wife—is less tolerable than the narrator's ongoing state of dying.

In the meantime, Beckett makes the reader party to the narrator's "telling" of a dream with all its elements: released from the reality of narrative time and compressing literary mentors Joyce and Flaubert while telling the dream's manifest content without the benefit of deconstructing the latent, but leaving it under the aegis of the reader.

If Flaubert represented for Beckett the incoherent conveyed within narrative form, Joyce represented the literary depiction of internal monologue. However, for Beckett, Joyce's articulation of the unconscious lacked the authenticity of the real thing. Knowlson cites Beckett's German Diary of 26 March 1937 in conveying Beckett's sense that Joyce's interior monologues within *Ulysses* presented an inauthentic rendering of unconscious process.

Disagreeing with Joyce that internal process emerges whole and fully formed, Beckett agrees with Flaubert that unconscious depiction must reflect incoherence. Here, Beckett's narrator plays with the reader. He "uses" the reader, who is probably unknowing of the author's divergence from Joyce on matters of interior dialogue, to contain a layered narrative, presumably an extension of *The End's* earlier narrative.

Certainly, the story has been told in a manner the reader will find internally consistent with *The End*. The narrator, both contemptuous and manipulative, toys with the taxi driver, while also assuring himself some temporary and dependent comfort. He finds temporary refuge in filth, and among animals, and bolts from the situation, suddenly ending the story without apparent resolution. But, here, Beckett has also illustrated the variegated levels of interior dialogue, their lies as well as their revelations, and, in the course of his cab-ride, playfully winks not only at psychoanalysis and Bion, but also at Joyce and Flaubert. He ends in *faux* innocence, disclaiming any intentional meaning, just as a patient might in a complex, circular session, "I don't know why I told this story, I could just as well have told another. Perhaps some other time I'll be able to tell another. Living souls, you will see how alike they are" (p. 60).

How like the concluding lines of *The End*: "The memory came faint and cold of the story I might have told, a story in the likeness of my life, I mean without the courage to end or the strength to go on" (p. 99).

Certainly, the purportedly living soul telling *The End* and *The Expelled* are so alike that they seem cut out of one another.

The Calmative

The Calmative begins in a manner determined to destablilise the receptive reader:

> I don't know when I died. It always seemed to me I died old, about ninety years old, and what years, and that my body bore it out, from head to foot. But this evening, alone in my icy bed, I have the feeling I'll be older than the day, the night, when the sky with all its lights fell upon me, the same I had so often gazed on since my first stumblings on the distant earth. (Beckett, 1995a, p. 61)

Is the reader to believe the narrator is dead? This would entail a very wide suspension of disbelief. Rather, while the narrator himself might be elderly, he is still alive and kicking. The clue for the reader is not to be found in this text, but in another, First Love. There, the more youthful narrator, visiting his father's cemetery plot, describes his own future epitaph. In part, it reads that the deceased "so hourly died that he lived on till now" (p. 26).

The narrator tells us that every living moment has been imbued with the torment of dying: unpleasant, perhaps exaggerated, but a summation of his experience. Yet, by beginning post mortem, the reader is necessarily disorientated. Orientation is possible only in two directions. The first is misleading: the narrator, narrating, lives. Later in Beckett's writing, as in the "trilogy" and *Texts for Nothing*, the idea of unconscious conceptions continuing as an ongoing physical stream following physical death would be considered.

The second undermines the psychoanalytic ideal advanced by the mature Bion, that each session be approached without "memory or desire". Indeed, Beckett makes it imperative that the reader *remember*. The reader's act of memory affirms the adequate maternal containment of the narrator's associations within the reader's mind. Throughout the novellas, Beckett has alluded, back and forth, across the boundaries of discrete stories, to elements explained or touched upon elsewhere. What seems to be a straightforward statement,

> One day I caught sight of my son. He was striding along with a brief-case under his arm. He took off his hat and bowed and I saw he was as bald as a coot. I was almost certain it was he. I turned round to gaze after him. He went bustling along on his duck feet, bowing and scrap-ing and flourishing his hat left and right. The insufferable son of a bitch. (p. 87)

is likely to be the fantasy of meeting with the child abandoned by the narrator in *First Love*, who wrote,

> What finished me was the birth. It woke me up. What that infant must have been going through! I fancy she had a woman with her, I seemed to hear steps in the kitchen, on and off. It went to my heart to leave a house without being put out. (p. 45)

Certainly, the narrator's reflection on his flight as being different from the more familiar expulsion fits our narrator as we know him. Were the novellas understood as multiple sessions, indeed, as different retrospective reflections of multiple points within a single life, the splitting of ideas and situations across stories makes both narrative and analytic sense. The reader must work to unify what the narrator has split, to unify it within the reader's own mind.

This, in fact, was Beckett's own declared sense of narrative closure. Lecturing about Racine to Trinity undergraduates, fifteen years before the novellas, Beckett explained that a play ends when, within recep-tive self-consciousness, the mind "faces facts" with an "integral awareness" of characters' fragmentary expression of a greater whole (LeJuez, 2008, p. 58). Beckett's description comes close to Bollas's notion of perceptive identification in momentary appreciation or the object's singularity (Bollas, 2006).

Across multiple free associational accounts in the novellas, Beckett demands that the reader integrate both repetitive narrative aspects of character as well as partial aspects, hints dropped in multiple places. Another example is in the title, *The Calmative*, itself. The reader's understanding of the calmative's nature is that it is cyanide, featured as a lethal dose both in *First Love* and in *The End*. But Beckett's trick of the mind is that the cyanide that appears in *First Love* and the phial of calmative swallowed in *The End* are physical potions, whereas *The Calmative* concerns the psychological act of storytelling. Beckett's narrator says,

So I'll tell myself a story, I'll try and tell myself another story, to try and calm myself, and it's there I feel I'll be old, old, even older than the day I fell, calling for help, and it came. Or is it possible that in this story I have come back to life, after my death? No, it's not like me to come back to life, after my death. (p. 61)

The receipt of such storytelling, of course, has been the reader's task. Not so ironically, that which calms the narrator disrupts the reader with its frequent incoherence or imposition of catastrophe. In this sense, storytelling within the confines of Beckett's one-way dyad is a mechanism for extruding the narrator's sense of chaos and catastrophe. A projective device that leaves the narrator calmer, it approximates what Anna O termed "the talking cure"—the confessional dimension of psychoanalysis.

The story unfolds with contents familiar to the reader, from previous novellas: "being thrown out"; a "den littered with empty tins . . . a ruined folly"; "I have changed refuge so often, in the course of my rout, that now I can't tell between dens and ruins"; and a dreamlike sense of unreality:

it is true that you often move along in a dream, houses and factories darken the air, trams go by and under your feet wet from the grass there are suddenly cobbles. I know only the city of my childhood, I must have seen the other, but unbelieving. (p. 62)

It is a frightening world he describes, of "assassins" in a "bed of Terror", as he tells "my story in the past none the less, as though it were a myth, or an old fable, for this evening I need another age, that age to become another age in which I became what I was" (p. 62). The reader is on familiar ground:[1] another retrospective view. As in *The End*, death by drowning is referenced. Again, as before, there is a bald man—once his son in *The End*—now a comedian. And just like the teller of this story, the reader sighs in the welter of references, "Its point escapes me" (p. 63). Again, the self-pity,

But it's to me this evening something has to happen, to my body as in myth and metamorphosis, this old body to which nothing ever happened, or so little, which never met with anything, loved anything, wished for anything, in its tarnished universe, except for the mirrors to shatter, the plane, the curved, the magnifying, the minifying, and to vanish in the havoc of its images. (p. 63)

But the fastidiously attuned eye once railing against physical symptoms as in *First Love*: "the corn, the cramp, the kibe, the bunion, the hammer toe, the nail ingrown, the fallen arch, the common blain, the club foot, duck foot, goose foot, pigeon foot, flat foot, trench foot" (p. 33) has turned to address the shattered hopes of life's representational mirrors.

The idea of story returns, remembering how his father calmed him, as a child, through the telling of stories, and how the specifics of calming were in its rituals, just as in psychoanalysis, with its iterative telling of one's life. For Beckett's narrator, what calmed was not simple storytelling, but the ritual of reading. Does the reader detect an empathic note, the hope of Beckett's narrator that somehow, despite all the projected material to be considered, the act of reading itself provides the reader's psychic retreat?

He writes,

> He had to read it to me, evening after evening, or pretend to read it to me, turning the pages and explaining the pictures that were of me, already, evening after evening the same pictures til I dozed off on his shoulder. If he had skipped a single word I would have hit him, with my little fist, in his big belly bursting out of the old cardigan and unbuttoned trousers that rested him from his office canonicals. (p. 64)

Thinking of father as he enters a strange and empty city, he is reminded of their ancient walks together through the meadows. His perception, as in *The End*, seems disorientated, "the very capstans this evening are out of order" (p. 65).

He considers a potential sexual encounter with a young boy, "holding a goat by the horn"; and thinks "can this base thought be mine?" (p. 66), but he is speechless and ashamed. Losing the moment of opportunity, he thinks to savour the goat's dung, "the pellets so soon cold and hard, sniff and even taste them" but decides not to. He runs, moving fast.

He emerges in a square, referencing again his foreign travels. He enters a church, lying before the altar then springing up a staircase, "mindless of my heart, like one hotly pursued by a homicidal maniac" (p. 68). Reaching his destination, a little dome, he flattens himself to the wall and inches around clockwise. He encounters another man, moving the other way and thinks, "how I'd love to push him, or him to push me, over the edge" (p. 69).

The dreamlike sequencing reminds the reader of the future Molloy. And, indeed, the narrator asks himself, "into what nightmare thingness am I fallen?" (p. 69). As in *Molloy*, the narrator seeks to find his way, but there is no one to ask where is "the Shepard's Gate for the love of God!" (p. 71). Dreaming, the narrator is certain that "I was still of this world", but "paying the price". His inner story is the opposite of calming; it is frightening and fearful.

He sits. Another man sits beside him and asks questions. The narrator is silent, but listens to the story of the other man's life. Somehow, the hearing of that story revitalises him. "Words were coming back to me, and the way to make them sound" (p. 71). One man's transmission of story revitalises the next. Perhaps the narrator is reminding the reader that there is more than the absorption of frustration in listening to another, however incoherent. The dyad itself, with its possibilities for human engagement, is life giving.

Age and aspects of sexual preoccupation are discussed, and in a manner reminding the reader of the narrator's habit of speaking freely, as if to shock:

> If it's not a rude question, he said, how old are you? I don't know, I said. You don't know! He cried. Not exactly, I said. Are thighs much in your thoughts, he asked. Arses, cunts and environs? I didn't follow. No more erections naturally, he said. Erections? I said. The penis, he said, you know what the penis is, there, between the legs. Ah that! I said. It thickens, lengthens, stiffens and rises, he said, does it not? I assented , though they were not the terms I would have used. (p. 73)

The man holds a bag, full of phials, on his lap. Thinking he wishes to buy one (the same sort of question put to the narrator by the taxi driver in *The Expelled*), the narrator says he has no money. The other man violently strikes him, speaking in a "caressing voice" as his fingers dug sharply into the other's neck. Pain and pleasure merged. He exchanges the phial for a kiss and asks himself or the reader, "have I been dreaming?"

He passes a horse-butcher's, imagining first a woman, then a young girl, who, like a former love, vanishes down a stair. As in *The Expelled*, the narrator contemplates, in his mind, a staircase. This time, he is not counting the steps down which he once fell, but considering the image: "On the steps of the loved one, who could not love and will not come back, and whose steps say so, that she could not love and will not come back" (p. 74).

The dream image is of a person who could not love and who shall not return. It is a self-directed thought, a depressed reminiscence of a loveless life, though momentarily lightened by another.

Images continue: a house "full of people", suggesting to the reader the houses before, from which he had been exiled. He thinks of asking for protection and shelter for the night, but does not, and is again on his way. He falls as others walk around him, extending him the courtesy of not stepping on him. Reality, he says, returns:

> And I had no need to raise my head from the ground to know I was back in the same blinding light as before. I said, Stay where you are, down on the friendly stone, or at least indifferent, don't open your eyes, wait for morning. (p. 76)

He recalls his father's storytelling, and again, as in *The Expelled*, but in vain, "I raised without hope my eyes to the sky" (p. 77), and continued.

The reader is only a witness, here, an analyst to an unanalysed dream. The dream is chock full of horror, of violence and sex, of humour and despair. It concludes with the narrator's engagement in another day: "for the light I stepped in put out the stars, assuming they were there, which I doubted, remembering the clouds" (p. 77).

What is meant to calm is terrifying. The life described in *The Calmative* is described looking backward, in dream imagery. It is the claustrophobic territory of the mind, knowing only itself, shut out against the world, but, however sceptical, hopeful that something in the multiply storied dyadic exchange between narrator and reader will alleviate the pain.

Note

1. Although the subject matter amplifies somewhat in its abstraction, suggesting the later *Trilogy* and beyond, to *Texts For Nothing* as the narrator describes the fantasy of physical deterioration.

CHAPTER TEN

Three essays on "the trilogy"

This chapter addresses three dimensions of Beckett's "trilogy". The first "The relation between writer and reader", addresses the centrality of the dyadic relation in Beckett's expansion of his free associational technique from the novellas to the trilogy. It is followed by a section titled "The last but one but one", addressing repetitive iterations within Beckett's *Molloy*. The third section, "Working through the trilogy", examines the process of Beckett's narrative clarification accomplished through the repetitive action of multiple narratives.

The relation between writer and reader

In the gap between writer and reader, what can be thought of as cohering, coming together, and how? Setting out, we suggest at least three "fields" of coherence: (1) the narrative elements, the story itself, told by the writer and apprehended by the reader; (2) the representation of the emotional lives of characters; (3) the processing of the story, in whole or part, by its audience. Each of these elements requires an intersubjective relation of back-and-forth between persons, of projection and introjection, to achieve meaning.

Within this implied back-and-forth, what breaks down, of course, is genuine real-time interpersonal communication. Unlike the therapeutic dialogue in which a patient's productions are met with the analyst's response, the act of reading proceeds in one direction, from the writer's characters to the reader's thoughts: there can be no continuation of the process. As we discussed earlier, in the discussion of Beckett's novellas, the assimilation into literature of the psychoanalytic technique of free association radicalises and cruelly intensifies the characters' pitilessly direct address to the reader.

Unbracketed by any contextualising comments, Beckett's stories are relentless in their demands upon the reader. The stories themselves as fields of coherence pale in comparison to the characters' investments not only in their own telling of narrative, but also to the implicit effect their telling has upon the reader. It is possible, as in *Molloy*, for the reader to impose order on the text. It may be roughly divisible into sections revolving around the narrator's changing preoccupations of mind—such as the introduction, the visit to mother, or the incident of Lousse's dog, but while such approximate coherence might satisfy, within each section, the reader is led circuitously and confusingly by the narrator. The reader proceeds at his own risk, as Beckett's narrator says explicitly:

> All I know is what the words know, and the dead things, and that makes a handsome little sum, with a beginning, middle, and an end as in the well-built phrase and the long sonata of the dead. And truly it little matters what I say, this, this or that or any other thing. Saying is inventing. Wrong, very rightly wrong, You invent nothing, you think you are inventing, you think you are escaping, and all you do is stammer out your lesson, the remnants of a pensum one day got by heart and long forgotten, life without tears, as it is wept. To hell with it anyway. Where was I? (Beckett, 2006b, p. 27)

The contradictions of "wrong, very rightly wrong" trip up the reader, taking in the stammered lessons, as reading proceeds. Also, the idea that "all I know is what the words know" is a purposive misstatement, because the words are directed, as pointedly as at the compulsion to repeat, towards an intended audience, the reader. For this purpose, words are not dead things, but enlivened projectiles— even if the appropriate empathic resonance is a desire to throw the book across the room. The writer's production is not so much in the conveyance of a "story" but in the action of words upon the reader. Is he living or dying or both? Is this a philosophical question or an element crucial to the telling, which goes on and on as the narrator says, "My life, my life, now I speak of it as of something over, now as of a joke which still goes on, and it is neither, for at the same time it is over and it goes on, and is there any tense for that" (Beckett, 2006b, p. 32).

The reader might tire of the aporia, of the statements and their oppositions. Yet, the reader's response does not affect the narrator. Indeed, this format ensures that the narrator's world remains narrowly private and cut-off from any benefit of human contact except for the excretory function of displacing worded content in the reader. The reader, through Molloy's narration, is often befuddled, much as Molloy is when attempting to communicate with his degraded, detested, and much desired mother: "I mean I knew more or less what she was talking about, and if I hadn't always taken part personally in the scenes she evoked, it was just as if I had" (Beckett, 2006b, p. 13). But, as Molloy, as narrator, is painfully aware, this approximation is hardly the clear and crisp communication of ideas. Rather, as pressures upon the other—paralleling Molloy's physical knocks upon his mother's head—the other often gets the wrong idea. "She must have thought I was saying no to her all the time, whereas nothing was further from my purpose" (Beckett, 2006b, p. 14).

The text's effect on the other might be anticipated or wished by Molloy; or, perhaps, the more appropriate attitude is that it simply remains ambiguous, understood or not. Mother attempts to babble, Molloy attempts to narrate. For the reader, the complete text stands alone, as the other's object, unaffected by reciprocal response. The writer's text does not change as a function of the reading audience. The reader, therefore, apprehends the textual object and does with it what he/she wishes: makes personal sense or nonsense of the text as a private act without link to the author, who has provided the object as stimulus. The reader attempts to construe.

Molloy's declaration above about his narration as invention, escape, or fragment of misremembered experience must ultimately frustrate. "To hell with it anyway" (Beckett, 2006b, p. 27) is the author's comment to himself in contemplating (mis)communication to the reader as other. Despite this negation from within the author's awareness of separation, the reader remains the object of desire none the less. Molloy depends upon the reader as absent interlocutor as he reorientates himself with "where was I?" (Beckett, 2006b, p. 27). The narrator claims that "there were no words for the want of need in which I was perishing" (Beckett, 2006b, p. 30) as he thrives in the telling of the miseries of both original maternal deprivation and subsequent human relatedness. Rather, in a slow and, for the reader, excruciating journey, the narrator sadistically imposes his need to be heard—despite the claim that he has no adequate words or language.

Two fields of sensemaking—in writing and in reading—meet in the text, and what coheres, therefore, can never be perfect in the sense of an author's intentional singularly, yet achieves a directed communication from author to reader, not only of the textual object as a whole, but primarily, as an assemblage of parts, within the reader's apprehension. The reader, in this sense, not only interprets the work read (without interrogation or discussion of the author), but also wonders at the meanings it conveys as a personal object interactive with the reader's emotional world. Critical within the communications seem to be embedded hints within the narrative—clues to the story of the character Molloy. What is important is related time and time again. As the character says,

> For the particulars, if you are interested in particulars, there is no need to despair, you may scrabble on the right door, in the right way, in the end. It's for the whole there seems to be no spell. Perhaps there is no whole, before you're dead. (Beckett, 2006b, p. 23)

The closest Molloy comes, in these particulars, is in approximation of his pensum, his life-task, more clearly defined as a positive virtue rather than non-productive repetition by the trilogy's conclusion in *The Unnamable*. This credo is

> Not to want to say, not to know what you want to say, not to be able to say what you think you want to say, and never to stop saying, or hardly ever, that is the thing to keep in mind, even in the heat of composition. (Beckett, 2006b, p. 23)

And, indeed, it mirrors the author's own comments, on interview, about the artist's work: "The situation is that of him who is helpless, cannot act, in the event cannot paint, since he is obliged to paint. The act is of him who, helpless, unable to act, acts, in the event paints, since he is obliged to paint" (Beckett, 1984, p. 43).

Despite helplessness and unknowing, inability and incapacity, life is lived in the obligation of the telling. Here, Molloy's narrating meets Mag's toothless and unconscious babbling in the human condition.

The last but one but one

The novellas establish the narrator's direct expression to the reader, and the effect of multiple stories parallels the effect of multiple psychotherapeutic sessions, layering linkages both said and unsaid within the recipient. The reader's rapt attention is demanded from the narrator as the four vignettes, each presently told as the recited memory of differing, related pasts.

The trilogy demands a similar dedication of the reader; but in adapting a different viewpoint regarding the narrator's monologue, it is both more exacting of attention and less emotionally demanding than the novellas. While presenting an enormously more complex situation, the trilogy's own self-absorption allows the reader breathing room. The trilogy begins with a brief introduction in *Molloy*, explaining somewhat elliptically that the written text to be told is a version of a text upon which the narrator has worked diligently. It is the authoritative text, approved by a committee of auditors who function interpretatively in reforming the narrator's recollections into a shape valid in their own assessment. If the narrator is unsure of the production which will be *Molloy*, his promised "last but one but one" (Beckett, 2006b, p. 4) telling of his story, it is because he is unsure of his own voice relative to the impositions of others. By the time the reader reaches *The Unnamable*, the third volume of the trilogy, he learns that this psychiatric committee is the author's fantasy. It is

> Inexistent, invented to explain I forget what. Ah yes, all lies, God and man, nature and the light of day, the heart's outpourings and the means of understanding, all invented, basely, by me alone, with the help of no one, since there is no one, to put off the hour when I must speak of me. (Beckett, 2006b, p. 298)

The fantasy has functioned as a vehicle for multiple characters and situations. It is a constructed fiction, a container of thought, to be studied both by writer and reader. Because it is a cohesive—if often seemingly incoherent—text, it allows the reader an emotional distance denied in the emotionally dependent novellas. Rather, like the author or narrator himself, the reader is positioned to contemplate the objects of the narrator's thought. While the narrator's psychological motivations extend to the use of the reader as container of emotion within the novellas, in the trilogy, the reader is enlisted as a trusting partner in the dyad, contemplating objects of narrated thought as the relational third, the object both of subject and reader's attentions. Here, Beckett focuses not so much on the behaviour of the narrator, which propels the novellas, or on the demands for a containing relationship necessarily provided by the reader, but reorientates from free associative direct address to description of how the mind works, in a world of thought without limitation.

Molloy lurches uncertainly, propelling the reader through time and confusion. Only at a stretch does its narration describe a conventional sequence of beginning, middle, and end. Rather, *Molloy* coheres as a succession of moments, descriptive of different mental states. These achieve cohesion through an integrative act of reading that is akin to the psychoanalyst's interpretive clinical listening. While the patient's objects of enquiry shift from subject to subject, the clinician's interest remains the patient's mind. So, too, does the reader's attention follow the narrative contours of Molloy, hovering before closure, wondering at the purpose and meaning of the text.

Molloy "begins" with an introduction informing the reader that the words to be read have already been written at great effort. They have been vetted and commented upon in a back-and-forth of writer and auditor suggestive of a structure resembling therapy. With the narrator's promise of a later beginning, the reader becomes aware of a doubling, a parallel process. Just as the narrator questions whether his own, organic telling is a beginning, against that which his auditors assume to be a different version, the textual beginning of *Molloy* serves as a prolegomena to what the narrator promises as his actual narrative beginning.

Suddenly, the penny drops for the reader. The narrator's introductory promise of a later beginning is for a story whose form is approved by auditors as credible. It is to be a standard edition, a single iteration among many. Its value in this regard is its authorisation through the eyes and diacritical marks of others. The narrator's introduction is purposive. It formally announces a literary contract with the reader. Soon, the reader is again thrown off by the narrator's assertion that the version to be produced is not definitive, but it is almost complete: "the last but one but one".

Beckett's shorter series of four novellas unfolded without this kind of formal framework. While linked through story elements and repetitions of similar situations at different moments of their narrators' lived experience, they resembled four different psychotherapy sessions of the same patient. Yet, unlike the casual remarks made by a patient to a listening other, broadly linking one day's recitation to another's, there are no links, no clues that "as I told you yesterday", or "you might remember when I . . .". Instead, somewhat uncannily, the reader is placed in a perfect situation reminiscent of the mature Wilfred Bion's clinical caution to approach each patient in each session with neither memory nor desire. Connections may exist—but are never definitive. As the narrator comments about the mental association with which he begins *First Love*, "That other links exist, on other levels, between these two affairs, is not impossible. I have enough trouble as it is in trying to say what I think I know" (Beckett, 1995a, p. 25).

If the novellas represent the unfolding of free associational direct address from narrator to reader's apprehension, then *Molloy*, the beginning of Beckett's trilogy, suggests the offering of a clinical write-up, a narrative case study, by the patient himself. Beckett's 1935 letter to Thomas MacGreevy provides an example. Beckett wrote,

> For me the position is really a simple and straightforward one, or was until complicated by the analysis, obviously necessarily. For years I was unhappy, consciously and deliberately ever since I left school and went to TCD, so that I isolated myself more & more, undertook less & less & lent myself to a crescendo of disparagement of others & myself. But in all that there was nothing that struck me as morbid. The misery & solitude & apathy & the sneers were the elements of an index of superiority & guaranteed the feeling of arrogant "otherness", which seemed as right & natural & as little morbid as the ways in which it was not so much expressed as implied & reserved & kept available for a possible utterance in the future. It was not until that way of living, or rather negation of living, developed such terrifying physical symptoms that it could no longer be pursued, that I became aware of anything morbid in myself. In short, if the heart had not put the fear of death into me I would still be boozing & sneering & lounging around & feeling that I was too good for anything else. It was with a

specific fear & a specific complaint that I went to Geoffrey, then to Bion, to learn that the "specific fear and complaint" was the least important symptom of a diseased condition that began in a time which I could not remember, my "pre-history", a bubble on the puddle; and that the fatuous torments which I had treasured as denoting the superior man were all part of the same pathology. That was the picture as I was obliged to accept it, and that is still largely the picture . . . If the heart still bubbles it is because the puddle has not been drained, and the fact of its bubbling more fiercely than ever is perhaps open to receive consolation from the waste that splutters most, when the bath is nearly empty. (10 March 1935)

However well crafted, even this definitive statement would be subject to change. Like Beckett's shift from viewing a "specific fear and complaint", its future vicissitudes, its elaborations, turns, and reversals, mark it only as a single member in Beckett's own interpretative series as patient, an example in personal correspondence of "the last but one but one".

In *Molloy*, as in therapy itself, the narrated story addresses the complexity of narrative construction, multiplied by the dyadic enterprise. The "beginning" promised to the reader is a reflection of the narrator's efforts, validated through reward by his auditor. The narrator makes no assertion of his own trust in the telling, merely noting that others have found it acceptable. His contractual assumption is that because his narrative has been found acceptable by others, the reader will find it acceptable as well. Anyway, for him as storyteller, there will be other versions. In this, it heralds what will be Beckett's trilogy. "This time, then once more I think, then perhaps a last time, then I think it'll be over, with that world too. Premonition of the last but one but one" (Beckett, 2006b, p. 4). As is the case in the novellas, the reader is free to proceed or not, as he pleases.

While promising a "beginning" vetted by others and so suggesting a coherence of content, the beginning of *Molloy* delivers something rather different. It is the first of at least three tellings, revealing of something beyond the simplicity of tales told. This is Molloy's private theatre, or really the private theatre of Beckett, refracted through his Molloys, Murphys, Malones, Mahoods, Watts, and Worms, as actors whose burdens become the object of both the author's and the reader's contemplation. The reader and author are bound, in this way, focused upon the third, which is the author's projective use of character.

Through the third, Beckett expands the reader's experience from simple receptivity of the narrator's direct address to a linkage with the narrator in contemplation of different mental objects, including the actions of others, past history, fantasy, morbid humour, and philosophical reflection.

The beginning of *Molloy* is hardly a beginning at all. It is the narrator's dreamlike observation of two men, momentarily greeting each other in a manner that will endure, for each of them, forever. This might, in parallel, represent the author's wish for relatedness with the reader, or the reader's action in projecting himself within the blank screen of the author's projected narrator. It also suggests the projection of a memory and a desire, the crossing of paths in time, of Beckett and another significant traveller in his life, Wilfred Bion. There is, of course, no way to know, but all these possibilities seem to lurk within the image.

The human objects of the narrator's telling are anonymous everymen who function as the containers of the narrator's anxiety and apprehension as he uses them to describe his own mental state. What is observed might not even be "true" in the sense that, disbelief suspended, it is "meant" by the author to be the narrator's "truth". The narrator says,

> And I am perhaps confusing several different occasions, and different times, deep down, and deep down is my dwelling, oh not deepest down, somewhere between the mud and the scum. And perhaps it was A one day at one place, then C another at another, then a third the rock and I, and so on for the other components, the cows, the sky, the sea, the mountains. I can't believe it. No, I will not lie, I can easily conceive it. No matter, no matter, let us go on, as if all arose from one and the same weariness, on and on heaping up and up, until there is no room, no light, for any more. (Beckett, 2006b, p. 10)

Rather, these are compositions of the mind, constructions relating to what we take to be the psychology of the teller. The truth of the narration is narrative truth, the truth of a created fiction. It is imperative and dreamlike—its manifest elements fused composites of other people, other days. It even concludes, as if within a dream, with the narrator's location of a bicycle he did not know he had, oddly left in a place he remembers. What the reader takes from the section, what coheres, is the picture of an "innocent", extremely lonely and demeaned, telling a story while yearning for the story of another. Seeking human contact, he seeks out his highly absent and regressed mother. Later, we learn that while disclaiming need, the narrator's motivating drive is in return to the mother. Need is everything and its intensity is mirrored negatively in the narrator's statement of "no words for the want of need" in which the narrator continuously suffers and is lost. Ironically, within *Molloy*, the singular coherent plotline from which the narrative begins is his success in achieving this regressive mission: the work begins, the reader is told, in his mother's house.

What is the author doing through his characters? Contemplation of authorial intent is the reader's reflexive understanding of what the object signifies to the reader. Once text is created, the question of intent shifts to the question of interpretation: what does this thing mean to me?

The movement of thought begins with external projection which is then internalised, making any aspect of the textual object—whether part or whole—relevant in our making sense of our worlds. What of me is projected into the text and, together with the text, reintegrated in my understanding? The location of coherence begins with the written text as object, but demands the participation of the reader as other. Beckett himself meditates upon the difficulty of such action. He questions the possibility either of getting the particulars correct or of getting the whole correct. And, in his narrator's exchange with the policeman during the incident of the bicycle, which lands him in jail, he proves his point. The officer makes a complex statement. The narrator replies to one aspect of the statement and, though the response might be correct, misses the point, infuriating the other:

> there are not two laws, that was the next thing I thought I understood, not two laws, one for the healthy, another for the sick, but one only to which all must bow, rich and poor, young and old, happy and sad. He was eloquent. I pointed out that I was not sad. That was a mistake. (Beckett, 2006b, p. 16)

The textual object—whether a person, an idea, or a complex action—serves as a "third", a point of triangulation created by the author, imagining and related to reciprocally by the reader, whose own surmise about the author's meaning is completely free for contemplation. At its best, contemplation might lead to the mind(s) of the characters, the mind of the author, as well (and more philosophically generalised) as the capabilities of mind in apprehending the human condition. And *Molloy*, engaged in a tightly bound, controlling dyad with the reader, introduces both himself and reader to the contents of this mind.

The concept of the "third" is implicit in the therapeutic model from which Beckett's free associational technique is derived. It inheres in the mental state, the latent contents, of the associations shared by the patient with the analyst. Concretely, in Beckett's own therapeutic experience, this implicit third was made explicit through Beckett and Bion's joint attendance at Jung's Tavistock lecture on 2 October 1935. Beckett's own correspondence to Tom MacGreevy suggests his concern about the effect of this joint attendance on the work of psychotherapy, so probably it was discussed, at least to that degree, within the therapeutic pair.

Beckett's authorial act of creation necessarily bestows a structure upon writing. The written object's parts, taken together, represent the formal cohesion of composition. This is the necessary outcome of presentation. As a starting point in describing Beckett's cohesions of meaning, it is not trivial. Rather, it roughly corresponds to a patient's narrative in psychotherapy, from the perspective of different hours on different days, as circumscribed by a finite period of time.

Beckett himself recognises such unity in his written correspondence during psychotherapy, when, like other patients, he describes therapy in terms of sessions attended. Yet, this is simply an ordinal suggestion of coherence, as if, in the domain of meaning, ten times were more meaningful than one. It corresponds more to the patient's consistency of attendance than to meaningful communication or change. Beyond this ordinal cohesion, Beckett's *Molloy* presents the cohesion of a character's successive mental states within discrete time periods. This coherence of a mind-in-time presents a struggle corresponding to William James' classic description of consciousness as the movement of a bird between flight and temporary rest (James, 1981).

This is neither a coherence of selfhood felt subjectively by Molloy nor a coherence of Molloy's character viewed by reader, audience, or external judge. It finds its analogies both in the reader's anguish in having dedicated many hours to the project of reading and in the narrator's conviction that the narrative telling is neither the last nor the first, but a version, not yet complete, and influenced by the "readings" of others, suggested, finally, in *The Unnamable* to be Basil/Mahood.

As Molloy demonstrates to the reader, this cohesion of elapsed time guarantees nothing. It simply describes the passing of time in pursuit of activity. What seems to count is the "pensum" or task—the ongoing challenge of articulation, despite difficulty, of one's own experience—caught first in the defensive confusion of repetition rather than creativity and next in the contradiction of being both first person and humanly influenced by the stories and actions of others.

Both Parts I and II of *Molloy* present the reader with this problem. Part I sets the stage with Molloy's writing of his narrative. Is he alive, dead, in purgatory? Irrelevant. What concerns the narrator is that the words, written down and submitted to an external auditor, are conveyed to the reader. Directly, the reader is confronted by Beckett with both the internalising action of reading and the relation of reader to writer. The reader, as external auditor, retains parts of the presented object as meaningful; others are rejected. Very literally, the coherence of the narrator's whole object is assimilated by the reader as partial, both piece by piece and not at all. This very natural process of internalising the object resounds across the boundary of writer–reader as judgement. Beckett, long before, in *Proust*, anticipated such partial steps in the assimilation of meaning within the changing nature of thought.

Freud's tripartite model of ego, mediating the demands of id and superego, approximates this judgement. Part II of *Molloy* begins with a hierarchy of demand upon Moran, whose action as messenger is externally motivated by a supervisor and the supervisor's boss. The ego must accommodate the demands of the id, superego, and external reality, as well as the defensive developments and habits of its past actions (Waelder, 1976). Attempting to satisfy as many of these multiple functions as possible, ego activity, if successful, as much as writing, is subject to the disappointment of insufficiency in attaining its full range of possibility. The reader cannot take in all the narrator intends, just as the narrator cannot convey to the reader all that he intends. Like the therapist and patient, only a rough approximation of apprehended particulars and wholes is possible; the impression of one's actions upon the other, of the interpersonal relationship implied in their meeting, remains.

Anxiety functions not only as radical and destabilising doubt, but also in the destabilising shift of mental states. The catastrophic action of anxiety breaks momentary coherence, yet the certainty of cohesive thought in its relation to its regular effacement in anxiety provides, for Beckett, a dominant and reliable variety of coherence. At least catastrophe is consistent. This alteration of subjectively meaningful fragmentary thought and its destabilisation by anxiety is Beckett's strong and singular attestation of coherence in *Molloy*. Beckett's familiar rhetorical vehicle is aporia, the juxtaposition of a positive statement and its opposite. Aporia's correlate as a psychological mechanism of defence against anxiety is "undoing": the dismantling or taking back what has been said or thought.

Throughout *Molloy*, Beckett employs this negation as punctuation. Not only is it marshalled in the familiar ironic form of I can't go on—I'll go on, but also, more perniciously, as negation of long passages, difficult for the reader to understand because of their complexity and meaningfulness solely to the narrator, "To hell with it anyway. Where was I?" (Beckett, 2006b, p. 27).

While such negation frustrates the desire for a simple, linear storyline, it also reflects two additional forms of coherence. The narrator's engagement is with narration itself as the object of desire. Within the power of this telling is the authorial self-consciousness of a listening other, resonant at some level—at least in the veiled hopefulness of the narrator—of hearing. The narrator, cannily, enquires of the reader, "where was I". The assumption is that, despite the stops and starts, the reversals and dead ends, someone is following.

Here, then, cautiously denied in *Molloy*, is the hope of human affirmation. The reader as superego, or as discrete sense-making other, is always self-interested. Like an earlier character, Murphy, a psychiatric aide whose need for the schizophrenic patient was greater than that patient's need for him, Molloy is suspicious of others' helping motivations. Discounting human compassion Molloy says,

> Let me tell you this, when social workers offer you, free, gratis and for nothing, something to hinder you from swooning, which with them is an obsession, it is useless to recoil, they will pursue you to the ends of the earth, the vomitory in the hands. The Salvation Army is no better. Against the charitable gesture there is no defence. (Beckett, 2006b, p. 19)

Irony, in itself, is insufficient in destroying something freely given. Beckettian undoing must literally turn desired interest both into vomit and shit: "You sink your head, you put out your hands all trembling and twined together and you say, 'Thank you, thank you lady, thank you kind lady.' To him who has nothing it is forbidden not to relish filth" (Beckett, 2006b, p. 19).

The reader learns slowly that the extension of effort in the reading of Beckett, while both desired and repudiated as need, is also folded into the concept of maternal charity, which, according to the narrator, "kept me dying" (Beckett, 2006b, p. 18).

Although the reader's selfless giving might be a fiction, Molloy's distrust of the other's attentions also anticipates desires and toys (sometimes cruelly) with the reader's desire to listen. His narrative lurches from strong conviction to its negation and to general confusion. Throughout, the coherence of this process, of words representing thoughts now passed and dead, but necessary to be heard by the other in appreciation of the self, mirrors the patient's position in the psychoanalytic dyad. The reader, witting or unwitting, has entered into a transferential relationship with the narrator. There is nothing to be done about it: the necessary and desired act of reading is itself demeaned by the narrator as charitable. Unlike the analyst, the reader's only hope is that the narrator, alone, will work this relation through. Remarkably, Beckett conveys this shift in the movement of the "pensum" from burdensome weight to freeing goal in *The Unnamable*, and, in this, reflects the therapeutic action of transference resolution.

Working through the trilogy

The narrator's motivation in *Molloy* is simply put: a repetition of something worked upon, vetted by auditors, and so authoritative according to others, if not to the narrator himself. But it is incomplete. The introduction to *Molloy*, in which the narrator presents this telling to the reader, makes clear both that its cohesion has cost the narrator effort and that others have approved it. Significantly, this lacks the narrator's own conviction. Rather, his own unstated hope is that the present telling, which will be followed by at least two more ("the last but one but one") might do the trick—either eventual exhaustion or arrival at sufficient, if ambiguous, conviction.

The narrator's ruminations, while purportedly based in that character's past experience, are not generally reflective in that they are not purposively goal directed. Here, Beckett displays an act of literary virtuosity. While the depiction of rumination mirrors extended talk with no clear goal except in the telling, the very conception of this display demands the author's experiential reflection upon the psychoanalytic process. The narrator's constructed document, arrived at painfully, told and retold, is meant to reflect the outcome of that reflexive, dyadic work. While the projections into the reader within the novellas approximate the patient's emotional demands upon the therapist, within the trilogy, the reader is assumed to be in alliance with the narrator in contemplation of the completed, if often incoherent, work.

According to John Dewey, reflection is achieved when belief is arrived at not through thought's "own direct account" but through signifying "witness, evidence, proof, voucher, warrant", pointing to conviction of belief through effortful, sometimes painful, goal-orientated work (Dewey, 1910). The psychoanalytic gathering of evidence underwriting the analyst's interpretative position relative to the patient is illustrative of this effort. While providing the raw material of his own analysis, the patient is not required to assimilate the analyst's reflections. Indeed, the patient's resistance to such suggestion or external imposition often signals his engagement of the analyst within transference.

This is the narrator's fictional position at the beginning of *Molloy*. He has provided data. He has reshaped it along the lines of others' interpretations. He is repeating it yet again, but without firm belief in its emotional truth for him. Rather, while self-interested and reflexive, the narrator's productions are meant to yield something for him through an alternative path. Beckett's trilogy traces a Freudian process beginning in memory, proceeding to repetition, and then the working-through of resistance. Freud writes,

> One must allow the patient time to become more conversant with this resistance with which he has now become acquainted, to work through it, to overcome it, by continuing, in defiance of it, the analytic work according to the fundamental rule of analysis. (Freud, 1914g, p. 155)

He cautions that the working through "may in practice turn out to be an arduous task for the subject of the analysis and a trial of patience for the analyst". This trial is certainly represented in the trilogy. "Nevertheless", Freud writes, "it is a part of the work which effects the greatest changes in the patient and which distinguishes analytic treatment from any kind of treatment by suggestion" (Freud, 1914g, pp. 155–156).

Does it succeed? The emotional weight of the narrator's telling in shifting his world view is best illustrated by the fate of his "pensum", described as a repetitive burden in *Molloy* but evolving to the affirmation of personal voice in *The Unnamable*. The pensum is Beckett's proof text in his narrative process of remembering, repeating, and working through, and so stands within the present reflective reading as our interpretative "witness, evidence, proof" of the "trilogy"'s analytic goal:

> I was given a pensum, at birth perhaps, as a punishment for having been born perhaps, or for no particular reason, because they dislike me, and I've forgotten what it is. But was I ever told? Squeeze, squeeze, not too hard, but squeeze a little longer, this is perhaps about you, and your goal at hand. After ten thousand words? Well, let us say one goal, after it there will be others. Speak, yes, but to me, I have never spoken enough to me, never listened enough to me, never replied enough to me, never had pity enough on me. (Beckett, 2006b, p. 304)

The narrator's transformative understanding of this life "punishment" results in recognition of the need not only to speak to himself as apart from others, but also to listen to himself, and with sufficient compassion. This working through unpacks a psychological construction, operative since "birth perhaps", but with its impact levelled squarely in relation to his analytic auditor, who is seen, at first, as cruel. Is the auditor genuinely cruel, or is it the narrator's projection, as he writes of his hatred for the man who "without opening his mouth, fastening on me his eyes like cinders with all their seeing, he changed me a little more each time into what he wanted me to be. Is he still glaring at me from the shadows?" (Beckett, 2006b, p. 292).

But, opposing this hatred, the narrator is also aware that this is the same man had "told me stories about me", interpretative works that "lived in my stead, issued forth from me, came back to me, entered back into me, heaped stories on my head" (Beckett, 2006b, p. 303). While intrusive, penetrating the narrator's omniscient demand for separateness through interpersonal insistence, he was, nevertheless, transformed.

By what action did this occur? His auditor was worried that neither of them understood the process sufficiently. Yet, there was something in this contact, of the analyst's voice interpreting the narrator's experience, that would confuse him. Here, in *The Unnamable*, the reader is swept back to the introduction to *Molloy* and to the narrator's original question: whose "beginning" is more valid? Is it the organic telling of life's story, or is it the revised, consensually determined location of life's images and events in an analytic framework? Perhaps in the working through facilitated by repetition, "this time, then once more I think, then perhaps a last time", his "premonition of the last but one but one", there will be understanding. Through the retellings in *The Unnamable*, the narrator writes of his analytic auditor,

> It is his voice which has often, always, mingled with mine, and sometimes drowned it completely. Until he left me for good, or refused to leave me any more, I don't know. Yes, I don't know if he's here now or far away, but I don't think I'm far wrong in saying that he has ceased to plague me. When he was away I tried to find myself again, to forget what he had said about me, about my misfortunes, fatuous misfortunes, idiotic pains, in the light of my true situation, revolting word. But his voice continued to testify for me, as though woven into mine, or preventing me from saying who I was, what I was, so as to have done with saying, done with listening, And still today, as he would say, though he plagues me no more his voice is there, in mine but less, less. And being no longer renewed it will disappear one day, I hope, from mine, completely, But in order for that to happen I must speak, speak. (Beckett, 2006b, p. 303)

Here is the narrator's separation of his own experience of self from the interpretative, transferential power of the analyst, that Basil who, either as Bion or Mahood or Worm, insinuates his way through the narrator's thoughts, leaving an enduring presence that Beckett underlines with a winking reference to the British Psychoanalytical Society and Ernest Jones at the end of a ruminative association concluding with, "Stop, spare me that, have compassion and let me stop", as if once again reliant on his analyst's intervention (Beckett, 2006b, p. 333). At this point of arrival is his new understanding of his relation to that analytic proxy for Bion, "with more understanding and felicity than ever" (Beckett, 2006b, p. 333).

Because the trilogy is set as a retelling of recovered memories and the joint constructions of patient and analyst, the task before the reader shifts from the tasks within the novellas. The novellas demand an emotional relationship to the narrator, written through the direct experience of a one-sided free associational literary form. While arguably more difficult within the trilogy, the reader's tasks are more complex. They begin in attempting to locate the form and purpose of the recitation and continue in attempting to impose a sense of evolving coherence upon what is often incoherent rumination, unknowable except to the narrator. Each task is reminiscent of the analyst's task in relation to the patient at different stages of psychoanalysis.

The emotional cruelty of the novellas may be explained, in part, by location of cruelty in *The Unnamable* within Mahood as the object of transference, so resonant with the narrator's own experience of cruelty. It echoes both its author's own "savage loving" and his experience of the "London Torture". But because the trilogy is reflexive in its telling, the narrator is less concerned with the reader's response than in the novellas. It is as if, from the beginning of *Molloy*, having been assured of a hearing, having, in fact, been paid for it, as a writer is for his published works, the narrator has become more secure in the presence of the reader as a reliable container. The reader assumes the role of audience to the narrator's description of his internal world, and so suggests, together with hints of the author's own resolution of transference within the trilogy, Beckett's own freedom to shift the form of his writing to drama, which he does before he finishes writing the conclusion of the trilogy. Indeed, Beckett's transition to drama with the writing of *Eleutheria* immediately follows his novellas, while *Godot* functions as a reprieve in writing the trilogy. Beckett's shift to drama formally shifts the relation of narrator to reader from the dyad to the triad, with the reader now a member of the audience, focusing with others upon actors' enacted roles in a continuous present. The shift also represents a movement between author and audience from psychotherapeutically inspired psychological enactment to enactment in physical performance.

CHAPTER ELEVEN

The psychology of characters

A nother route to achieving narrative cohesion is inductive, accumulating the narrator's descriptions of his psychological situations toward a composition of character description. To a large degree, Beckett's narrated characters are what the narrator of *The Unnamable* describes as "puppets", containers of diverse aspects of the narrated self. Beckett writes,

> All these Murphys, Molloys and Malones do not fool me. They have made me waste my time, suffer for nothing, speak of them when, in order to stop speaking, I should have spoken of me and of me alone. But I just said I have spoken of me, am speaking of me . . . They never suffered my pains, their pains are nothing, compared to mine, a mere tittle of mine, the tittle I thought I could put from me, in order to witness it. (Beckett, 2006b, p. 297)

Together, they stand as partial objects reflective of the author, in alignment with what Beckett heard from Jung on 2 October 1935:

> Complexes are autonomous groups of associations that have a tendency to move by themselves, to live their own life apart from our intentions. I hold that our personal unconscious, as well as the

collective unconscious, consists of an indefinite, because unknown, number of complexes or fragmentary personalities.

This idea explains a lot. It explains, for instance, the simple fact that a poet has the capacity to dramatize and personify his mental contents. When he creates a character on the stage, or in his poem, or drama or novel, he thinks it is merely a product of his imagination but that character in a certain secret way has made itself. Any novelist or writer will deny that these characters have a psychological meaning, but as a matter of fact you know as well as I do that they have one. Therefore you can read a writer's mind when you study the characters he creates. (Jung, 1968, p. 81)

Beckett describes, both in the novellas and in the trilogy, a phenomenological world of projective identification, of communicating aspects of the self through inducement of mental states in another. The psychoanalyst Henri Rey eloquently describes this form of psychological presentation, sounding much like the narrator's world within Beckett's novellas. He writes,

They complain of an inability to make contact with others, and find it impossible to maintain any warm and steady relationship. If they actually manage to enter into a relationship it rapidly becomes intensely dependent and results in disorders of identity. They rapidly and transiently form an identification with their objects, and experience a loss of their sense of identity with the self. They seldom establish a firm sexual identity, and vacillate in their experience of maleness and femaleness. They are not homosexuals but have fears that they may be, and their choice of love objects, or attempts at choice of love objects, are just as vacillating. They are demanding, controlling, manipulative, threatening, and devaluing towards others. They accuse society and others for their ills and are easily persecuted. This may be associated with grandiose ideas about themselves. In fact, their feelings are dominated by phantasies of relative smallness and bigness. When threatened by feeling small and unprotected and in danger they may defend themselves by uncontrollable rages and various forms of impulse behavior. (Rey, 1994, pp. 8–9)

Rey continues his description, citing patients' complaints of futility, as well as deadened boredom and uselessness. He also recognises abnormal physical sensations and body-image disturbances, including depersonalisation and derealisation. Finally, Rey summarises, "their underlying state of perplexity and confusion is frequently apparent".

This claustrophobic and schizoid world is the psychic territory of Beckett narrators, a geographic world of mind. Molloy's homeland, always the same and always unknown, is internal, with thought vistas both expansive and constricted: "Molloy, your region is vast, you have never left it and you never shall. And wheresoever you wander, within its distant limits, things will always be the same, precisely" (Beckett, 2006b, p. 60).

While the clinical dimension of free association and the self-directed, often obsessional processing of unceasing internal, fragmentary thought characterise Beckett's narrators, certain aspects of their presentation need not have come directly from Beckett's personal experience. Beckett also read widely in psychoanalytic texts during the period of his psychotherapy with Bion. It is possible to infer, from reading the same texts, the emerging shape of Beckett's future characters. This shape advances Beckett's own notion of psychology within literature, as reflected in his *Proust*, and fills the uncertain premises of psychological change Beckett infers from Proust with an internal object assimilated from psychoanalysis.

Beckett, for example, read and took notes on Ernest Jones' 1920 manual for physicians, *Treatment of the Neuroses* (Feldman, 2006). Absent Beckett's own personal experience and suffering, Jones' book suggests itself as a provocative resource for framing the construction of a particular kind of literary character. It begins with an individual whose "inmost being is deranged" (Jones, 1963, p. 2). He is "torn by the conflicts warring in the recesses of his mind" and despairs of ever having a moment of psychological peace. The terrifying probability of another onset of dreadful symptoms, plunging him incomprehensibly into a state of fearful depression, leaves him with a terror of the present and future unknown—and the high belief that "some symptom, new or old, will suddenly take possession of his faculties" (Jones, 1963, p. 4).

Not only is Jones' patient uncomfortable in himself, but he is also deliberate in provoking "distress in the persons nearest the patient" (Jones, 1963, p. 7). Enormously porous to the intrusiveness of others in the world, he shapes his internal phantasies through introjection and it is the reciprocal projection of these internalised identifications, fused with love, hate, and sexuality, and often oblivious to the constraints of reality, that are transferred externally, in his rapport with the world (Jones, 1963, p. 79).

The patient described by Jones frequently experiences the symptoms of "constipation, diarrhea, flatulence and vomiting" (Jones, 1963, p. 30). His behaviours, such as frequent masturbation, suggestive of underlying perverse sexual thought, are disquieting in polite company. Fearful of how he responds to normal people and objects in the world, he is often frightened and uncertain of his perceptions and actions (Jones, 1963, p. 30). Jones provides an example of such confusion. He describes a man who confuses a doctor with a travelling salesman by focusing not on the individual, but on a piece of luggage, carried by each (Jones, 1963, p. 34):

> This individual's emotional reactions are always out of date. Over and over, the experience of the past is relived in the present. Because he has assimilated past relations within himself, fusing them with other loves and hates, he lives them repetitively, externalizing them in the presence of different individuals. Critical memories are dissociated. His symptoms themselves thrive, split off from consciousness. (Jones, 1963, p. 88)

Jones' character, seemingly desirous of wellbeing, seems to will his disease. "Sordid reality" is not to be preferred to malleable phantasy. In this sense, like Peter Pan, the Jones hysteric never grows up (Jones, 1963, p. 116). What others see in his behaviour, were they to look closely, is a repetitive circling of thoughts, "hovering about the painful spot" (Jones, 1963, p. 130). Empathically, inductively, the observer gets "unmistakable clues" about what is at "the back of his mind". While the goal of psychoanalysis is "to substitute harmonious peace for the turmoil of hidden conflict", this individual sufferer is never at peace (Jones, 1963, p. 146). His is a life of painful opposition, not only of generalised psychic conflict, but of the actual opposition of one thought by the other. He lives aporia.

Beckett's theoretical readings suggest his development of this general character type, extending the Dantean dysphoria of Beckett's beloved Belacqua through descriptive psychoanalytic dynamics. Yet, the struggles of Murphy and Watt, of Mercier and Camier, to find their authentic inner voices achieve the identifiable tang and feel of psychoanalytic process only in the novellas and the trilogy as they engage the reader as the container of projected narrative.

Beckett's characters reflect preoccupation within an inner world in which, following Klein, "excrements and bad parts of the self" intentionally attempt to injure and to control the object. Within psycho-therapy, the condition might reflect use of the analyst as if part of the self, use of the consultation room as the inside of an object containing the analyst, reversal of the adult–child relationship, with the analyst containing an alienated infantile aspect of the patient, and the patient's "exercise of omnipotent control over the analyst" (Meltzer, 1992, pp. 3, 35). Paralleling such processes in writing is Beckett's use of the reader as container, use of narrative as a vehicle integrating narrator and reader, the reader's apprehension of the narrator's repu-diated or extruded concerns, and omnipotent control over writing, itself densely challenging the reader's sense-making.

Like Beckett's highly literate but confused and confusing narra-tors, the schizoid claustrophobic clinical condition reflects an alter-nation between a false sense of adult competence and maturity, masquerading as omnipotence, and combative attack. Despite his tragedies and insecurities, Beckett's narrator, self-described as inno-cent, is also fierce. His hatreds for women, children, and the elderly are made explicit in *The Expelled*. He is a connoisseur of his own humiliation. Laughed at by others, he comments in *The End*, " my appearance still made people laugh, with that hearty jovial laugh so good for the health". Yet, his shame is anything but benign. Feel-ing himself demeaned, he is on continuous alert. Midway through *Molloy* he beats a man to death with his crutch. Cunningly, he admits "I stopped being half-witted and became sly, whenever I took the trouble" (Beckett, 2006b, p. 79). Controlling others, however limited his skill-set, he both fears and enacts violence. Accurate representa-tion of this kind of individual might account, in part, for the reader's sense of being attacked, oppressed, and overwhelmed by the narra-tive.

Cumulatively, Jones', Rey's, and Meltzer's descriptions of these individuals within the clinical setting reflect aspects of the narrator's presentation in the novellas. The pretentious "pseudo-maturity" is reflected in overly intellectualised passages—often revealing past education and foreign travel—meant seductively to appeal to the reader. A particularly witty example is in the contrasting cemetery descriptions at the beginning of *First Love*. Another example is Molloy's allusion to his educational experience. Facile and a bit smug, it suggests not so much a man who suffers the way he describes, but, rather, a jaded man of the world:

Yes, I once took an interest in astronomy, I don't deny it. Then it was geology that killed a few years for me. The next pain in the balls was anthropology and the other disciplines, such as psychiatry, that are connected with it, disconnected, then connected again, according to the latest discoveries. What I liked in anthropology was its inexhaustible faculty of negation, its relentless definition of man, as though he were no better than God, in terms of what he is not. (Beckett, 2006b, p. 35)

Called a "false self" in the Winnicottian tradition, pseudo-maturity reflects the

feeling of fraudulence as an adult person, the sexual impotence or pseudo-potency (excited by secret perverse fantasies), the inner lone-liness and the basic confusion between good and bad, all create a life of tension and lack of satisfaction, bolstered, or rather, compensated, only by the smugness and snobbery which are an inevitable accom-paniment of massive projective identification. (Meltzer, 1992, p. 17)

The projective identification emergent in treatment would find its target within the countertransference of the analyst, just as the narra-tor induces the experience of different, often unpleasant, mental states in the reader. However, given the structure of psychoanalysis in contrast to reading, the analyst has the opportunity to reflect, inter-pret, and confront the patient while the reader does not.

Molloy, as a character, writes of himself as if projected on to another. He locates his own sadness, his own anxiety, in others, whether real or in fantastic construction. Living in his thoughts, he locates his experience within the objects he describes. For example, unable to express self-pity directly, he locates it as if having compas-sion for someone else:

But now he knows these hills, that is to say he knows them better, and if ever again he sees them from afar it will be I think, with other eyes, and not only that but the within, all that inner space one never sees, the brain and heart and other caverns where thought and feeling dance their sabbath, all that too quite differently disposed. He looks old and it is a sorry sight to see him solitary after so many years, so many days and nights unthinkingly given to that rumour rising at birth and even earlier, What shall I do? What shall I do? now low, a murmur, now precise as a headwaiter's. And to follow, and often rising to a scream . . . (Beckett, 2006b, p. 6)

Continuing, he draws a clearer picture of himself, as seen in another's reflection. He is frightened and feels threatened, though aware superficially and non-productively that he has nothing to fear,

> the man was innocent, he had nothing to fear, though he went in fear he had nothing to fear, there was nothing they could do to him, or very little. But he can't have known it. I wouldn't know it myself, if I thought about it. Yes, he saw himself threatened, his body threatened, his reason threatened, and perhaps he was, perhaps they were, in spite of his innocence. (Beckett, 2006b, p. 6)

For him, anxiety is both ubiquitous and contagious: "I watched him recede, overtaken (myself) by his anxiety, at least by an anxiety which was not necessarily his, but of which as it were he partook. Who knows if it wasn't my own anxiety overtaking him" (Beckett, 2006b, p. 6).

Still, while self-pitying, he disbelieves in the charitable act or in genuine compassion. Another's giving always exacts its personal *quid pro quo*. Bitterly sardonic, he writes in *Molloy*,

> Let me tell you this, when social workers offer you, free, gratis, and for nothing, something to hinder you from swooning, which with them is an obsession, it is useless to recoil, they will pursue you to the ends of the earth, the vomitory in their hands. The Salvation Army is no better. Against the charitable gesture there is no defence, that I know of. You sink your head, you put out your hands all trembling and twined together and you say, "Thank you, thank you lady, thank you kind lady." To him who has nothing it is forbidden not to relish filth. (Beckett, 2006b, p. 19)

Within psychotherapy itself, work with this kind of patient poses an uphill struggle, as

> cooperation of an adult sort in the analytic process is replaced by a pseudo-cooperation or "helpfulness" to the analyst. This acting out shows itself in a somewhat slavish demeanour, a desire to convince, to demonstrate, to assist, or to relieve the analyst of his burdens. Material is therefore, often of a predigested variety, sometimes given in "headline" fashion or as superficial interpretations of mental states. All sense of the patient's wishing to elicit interpretation is absent, replaced by an evident desire for praise, approval, admiration or even gratitude from the analyst. When these are not forthcoming, the

analyst's activities are often felt to evince lack of understanding, envious attacks on the patient's capacities, mere surliness, or frank sadism . . . so skilled is the counterfeiting of maturity in thought, attitude, communication, and action that only the dreams make possible this teasing apart of the infantile, "pseudo-mature" items from the adult pattern of life. (Meltzer, 1992, pp. 17–18)

It is within dreams that claustrophobic aspects of the mind emerge, and the imagery within the novellas—both the specific dream imagery and the imagery in non-specific direct address—mirror these forms. Included are the idealisation of faeces as food—as in the image of smelling and eating goat droppings, scavenging and finding faeces—as in references to a valentine inscribed on a cow turd, places represented as dark, dirty, and foreign—as the cities in which the narrator finds himself, and the tumble down sheds and cattle stables in which he dwells. Beckett's narrator inhabits an internal world of ruin and filth. In *Molloy*, he writes,

And if I failed to mention this detail in its proper place it is because you cannot mention everything in its proper place, you must choose, between the things not worth mentioning and those even less so. For if you set out to mention everything you would never be done, and that's what counts, to be done, to have done. Oh, I know, even when you mention only a few of the things there are, you do not get done either, I know, I know. But it's a change of muck. And if all muck is the same muck that doesn't matter, its good to have a change of muck, to move from one heap to another a little further on, from time to time, fluttering you might say, like a butterfly, as if you were ephemeral. And if you are wrong, and you are wrong, I mean when you record circumstances better left unspoken, others, rightly, if you like, but for no good reason, as for example that new moon, it is often in good faith, excellent faith. (Beckett, 2006b, pp. 36–37)

The rectum, too, is idealised, as is the toilet. Frequent waterside references to river and sea, looking down below from a height, are, within the language of dreams, indicators of this fixation. So, too, is a preoccupation with anal masturbation—as when the narrator in *The End* tells the reader that he pleasures himself by thrusting his finger into his anus up to his knuckle. The generally dirty, soiled, and filthy self-description of the narrator's body completes this theme. A passage from *Molloy* similarly illustrates:

I would have hesitated to exclaim, with my finger up my arse-hole, for example, Jesus-Christ, it's much worse than yesterday, I can hardly believe it's the same hole. I apologize for having to revert to this lewd orifice 'tis my muse will have it so. Perhaps it is less to be thought of as the eyesore here called by its name than as the symbol of those passed over in silence, a distinction due perhaps to its centrality and its air of being a link between me and the other excrement. We under-estimate this little hole, it seems to me, we call it the arse-hole and affect to despise it. But is it not rather the true portal of our being and the celebrated mouth no more than the kitchen-door. Nothing goes in, or so little, that is not rejected on the spot, or very nearly. Almost everything revolts it that comes from without and what comes from within does not seem to receive a very warm welcome either. (Beckett, 2006b, p. 74)

Meltzer's descriptions of the claustrophobic character in treatment bear some correspondence to what we know of Beckett's personal characteristics, from his own letters. Beckett's caustic humour was a reliable and engaging vehicle for a sometimes scornful and pained world view. This is what Meltzer terms a capacity for "scathing mock-ery" and "laughing contemptuously" (Meltzer, 1992, p. 20). Writing to Mary Manning Howe, Beckett jokes bitterly, again focused on evacu-ation of the bowels, as he fulminates in frustration against editorial revision.

Reavey wrote enclosing a letter from Greensletandhindrance. I am exhorted to ablate 33.3 recurring to all eternity of my work. I have thought of a better plan. Take every 500th word, punctuate carefully and publish a poem in prose in the Paris Daily Mail. Then the rest separately and privately, with a forewarning from Geoffrey, as the ravings of a schizoid, or serially, in translation, in the Zeitschrift fur Kitsch. My next work shall be on rice paper wound about a spool, with a perforated line every six inches and on sale in Boots. The length of each chapter will be carefully calculated to suit with the average free motion. And with every copy a free sample of some laxative to promote sales. The Beckett Bowel Books, Jesus in farto. Issued in imperishable tissue. Thistledown end papers. All edges disinfected. 1000 wipes of clean fun. Also in Braille for anal pruritics. All Sturm and no Drang. (MMH, 14 November 1936)

Meltzer writes that during the early phases of psychotherapy, the focus of patient–therapist interest is in the relief of the patient's confusional states (Meltzer, 1992, p. 23). This kind of relief is reflected in *The Expelled* through resolution by narration of the narrator's panic related to losing an exact memory of stairs. Beckett himself, in his correspondence during 1934 and 1935, discusses moments of relief from panic gained in psychotherapy until he despairs entirely of the therapeutic project when panic returns.

Given the duality of a therapeutic transference split between Bion and Thompson, and mediated by the interest of both in furthering Beckett's intellectual knowledge of psychiatry and psychoanalysis, great store must have been placed upon Beckett's capabilities. Meltzer cautions that there is

> pressure on the analyst to join in the idealization of the pseudo-maturity so great, and the underlying threats of psychosis and suicide so covertly communicated that many of the "successful" analyses which break down months or years after termination may fall into this category. (Meltzer, 1992, p. 24)

Certainly, one way of construing Beckett's dissatisfaction with Bion and the "London Torture" immediately following termination, with the resurgence of symptomatic distress, follows this pattern. Indeed, while the relatively untrained Bion, still not psychoanalysed himself, was probably incapable of mastering a difficult countertransference. Meltzer further cautions that

> It is necessary therefore also to stress that the countertransference position is extremely difficult and in every way repeats the dilemma of the parents, who found themselves with a "model" child, so long as they abstained from being distinctly parental, either in the form of authority, teaching, or opposition to the relatively modest claims for privileges beyond those to which the child's age and accomplishments could reasonably entitle it. (Meltzer, 1992, p. 24)

Beckett, the young writer and confidante of Joyce, was certainly a prized patient, but, like the patients described by Meltzer, the seduction of his literary brilliance alternated with genuine tenderness—as suggested by Beckett's fond memories of Bion in his letters. Tragically, like the verdict of *The Calmative*'s narrator, a person who could never love or feel loved, in observation of another's final disappearance down the stairs, the claustrum patient lacks the preconditions for loving. As with the narrator in *First Love*, intense possessive desire alternates with denigration.

Meltzer also writes that the termination of analysis is "quietly pursued as a fiat for a non-analytic and interminable relation to the analyst and to psycho-analysis" (Meltzer, 1992, p. 25).

Often, this develops through a defensive concern about funding—the very complaint justifying both Beckett's and the early Bion's flights from psychotherapy.

Certainly, Beckett's intellectual recruitment of free association with its concomitant effect upon the reader suggests a creative and brilliantly interminable relation to psychoanalysis. Writing about another schizoid writer, Rilke, Britton observes that the creation of literary writing, itself—even writing about schizoid states—reflects a healthier capacity for integration than the state described (Britton, 1999). Similarly, Beckett's depiction in writing of the claustrophobic condition itself conceptualises and, thus, facilitates a method for movement from it.

However, movement from internal entrapment is no easy task. Meltzer cautions that analytic success in emergence from it will mean "a prolonged period of violently negative transference and uncooperativeness". Not only did these attitudes mark Beckett's own psychotherapy, but they also inflect the reader's experience within the free associational novellas and the trilogy. Within the novellas, Beckett conveys to the reader the markers of schizoid withdrawal: intolerance of separation, as in the continuous trauma of displacement from dependent relations; omnipotent control, as in the very form of narrative direct address, without context or explanation to the reader; envy and jealousy, as in the narrator's malevolent reflections on children and the elderly and even horses, treated better by charities than he; excessive persecutory anxiety, whether from the nameless "they" of institution or home, or thieving landlords or "assassins"; and nameless dread: "paranoid anxieties which are fundamentally unbearable in quality have been described, as distinguished from other forms of persecution which may rise to an intensity which is unbearable in quantity" (Meltzer, 1992, p. 35).

The claustrophobic internal world, though never diagnosed, is the mental homeland of Beckett's characters in the novellas and the trilogy. In their pursuit of the relief of psychic pain, these individuals require objects in the outside world who are capable of containing their projections. Beckett's literary brilliance is in the fictional depiction of such states of mind, authentic reproductions of internal monologues that depart definitively from the internal depictions of Beckett's literary mentor, James Joyce. For the reader, containing this narrated internal world, the experience of reading Beckett might itself become dreadful.

It begins in description of catastrophic destruction, its ruins congruent with a post-war European landscape after both the First and Second World Wars. Yet, this ruin is also psychic. It is internal:

> a place with neither plan nor bounds and of which I understand nothing, not even of what it is made, still less into what. And the thing in ruins. I don't know what it is, what it was, nor whether it is not less a question of ruins than the indestructible chaos of timeless things, if that is the right expression, It is in any case a place devoid of mystery, deserted by magic, because devoid of mystery. And if I do not go there gladly, I go perhaps more gladly there than anywhere else, astonished and at peace, I nearly said as in a dream, but no, no. But it is not the kind of place where you go, but where you find yourself sometimes, not knowing how, and which you cannot leave at will, and where you find yourself without any pleasure, but with more perhaps than in those places you can escape from, by making an effort, places full of mystery, full of the familiar mysteries. (Beckett, 2006b, p. 35)

The repetitive iterations of the narrators' stories are meant to achieve a purpose, to gain some meaning as humans endure life cast as a continuous deterioration or dying, until the body and mind are extinguished:

> But it is only since I have ceased to live that I think of these things and the other things. It is in the tranquility of decomposition that I remember the long confused emotion which was my life, and that I judge it, as it is said that God will judge me, and with no less impertinence. To decompose is to live too I know, I know, don't torment me, but one sometimes forgets. And of that life too I shall tell you perhaps one day, the day I know that when I thought I knew I was merely existing and that passion without form or stations will have devoured me down to the rotting flesh itself and that when I know I know nothing, am only crying out as I have always cried out, more or less piercingly, more or less openly. Let me cry out then, it's said to be good for you, Yes, let me cry out, this time, then another time perhaps, then perhaps a last time. (Beckett, 2006b, p. 21)

If such monologues have a generalised goal, it is the attempt to approximate a sense of wholeness, of personal meaning:

> Yes, it's all easy when you know why, a mere matter of magic. Yes, the whole thing is to know which saint to implore, any fool can implore him. For the particulars, if you are interested in particulars, there is no need to despair, you may scrabble on the right door, in the right way, in the end. It's for the whole there seems to be no spell. Perhaps there is no whole, before you're dead. (Beckett, 2006b, p. 23)

Without a sense of the whole, success is otherwise measured as incremental change: "The fact is, it seems, that the most you can hope is to be a little less, in the end, the creature you were in the beginning, and the middle" (Beckett, 2006b, p. 28).

Meltzer writes that the mature Bion understood the development of mind as

> a complicated process which has to be structured every step of the way and cannot therefore be compared with the biological forms of growth that are determined by genetic history and implemented by hormonal systems. He thought that mental development was in a sense autonomous: that the mind builds itself, bit by bit, by "digesting" experiences. (Meltzer, 1992, p. 49)

Beckett's narratives relate this process of digestion, congruent with the metapsychology of incremental change advanced in his early monograph on Proust. Any and all hope resides here, as do catastrophe and dread. Beckett's narrators very slowly metabolise their understanding. Molloy says, "Divine analysis that conduces thus to knowledge of yourself, and of your fellow-men, if you happen to have any" (Beckett, 2006b, p. 30).

While purporting to be unsuccessful in his use of words, Molloy is both correct and incorrect. In fact, whether formally silent or speaking, he fairly screams,

> it often happened to me, before I gave up speaking for good, to think I had said too little when in fact I had said too much and in fact to have said too little when I thought I had said too much. Yes, I was never silent, whatever I said I was never silent. (Beckett, 2006b, p. 30)

This hinting at his own ambiguous fund of knowledge exactly conveys pseudo-maturity, using, as it does, words that might appear to make sense if not thought about too closely: "Elliptically speaking, for it was only later, by way of induction, or deduction, I forget which, that I knew what it was" (Beckett, 2006b, p. 16).

The recurrent focus of Beckett's narrator is his own experiential view into thought and feeling, a reflection of the persistent activity of the claustrophobic mind:

> And these different windows that open in my head, when I grope again among those days, really existed perhaps and perhaps still do, in spite of my being no longer there, I mean, looking at them, opening them and shutting them, or crouched in the corner of the room marveling at the things they framed. (Beckett, 2006b, p. 47)

Throughout, he is a connoisseur of despair. He writes, "I was out of sorts. They are deep, my sorts, a deep ditch, and I am not often out of them. That's why I mention it" (Beckett, 2006b, p. 16). Yet, even these depths have their own depths, and his tolerance waxes and wanes: "You think you have your bellyful but you seldom have it really, It was because I knew I was there that I had my bellyful, a mile more to go and I would have had my bellyful an hour later" (Beckett, 2006b, p. 30).

He laughs sardonically at his own existence: "My life, my life, now I speak of it as of something over, now as of a joke which still goes on, and it is neither for at the same time it is over and it goes on, is there any tense for that?" (Beckett, 2006b, p. 31).

Still, underneath this bitterness, real emotion feels lost to him: "tears and laughter, they are so much Gaelic to me" (Beckett, 2006b, p. 32).

Doggedly, painfully, he continues, both railing at life and struggling for some understanding. What is left is "dreaming and farting" (Beckett, 2006b, p. 8), one elegant, one crude, both mostly involuntary. Stuck in recursive cycles of projection and attempts at thinking, his credo is

> Not to want to say, not to know what you want to say, not to be able to say what you think you want to say, and never to stop saying, or hardly ever, that is the thing to keep in mind, even in the heat of composition. (Beckett, 2006b, p. 23)

Life, according to Molloy, is painful repetition and delusion:

> Saying is inventing. Wrong, very rightly wrong. You invent nothing, you think you are inventing, you think you are escaping, and all you do is stammer out your lesson, the remnants of a pensum one day got by heart and long forgotten, life without tears, as it is wept. To hell with it anyway. Where was I. (Beckett, 2006b, p. 27)

The cruel and catastrophic world described by Beckett's narrators travel—like Watt along the old Harcourt Street train line—between two poles, described by psychoanalyst Britton as "incarceration" and "fragmentation" (Britton, 1992, p. 112). Interpreting Bion's 1967 paper, "Catastrophic change", Britton explains the individual's attempt to integrate recurrent change within a continuity of self. As discussed earlier, this is also a hallmark of Ericson's "identity crisis", painfully experienced by the young Beckett. Its dynamics correspond almost exactly with Beckett's own written metapsychological interpretation of Proust. Indeed, it is as if in this context, Beckett's articulation had identified within Proust his own painful experience. Beckett termed this catastrophe "indifference" (Beckett, 1931), which Britton interprets through Bion's understanding of the self as a container of continuous personal identity, disrupted

> by self-development or new self-discoveries, then psychic change is experienced as catastrophic, since the changes disintegrate the sense of self-continuity. When this happens the subjective experience is one of fragmentation. (Britton, 1992, p. 112)

The result is often paralysis. Certainly, as read through Beckett's narrators, it is often repetitive and painful. This fits with Jones' observation of neurotic patients' repetitive circling around indications of their all-consuming conflicts. Yet, in the course of working through that is described by Beckett in the novellas and the trilogy, the shuttle between claustrophobic incarceration on the one hand and fragmentation on the other yields new and productive experience. This emerges reparatively. It takes two forms: on the one hand, a literary product in a newly positive relation to the internalised presence of a Bion character in resolution of a charged transference relationship, and, on the other, enacting Beckett's new-found freedom in moving from the rather brutal use of reader as containment for projective identification in novella and novel to the dramatic enactment of interpersonal engagement with the reader free to experience with others, as a member of an audience.

Remarkably, as Beckett proceeds beyond the trilogy, the clinical reader of Beckett discerns a shift corresponding to the structural changes emergent as strong outcomes of effective psychoanalytic psychotherapy (Kernberg, 1988). Such change in psychic structure is prominent in new depictions of interpersonal engagement between Beckett's characters following the working through of the narrator's hostile relation to Basil.

The most striking example is in the transformation of the malevolent "fuck you" mother of *The End* to a mother who disappoints both herself and others in her inadequacy (Beckett, 1995a, p. 156). While a sanitised reprise of the earlier example occurs late in Beckett's writing (Beckett, 1996), this reflects the long-standing tenacity in the recipient of such maternal outrage.

However, by then, the familiar miseries of the generic Beckett character have included both men and women. The reciprocal savage loving of Beckett's earlier work, as in the son's adhesive desire for Mag, sunk in her autistic world in *Molloy*, joins the other disappointing characteristics of humankind.

In *From a Forgotten Work*, the once malevolent maternal character has become merely sad, a disappointment to herself and others. Yet, by the time of his writing *From a Forgotten Work*, Beckett himself had turned from prose to the theatre, as if both to free the internal psychic probing represented in prose and to nourish it with the interpersonal engagement between characters embodied by actors in his drama. Mother becomes merely flighty, unable to root herself firmly in her hobbies. Judgemental malevolence shifts to "no tenacity of purpose" as borderline rage shifts to neurotic unpleasure (Beckett, 1995, p. 156).

If psychoanalytic structural change is not reflected in this shift within interpersonal relations, then certainly the writer's descriptive attitude towards women has been transformed. While remaining as wretched as male characters, they emerge from earlier dimensions of malice and desire. If inadequate, as in *From a Forgotten Work*, or sparsely drawn yet self-sustaining, like Nell in *Endgame*, a broader human quality has now been attributed to women. Certainly, this is reflected in the emotionally resonant and sympathetic character of *Footfalls*, called May by Beckett, the name of his own mother.

Just as Beckett brilliantly depicted a particular character type, described early in the twentieth century by Jones, so did he also depict a developmental evolution in how his narrators, in their partiality and conflict, work through aspects of their savage loving to arrive at more manageable disappointment. Winkingly or unwittingly, the development of Beckett's characters illustrate the internal human shift between Klein's paranoid–schizoid and depressive positions.

CHAPTER TWELVE

Reaching the limit of free association

If free association, developed as a literary form, characterises the novellas, it reaches its stretching point in the trilogy. The reader, lost in association, remains as the abstract object of authorial intent, but vanishes as the author's auditor, attempting to contain or to clarify incoherence. By the conclusion of the trilogy, with *The Unnamable*, not only relation to the reader, but also to characters, as the part-object creations of the author, have vanished from within the flood of consciousness articulated by narrational voice. Yet, the unceasing process of mental activity remains. Its back-and-forth rhythm is familiar, evoking the obsessional process, in its tangential advance and undoing. It begins, "Where now? Who now? When now? Unquestioning. I, say I. Unbelieving. Questions, hypotheses, call them that. Keep going, going on, call that going, call that on" (Beckett, 2006, p. 285).

Questions linked to unquestioning, an affirmation of I—if only said without conviction—and the deconstruction of the phrase "keep going", as if each word were simply an object, meaningless, to be contemplated as it is uttered, "call that going", "call that on": in part obsessive compulsive, in part, recalling the arbitrary naming of objects in Genesis 2: 19b "and whatever the man called each living creature, that would be its name". Ruminative, madly undoing each clause as it lurches forward, Beckett writes, "Can it be that one day, off it goes on, that one day I simply stayed in, in where, instead of going out, in the old way, out to spend day and night as far away as possible, it wasn't far" (Beckett, 2006b, p. 285).

Off goes on, staying in contrast with out as one day clangs with the old way, linking and undoing day and night, far and not far. Beckett asks how to proceed and wonders, "By aporia pure and simple? Or by affirmations and negations invalidated as soon as uttered?" (Beckett, 2006b, p. 285).

So absorbed is the narrator that the reader is negated; in narration, the reader becomes Beckett's yearning Murphy, desirous of attention as the narrational voice itself imitates Mr Endon, for whom connection is subordinated to the dominance of a personal inner voice. Or, perhaps, viewed from the vertex of projective identification, it might be that the narrator achieves a perfect fusion, a perfect confidence in being contained to the point where other as other ceases to exist.

In this sense, *The Unnamable*, rather than *Malone Dies*, as once suggested by Beckett, really does conclude the series of works begun with *Murphy* (Craig, Fehsenfeld, Gunn, & Overbeck, 2011, a letter to G. Reavy, 8 July 1948). Beckett's literary series begins in philosophical contemplation of mental activity concluding in the physical safety of the psychiatric hospital. It lurches forward into freely associational projection, using the reader as a containing other, until the process of thought requires only its self observation in the waxing and waning of thought's preconceptions, sometimes coalescing as understandable coherence. Finally, it remains wholly private and unknowably opaque to the reader as other, whose resonance with it is in his own, personally evoked, emotion.

It is not the narrator alone who asks, "what am I to do, what shall I do, in my situation, how proceed?" It is the reader, too, nearing saturation in *The Unnamable*, befuddled by incoherence. Beckett's pretentious use of philosophical terms, aporia and ephectic—do not signal a narrative superiority as much as the frantic grasping in display of fragmenting authorial omnipotence. Trying to understand is hard enough, until it becomes necessary to find a dictionary. Here is Beckett's fictional regression to an earlier edition of Beckett as author in the shadow of James Joyce, while the reader recognises that, at least, in finding a dictionary, there is some point of orientation. The reader learns that aporia suggests negation and that ephectic is the habitual suspension of judgement. This becomes less and less possible as the reader is stressed by a narrational voice promising "like a bird to shit on them all without exception" (Beckett, 2006, p. 285).

Within a page, the omnipotence of authorial control triumphs. Focused wholly internally, the author affects a blind eye turned to the reader. Its empathic resonance in the reader succeeds in achieving Beckett's limit, now tested against the reader's willingness to endure any punishment. Each reader is different, but confronts the challenge of indifference with a closing of the book.

The author promises a compulsion to speak and delivers in quantity. Yet, his narrator reaches the end of a complex sentence, disclaiming its absent object with an undoing, "I forget, no matter". All this before the end of page one. For the reader, the choice is abandonment of text or the abandonment of hope with descent into Dantean hell. In a moment, though, as if anticipating the reader's despair, Beckett writes, "hell itself, although eternal, dates from the revolt of Lucifer" (Beckett, 2006b, p. 289). So, yes, it is possible to hang on, but at the cost of personal frustration. The reader is alone.

Perhaps he is more than alone: rather, alone and rejected. The narrational voice says, "I shall not be alone, in the beginning. I am of course alone. Alone". He describes clearly that "I shall have company. In the beginning. A few puppets. Then I'll scatter them to the winds if I can" (Beckett, 2006b, p. 286).

Not only are Beckett's narrators his puppets, but so, also, is the reader, first companion to the narrator as container for unpleasant narrational projections and next scattered to the wind in abandonment.

While the narrational voice summons Malone, Molloy, and all characters, those Jonesian or Jungian expressions of part-selves, his "troop of lunatics" (Beckett, 2006b, p. 302) from *Murphy* onwards, it is in the context of reaching their point of obliteration, "the place where one finishes vanishing". The deterioration in vanishing is a descent into fragmentation, with cohesive thought in bits.

And the reader "gets it": staying on is possible, if only to test the reader's own vanishing point, the point at which indifference to incoherence is mastered and one simply continues, reading, attempting to link, through to the end. Yes, the reader, like the vanishing characters themselves, is to be a "puppet", scattered by the author, and the voice's intent is to affirm a solitary aloneness. From here, it becomes the reader's choice to remain in the presence of an inward authorial density reaching the vanishing point of human relatedness in the collapse of the dyad for the psychology of a singular mind outside relatedness. Within pages of beginning *The Unnamable*, Beckett approaches the limit of free association in dissolution of the dyad through its attack on the reader's capacity for containment of mental contents.

Quietly, regressively, Beckett slips across the line from a psychology of two to a psychology of one, of which Rickman, who, after Beckett's work with Bion, would become Bion's first psychoanalyst, wrote,

> 'one-person psychology' concerns itself with what goes on inside one person taken in isolation. . . . In the language of two-and-three person psychology the ego ideal of the observer in one-person psychology is a robot. (Rickman, 2003)

Made robotic, the reader either proceeds or does not. Beckett triumphs over his earlier dependent dread of interpersonal indifference through exquisitely narcissistic self-absorption.

However, the one-person psychology is incomplete. Throughout, the reader remains a stalwart other, despite apparent narrational desire to know his speech, alone. Despite Beckett's every attempt to scatter the reader, within the dynamic of reading, the reader remains essential to the novel as containment for narrational projection. But this raises a problem if writing is to continue. If the reader becomes negligible for the narrator, who shall listen, who shall contain, who shall read when there is no longer a reader?

Theatre would provide an answer. At the same time that Beckett struggled with prose writing, he found relief in the writing of plays. The first, *Eleutheria*, followed Beckett's writing of the novellas by several months. *Waiting for Godot* followed in two years, itself a diversion from the trilogy. The storyline of *Eleutheria*, with depressed and avoidant son, dying father, and over-involved mother, is familiar landscape in Beckett biography. Additionally, there is mention of a psychiatric patient who, on recovery, sends his therapist a postcard from time to time, not unlike the writer himself in the years before the Second World War. That war is also present, in the continuous work of repair by a character called "the glazier" and in the contemplation on euthanasia, death, and the grim task of living in the wake of humanity's self-destructive assault.

Eleutheria is a literary coda to Beckett's letter to Thomas Mac-Greevy of 10 March 1935. It is an abstraction of Beckett's own identity crisis, compressed and denatured. Even the solution, thinly drawn and tedious, of an individual's arrival at a state of freedom which itself is boring, mirrors both Beckett's own self-styled trajectory as well as his Dantean role model, Belacqua.

However, more importantly, *Eleutheria* represents a first step in Beckett's explicit shift of action from projective identification to stage direction. *Eleutheria*'s stage notes, for example, underline a fundamental tension between consciousness and what is not seen. Rather than embedding this ambivalence within a character's thinking, as in his prose, Beckett shifts its representation to physical enactment. His staging contrasts "main" and "marginal" actions, the latter described as "less an action than a site, often empty". While the script focuses entirely on the main production, Beckett explains the marginal pressures as "the actor's business, within the limits of the directions" given by the author (Beckett, 1995b).

Together with the trilogy, *Eleutheria* narrates Beckett's literary process of working through. Its unique role is in the explicit literary reclamation of narrative tension from its placement within the reader. From here on, Beckett's work will mine two fields. The first, continuing to probe internal depths, as in *Texts for Nothing*, retains Beckett's established relation to the reader. The other, shifting enactment from the internal work of the reader to the field of stage direction and acting will be realised in physical enactment, increasingly fusing the field of internal experience with external dramatisation, as in *Not I*.

In a profound sense, *The Unnamable* represents the conclusion of Beckett's psychiatric series—from Bethlem to Tavistock—in probing the possibilities and limits of the individual with the literary dyad of free association. With *Godot*, Beckett achieves not only critical success, but also release from the dyad of writer and reader, perhaps, not unlike his Mercier and Camier, a "pseudo-couple" not fully acknowledged as discrete individuals, but fused in the relation of container–contained, before emergence into the embodied interpersonal enactments of theatre.

Godot's characters, Vladimir and Estragon, emerge full and complete in their interpersonal interactions, within both their pairing and in relation to the pair of Pozzo and Lucky.

Where the reader's only escape from authorial demand of interested containment had been indifference and a closing of the book, Beckett's shift in format allows for a very different possibility. One character might say no, or even the capitalised "DON'T TELL ME!" to another, as Vladimir tells Estragon, and the ensuing discussion is welcomed. Indeed, the relation between an individual's statement and another's response, negative or positive, exists in the reality of a complete human relationship rather than in the enforced ideal of perfect receptive containment. Estragon replies, "It's not nice of you, Didi. Who am I to tell my private nightmares to if I can't tell them to you?" (Beckett, 2006b, p. 10). And Didi can say, directly and straightforwardly, "Let them remain private. You know I can't bear that".

Despite Estragon's threat in wondering "if it wouldn't be better for us to part", they do not, and the play goes on. Indeed, the responsiveness within this relationship, absorbent of human longing, is more representative of the therapeutic give-and-take than Beckett's earlier idealised and hostilely enforced containment of the reader. Rather, the give-and-take becomes both subject and object as the reader, now audience, observes.

The emphatic nature of individual personality continues to be affirmed. This is Beckett pure. "One is what one is", says Vladimir, to which Estragon adds, "Nothing to be done" (Beckett, 2006b, p. 15). But an earlier pugnaciousness seems to evaporate as the idea is bandied about on stage. It is no longer direct address, as in Beckett's 1934 letter to Nualla Costello, "But there it is. One is not what one is not", or in *First Love*'s "But there it is, you either love or you don't". Declared almost antiphonally by Didi and Gogo, the finality and intransigence of Beckettian affirmation is defanged.

The reader, raising his head from the trilogy, is momentarily disorientated, having waited without knowing for this *Godot*. There is nothing to contain. In the place of the reader's thought, the actor now occupies the character. The reader is now the audience, and the relaxation of thought allows thought to float free—exactly the observational position of the analyst's position under Freud's classic model of psychoanalysis. Yet, having been so tenaciously focused in the act of reading by the containing demands of Beckett's narrational voice, the shift from reader to audience is exhilarating.

So must it have been for Beckett, as well. *Godot* begins with a familiar image from *Proust*, through *Watt*, and Thompson's young man at Bethlem, waiting for his mother—the boot. But the richness of possibility for focus by the recent reader, now audience, is extraordinary: shall it be Estragon's sitting?; the stage setting itself?; Vladimir's entry?; Estragon's familiar Beckettian "Nothing to be done"?; the similar familiarity of Vladimir's associational gloss on the content, or the humour implicit in the gag—that he is not relating to the shoe at all when he says, before turning to Estragon, "I'm beginning to come round to that opinion. All my life I've tried to put it from me, saying, Vladimir, be reasonable, you haven't yet tried everything. And I resumed the struggle" (Beckett, 2006b, p 3).

The reader, released from containing, has a moment to reflect that Estragon has begun a thought and that its elaboration has continued not through extension and negation by the same character, but, rather, by another character, Vladimir. And further, that the dynamic effect of statement and its elaboration in defensive association has, within this unpacking, allowed not only for the declaration of different viewpoints, but the enjoyable humour in contradiction. A holding of conflict in precious aporia has dissolved into dramatic contrast. Where laughter was not possible within the tensions of the reader's containment, the reader's new role as audience, together with the location of complex thought within several characters rather than in the mind of one, allows for comedic distance.

Relative to the dyadic action of containment, or holding narrational contents, the action of audience participant is relatively passive. In this, it allows a freedom of motion. It allows for some members of the audience to hear and to internalise the seriousness of lines such as, "people are bloody ignorant apes" (Beckett, 2006b, p. 7), the hatefulness of which reminds the reader of the novellas, while allowing it to float away in the moving flow of dialogue. Softly. Softly. Hate becomes linked with compassion as mutual contemplation of suicide becomes linked with humour in a meaningful composite.

Because the dramatic form also shifts another aspect of Beckett's free associational experiment, its coherence, *Waiting for Godot* reacts against the incoherence of the trilogy with a coherence even an "eejit" could not miss: the actions of the first act are repeated, in small variation, within the second. Yet, the repetition of the first within the second also extends the repetitive linearity of individual thought that has been Beckett's mainstay, as it is the basis, too, of free association within multiple psychoanalytic sessions. The genius, of course, is that the waiting entailed is no waiting at all, but a literal enactment of this human condition.

The physical shift from reader to audience works two changes on the observer. The first shifts his observational focus from the intellectual to the experiential. The second provides him with a measure of comfort or safety from both authorial projection and the difficulties of Beckett's direct evocation of incoherence within the attentive reader.

In a profound literary sense, these shifts both expand the possibilities of the dyad and expand the dyad to include a third, fourth, and group. While Beckett develops a "one person" psychology within the concluding work of the trilogy, and beyond to *Texts For Nothing*, he also expands the full relational range of dyadic, triadic, and group relatedness on stage while extending a measure of observational security to the audience. The containment of individual psychology becomes the province of the individual alone rather than the specialised maternal caring or containing of the narrator–reader dyad. This expands the dyad's capacity for different aspects of relatedness. It is fitting, therefore, that Beckett comments on the resolution of his transference to Bion as Basil–Mahood–Worm as an integration of experiencing that other, within the authorial self. The developmental triumph in the fictional working through depicted by Beckett from his short works through to his trilogy reaches the limit of both the reader and of the narrator's self absorption. Remarkably, as an ambivalently remembered analytic experience is now kindly remembered, Beckett as writer proceeds from self-absorption to the full depiction of human relationships. The intense investigation of psychological claustrophobia enlarges to the writer's consideration of interpersonal object relations.

In a profound literary sense, *Waiting for Godot* signals an arrival in relationship larger and more responsive than the dyad. The dyad is preserved in all its glory in the interactions of characters. But characters now are free, within role, to respond to one another, not held hostage as containers of hostile projection through narrational intent. Vladimir disturbs Estragon and Estragon tells him. Hearing this, the reader-who-is-now-audience experiences terrific relief. Unlike the resonant evocation of emotion of catharsis, the reader experiences a delicious freedom in the relaxation of focused attention. No longer the container of projection, the reader as audience becomes merely an observer as projections move back and forth between the actions of actors, themselves vitalising both the meanings of author and director.

The reader is freed, much like the therapist released by the patient from the violence of aggressively focused dependency, as when discussion of a third becomes acts to ease therapeutic impasse, as when Jung could become the subject of discussion between Beckett and Bion, linking their thinking across a divide created by the Beckett–Thompson split. Bion really does get it right when, in "The imaginary twin", he notes the patient's behaviour "as if he were saying, 'Go on; it's your turn.'" (p. 5).

The liberating joy of the reader must reflect Beckett's own. *Godot*, in this sense, is not waiting, but, rather, an arrival. It emerges as a solution for Beckett, bogged down in the trilogy's deep dive into the preconceptions at the door of the unconscious. In *Godot*, there are familiar themes, but in a cohesive story: a story so cohesive it doubles itself. *Godot* waits for the once-reader, now audience, in plain sight: the responsive engagement of a dyad, their meeting with a second dyad, the relations of two, three, and four. All and each to be observed, from humour to viciousness, in the company of other audience members, paying attention to the unfoldings on stage without an authorial demand to contain either projected detritus or ambiguous apprehensions.

With *Godot*, Beckett transforms his work. He makes it accessible to all. Certainly, it demands thought, but dances a sommersault of relief for its recipient after the novellas and the trilogy. *Godot*'s Act II mirrors Act I, following the Second World War as Richard Aldington's earlier paen to the two tramps, Bim and Bom, in his epilogue to *The Colonel's Daughter*, follows the First World War. While Vladimir and Estragon are also mid-century descendants of Synge's Wicklow tramps, they breathe the same air as Aldington's Bolshevik Marx Brothers, Bim and Bom, caustically surveying post-war devastation (Aldington, 1931, pp. 323–335). Even Aldington's "Shelleyan paper-boat of the moon" and "huge solitary elm" are echoed in Godot, both a radical statement and departure from the claustrophobic constraint of the analytic dyad and a homage to the learning from an earlier generation of warriors, the generation of Aldington, MacGreevy, and Bion. Destruction, perhaps, but also the post-war joy of being alive.

Somehow, reaching the limit of free association within the dyad, Beckett himself was also liberated: he could extend kindness and protection. The shift, of course, was familiar: the same elements had been present in Beckett's psychoanalytic explorations, from an intolerance to the dyadic form of therapy to its expansion through another dyad with Thompson, together, as a pair, observing the psychotic patient as a "third", and forward, with Bion, toward the construction of the same triadic relationship to Jung. With *Godot*, this relationship came full circle, with the action on stage—whether of one, two, three, four, or more—occurring in relation to the audience as "third". With *Godot*, too, as Beckett's relation-filled human address to the trilogy, it develops his writing from claustrophobic self-absorption to the dialogic freedom of dramatic discourse.

CHAPTER THIRTEEN

Patient Zero: learning from the Beckett experience

Long after the conclusion of his London torture, Samuel Beckett began to produce the series of dramas that made him celebrated. One of the extraordinary features of these works is that they represent an enactment and elaboration of the later work of Wilfred Bion. How did this come about? In literary terms, the chronology of influence is obscure. Bion certainly was no Bionian when he was seeing Beckett. He was a very inexperienced psychiatrist and psychotherapist when he had Beckett in treatment. In the 1930s, his tools were Hadfieldian, and he was conflicted about his psychotherapeutic education. His distinctive writings were twenty years in the future. Moreover, Bionian theory is built upon the work of Klein, and she had written little of her distinctive work in 1935. Bion's biographers say relatively little about his life during the years between the two world wars: they seem to have a "warm-up" quality, as of a protracted early adulthood. Indeed, although Bion was nearly forty when he saw Beckett, he does seem to have been in the last stages of early manhood. He had undergone some psychotherapy, but had not experienced the psychoanalysis he so desired and needed; he was improving himself, studying, training, even taking piano lessons; he was not yet married. His difficult childhood, painful separation from

India and his family, and terrible experiences at the Western Front seem to have simply been put on hold until he could attend to them psychologically, while he was building a career he could stay with and just getting on with living.

In his dealings with, and long-term response to, Samuel Beckett, however, Bion showed the first flash of his confronting, moody, and sometimes frightening genius. A patient of literally unique gifts, Beckett seems to have forced Bion to fight towards a grasp of the basics of the interpersonal work that he would spend a lifetime working out. Many of the insights of Bion's later works, such as the writings on interpersonal storms, the description of attacks on thought processes, the preoccupation with thought itself, and even the notorious Grid, appear to have had their roots in the work with this very early patient. In Beckett's particular combination of disturbance, somatising, furious silences, boringness, limpness, thought disruption, intellectual power, and the powerful ability to project, in the necessity of making the patient part of his own subjectivity to the extent of recasting the case as fiction (as he notes when reprinting it nearly twenty years after first presenting it, and some thirty years after working with the patient), and in the effect on his own thinking and feeling, Bion found the patient zero of postmodern psychoanalysis. That is to say, Bion found himself in this patient, even perhaps to the extent of overwriting the patient's actual story. Beckett, too, was able to take this as-yet-unwritten set of understandings into his separate future.

The provocative term "postmodern" signifies that, unlike earlier masters of psychoanalysis, Freud and Klein in particular, Bion's concept of thought and mind was radically interpersonal, or, more exactly, transpersonal, in the sense that he understands mind and thought to be dynamic and experienced across and between persons in a dramatic shuttle. In a sense, this almost undermines the psychoanalytic enterprise: Bion did not work with the model of a one-person psychology which Freud had developed, a model in which the detached analyst uses his unconscious to consider the unconscious of the patient and the two individuals are conceptualised as psychological systems that are similar but separate. In Kleinian countertransference theory (rather objected to by Klein), there is some degree of interpenetration: the analyst's unconscious is available to be affected by the patient's, and, to some extent, vice-versa, and this must be used diagnostically. These ideas have grown out of the work of Ferenczi. Bion, however, takes these theories a great deal further. He actually conceives of mind as inter-mind, expounding these ideas fully in his mature papers. Freud's early metapsychology had a nineteenth-century scientific vision of minds as engines, reservoirs, quantities of energies, and Freud's modernist metapsychology imagines sympa-thetic but separate minds which could interrogate each other, some-what hierarchically, in that the superior mind generally considered the inferior one. Literary production follows the same path: Victorian novelists such as George Eliot imagining the mind as separate, walled; modernist novelists, prototypically Virginia Woolf, depicting separate minds contemplating each other's functioning. The postmodern inter-subjective model, seen prototypically in Beckett post-Godot, with the linked dependent hate-filled couples, and Toni Morrison with her murderously loving mother–child dyad, begins to be represented in literature around the mid twentieth century. Bion's high theoretical period fits squarely into postmodern psychoanalysis.

The idea of a truly postmodern psychoanalysis is confronting precisely because it critiques the "rules" and goals of psychoanalysis, including the strict division of healer and patient, and the sancity, indeed the actuality, of patient experience. Reporting the Plenary Panel on Postmodern Psychoanalysis, Robertson (2002) notes,

> The modern world has cultivated the myth of progress, extolled the quantitative experimental method of science and accepted the power of universal reason; postmodernists challenge these beliefs. In contrast, they privilege diversity, pluralism, extreme relativism and the fragmentation of political groups. (Pp. 468–472)

This is not inaccurate, but as a description has a somewhat rote quality to it, and its relevance to clinical psychoanalysis is not obvious. In this report, Amati Mehler is reported as noting that there are "two types of postmodernism: one invented by artists, architects and then adopted in literature; the other invented by philosophers" (Robertson, 2002, p. 468).

All disciplines have distinctive epistemologies, including psycho-analysis, and the development of countertransference as a clinical and epistemological tool destabilised the idea of the bounded subjectivity for psychoanalysis. Relational psychoanalytic theories operate in the same epistemological universe as postmodern literary criticism, congruent with the postmodern idea of truth as constructed and relational, and selfhood as shifting, contingent, and always-in-process (Bollas, 1987; Casement, 1990). This is not to say that postmodern psychoanalysis has concluded its business with modernist versions of itself; as Zygman Bauman says of postmodernism in general, it remains in dialogue with them, using them, extending them, dropping them while continuing to bear them in mind (Bauman, 1997). The existence of interself does not mean that there is never an intraself. It is precisely that personal interself that is Beckett's point of arrival in the novellas, first existent under, and then beyond, the dyadic tool of free association. The mature Beckett, as in *Not I*, can be thought to have turned to the interself until reaching its vanishing point and turning yet again in emphasis to the intraself.

Postmodern insistence on the constructed nature of reality is perhaps its most confronting aspect. While in one sense this idea provides the basis of psychoanalysis, in another, it challenges the very idea of an actual patient experience—something that has tended to exasperate patients since Dora—and the mutuality of the experience perhaps raises questions about the treatment experience. But it is into this territory that Bion plunges with his post-therapeutic conception of Beckett. That early patient was taken deep into Bion's mind, and wrestled with for years, surfacing as an acknowledgedly fictional composite in "The imaginary twin". Bion is able to use the profoundly remembered experience with Beckett as countertransference theory develops over the 1930s, 1940s, and 1950s: the most basic thing his Grid tells us is that thought involves the intersection of subjectivities, the horizontal and vertical axes (Bion, 1989). Likewise, Bion and the experience of the Jung lecture were taken deep into Beckett's creative life, finally emerging in his greatest works where dyads fight it out in despair, affection, and frustration. Bion's final position, requiring that psychoanalysts decline to name the goal of psychoanalysis, giving the various components of the psychoanalytic enterprise algebraic "names" (O, K, $-K$, and so on) seems to pay tribute to this long engagement with Patient Zero: who knows what will come of decades of wrestling with, and ruminating on, the analytic space?

The reason that the much-celebrated difficulty of the work of each man seems much less when they are considered together must be because, though completely separated for all but two years of their lives, their work began as dyadic thinking. The cataclysmic experience of having a distressed genius in treatment when one is barely qualified, and when the technical approaches for dealing with this level of distress have not yet been developed, reverberates through Bion's work for decades. Such famous comments as his suggestion that if there are not "two rather frightened people in a consulting room, the patient and the psycho-analyst . . . one wonders why they are bothering to find out what everybody knows" (Bion, 1990, p. 5), and his remarks about the emotional storm created when two personalities meet (Bion, 1994) bear the marks of that early experience.

Many of the insights which Bion systematised through Kleinian theory, and through which he systematised some Kleinian ideas in return, were arrived at in his work with Beckett in this way, personality-to-personality, as it were. In a profound sense, Bion summarises this in Section 12 of "The imaginary twin", when he remarks, "These details were not at the time important, but belonged rather to the periphery of the main stream of his associations".

In the context of Bion's technique at the time, Hadfieldian reductive analysis, the unarticulated and unnoted experiences of 1934–1935, obscurely jettisoned beyond the clinical focus, would remain to germinate in Bion's seminal 1950 paper, "The imaginary twin", read to the British Psychoanalytical Society on 1 November 1950 (Bion, 1967). Beckett's ideas about isolation and thwarted communication likewise have derived from his time on the couch. Beckett and Bion develop these insights fully in independent work in the 1950s and 1960s: Bion's papers written in the 1950s and early 1960s and collected in *Second Thoughts* (1967), and Beckett's plays *Waiting for Godot* (1952) and *Endgame* (1958) (Beckett, 2006b). The parallels between what Bion develops as post-Kleinian theory and Beckett turns into his great plays arise from profound correspondence between them (Bléandonu, 1994; Simon, 1988). We know nothing specific about Bion's ideas about the links between the two men, as, quite properly, he took Beckett's confidences to the grave; but Klein, Bion's own analyst and mentor, and thus privy to his confidences, comments (in her only reference to Bion's work) that the twin represents "un-understood and split-off parts which the individual is longing to regain" (Klein, 1975, p. 302). It seems likely that Beckett might have represented a split-off artist part for Bion. Throughout his life, Bion wrote prolifically; he also painted late in life. Bion wrote a mammoth sub-Joycean work of autobiography, *A Memoir of the Future*; as Beckett's working through in the trilogy suggests, Bion might represent a sort of Godot figure for Beckett, a sober and potentially empathic auditor who cruelly withheld himself, but could make all meaningful if he chose.

The crucial issue is that the inadequately theorised and truncated course of psychotherapy, which was all Bion had to offer at the time, did indeed stabilise Beckett, and the young writer seems to have developed a clearly defined internal psychotherapeutic object which he was able to draw on, both aesthetically and personally, for the rest of his life. The outcome is mystifying: how did the distraught somatiser who spent his early manhood producing works that are simultaneously horribly boring and intolerably upsetting turn into a Nobel Prize winner? The answer lies in the deep correspondence between the two men, and the fit between their fantasies, strengths, and rivalries. At the deepest level, Bion's adequacy as a psychotherapist comes down not to technique or clinical understanding, but to his celebrated courage under fire. Bion's war experience was extensive. He had gone straight from school to the horrors of the Western Front, as a teenage tank commander for three years, until the armistice. His experiences there were unsurprisingly terrible, and it is clear that what he took away from it is that bravery is a matter of standing one's ground (Souter, 2009). The famous incident where he was recommended for the VC involved his seizing another's weapon when his own had jammed. Bion himself was characteristically dismissive of his heroism, describing bravery as being often a matter of running in one direction rather than another. The Winnicottian principle of the analyst's adequacy, not yet theorised, was foundational to Bion's treatment of Beckett. He neither fought with nor ran away from his difficult patient. He was open to the extremely hostile projections. He did not direct Beckett to "fuck off", as Beckett felt that his mother had done. In addition, Bion's war experience had given him precocious understanding of the horrible nature of some of the projections that might come his way, graphically shown in the repeated reconstructions he gives of his revolted response to the communicative efforts of the dying soldier he calls Sweeting (Souter, 2009). By the time he was working with Beckett as a newly minted psychiatrist in the 1930s, Bion had long ago learnt how to stay with hostile projections. This was of crucial importance to Beckett, who seemed determined to try his therapist's stamina to the utmost, not only through splitting the transference and withholding material in ways that must have been annoying to the therapist, but also through continuous demand for untimely termination. In addition, the complementary strengths and points of weakness between them would develop. The loss of the reliable mother in childhood—Bion's through literal distance, Beckett's through emotional distance—might perhaps have been a point of origin: each was fearsomely taciturn, had a certain lack of facial expressiveness, clearly seen in photographs, had difficulties with beginning adult sexuality, and, most surprisingly, had careers as war heroes. Both men had strange combinations of physical courage and cowardice. Bion's had been formally tempered on the battlefield; Beckett's was more openly a matter of running away, famously walking out of Paris just steps ahead of the Gestapo.

In the event, the uncanny series of complementary gifts and deficits, plus Bion's capacity to bear attack without flinching, and their deep investment in each other's specialities, provided the very distressed young artist-manqué (at that time) with a reliable and empathic auditor, from whom he was able to introject a usable internal psychotherapeutic object.

We turn now to the theoretical elements in Klein and Bion that can be seen to shape Beckett's work. Unlike most psychoanalysts, Bion had some training in philosophy (as part of the Arts degree he completed before beginning medical studies), and, as a result of his time at the Front, building on his shocked transition at eight years of age from India to a British boarding school, he also had a deeply felt sense of the cruelty and random nature of social life. The background in academic philosophy might explain Bion's concern to extend Kleinian ideas so that they make formal sense, and his traumatic time at the Front is perhaps related to his interest in the impact of a psychotic environment. Like Winnicott, Bion pays much more attention to the interpersonal situation than Klein. Klein is almost uncannily concentrated on the intrapsychic: hatred, rage, greed are all, as it were, "in" the infant, and the relationship between infant and world is irrelevant to her consideration of psychic events. Klein's major contributions to psychoanalytic theory include her investigation of the primitive psychic mechanisms and emotions, especially splitting, projection, and envy, and she concludes that the earliest direct manifestation of the death instinct is envy. This is because (if it is impossible for the self to be as good as the object) the self aims to spoil the goodness of the object, and, thus, attacks the source of life (Segal, 1988, pp. 40–42). What we concentrate on here is Bion's response to Klein's elaboration of the Freudian theory of the death drive. Bion's reformulation of Kleinian envy in the late 1950s and early 1960s make it plain that mental activity depends on an individual being able to tolerate the idea of contact and communication: that is, he is interested in the role of envy in so far as it interferes with this. In essence, he considers the function of relating, rather than the inside of one or the other parties.

In two seminal papers, "Attacks on linking" (1959) and "The psycho-analytic study of thinking" (1962), Bion argues that in order for communication and mental activity to proceed, envy needs to be manageable enough for a link between two minds to be tolerated. He imagines this potential "link" as erotically charged: "The prototype for all the links of which I wish to speak is the primitive breast or penis" (Bion, 1967, p. 93). Via what he terms "normal projective identification", a non-pathological use of projective identification to communicate, minds need to come together in creative exchange. In the case of a parent and baby, the "stronger personality" has to be able to accept and "contain" the child's split-off terrors and rages, modify them, and return them to the child in a less toxic form. If this does not happen, the child has to accept its own frightened self back unmodified, and experiences, Bion says, in what is perhaps his most striking phrase, "not the fear of dying made tolerable, but nameless dread" (Bion, 1967, p. 116). There are two main reasons that a link might not be established and the child's projections cannot be accepted, modified, and returned for reintegration: first, because the parent cannot manage to do it, because she is too depressed, too busy, too psychotic, or whatever, and second, because the child enviously attacks the idea that the mother has this capacity. When a creative mental link cannot be forged between two parties, "two objects cannot be brought together . . . to produce a new mental object" (Bion, 1967, p. 50), and dynamic or creative thought becomes impossible. Instead, a world where creativity is possible is replaced by a world dominated by "minute links which, being impregnated now with cruelty, link objects together cruelly", and the mental processes are "perverse, cruel and sterile" (Bion, 1967, p. 109). An individual caught up in this process reverts, in Bion's schema, to ever more malignant projective identification, where unwanted parts of the mind are violently projected into the outside world, and the end result is a self left damaged and depleted.

When the process does "work", that is, when an individual's projections can be modified and returned so that they can be integrated, the individual is left strengthened rather than depleted. However, Bion considers the idea of mental "health" in a different way from Klein. Where Klein thinks of the paranoid–schizoid position as a primitive one, and progression to the depressive position as a good thing, generally speaking, Bion thinks of a shuttle, often quite rapid, back and forward between the two positions. He calls this PS↔D. An individual continually lurches between paranoid–schizoid terrors on the one hand, which a containing object would modify, and depressive insights on the other, only to have, as it were, another terror, which would have to be contained, modified, reintegrated, and so on. In this schema, mental health is not an ego-based stuckness in depressive sanity, but the ability to move between the two positions, to grow and learn, to reach one's anxieties, manage them, move on to new ones, and so on. It is out of PS↔D that "thinking", the capacity to manage the thoughts that come one's way, develops. This is surprisingly consistent with Beckett's own metapsychological thesis, *Proust*, written in 1931. In this work, continuous integration and disintegration are the products of the ongoing human thought process of consciousness, mediated by the catastrophe of indifference—a kind of dead end or cliff of meaninglessness. In his disconcerting algebraic system of psychological notation, Bion refers to thinking as "K", or knowledge, and defines it as "the mating of a preconception with a frustration" (Bion, 1967, p. 111). The opposite of this, " – K", an attack on thinking, is a mental absence, an encounter with what Bion calls a breast which, instead of feeding the self, sucks and strips it, a "greedy vagina-like breast", as he puts it (Bion, 1967, p. 115). Creative mental work, thus, consists of a series of terrible shocks and recoveries, a coming together of two minds in a sort of mutually destabilising dialectic. Bion goes so far as to describe these events as "catastrophes" (Bion, 1967, pp. 7–11, 89, 101, 108).

This idea of "nameless dread", the result of the thwarting of the need for a projection-modifying object, seems to contain the kernel of much of Bion's work as a post-Kleinian theorist, but it is in some ways difficult to comprehend fully what he means by the expression. The situation is, however, made remarkably clear in Beckett's mature work. The short play, *Not I*, for example, is a sort of couch monologue exploring "nameless dread" precisely: the patient's associations go on and on unanswered and the auditor's efforts to communicate are violently rejected. The link between pain and self that the auditor seems to be trying to stuff into Mouth is spat straight out every time. In this play, the auditor seems to be anxious to form a link, but Mouth will not take it in, hungry though she is. The essential feature of this character is that she is expulsive, communication rejecting, and suffers accordingly. The early literary prototype for this dynamic is depicted in Beckett's action upon the reader in the novellas.

Waiting for Godot and *Endgame* show a world where continuity of thought or meaning cannot be established, and where despised or feared parts of self are violently expelled into others and reintrojected with mounting terror. Mental functions seize up, $-K$ reigns. Characters are baffled by the inability to understand each other or to interpret signs accurately. Actions are robbed of meaning, and repeated over and over. In fact, all the characters seem like part-objects, despised and rejected bits of people stuck in more or less malignant pairs, "linked together cruelly", as Bion puts it, in hate-filled, mutually uncomprehending couples. These plays elaborate the effects of corrosive envy where nothing can be taken or given freely. The effects are particularly malignant in *Endgame*, where scarcity and cruel deprivation reign. The keys to the kitchen are withheld, painkillers have run out, a rat cannot be allowed death in his own time. The withholding effects of envy give the plays their jerky, almost strobe-like, effect: nothing develops between minds; dialogue peters out, irritably.

These characters show an alienation from each other, mutual belief that the other's mind is completely unavailable for understanding or use. But, despite this, we argue that, for several reasons, the plays are not hopeless or tragic. Indeed, from the developmental trajectory of Beckett's own work, they are a triumph of hope: a movement from solipsism in the seeking of the intraself to interest in the external world of others in the interself. They are, therefore, in a personal sense, Beckett's signification of therapy's efficacy in thriving beyond the privileged, if somewhat claustrophobic, pressure cooker of the consulting room, actual or internalised. First, we think a PS↔D shuttle—where the audience moves between despair and confusion, and laughter and illumination, and back again—is set up for the reader/

audience by the structure and actions of the plays. The prime example of this is the repeated structure of *Waiting for Godot*, where "nothing happens twice" (Connor, 1988, p. 119); the alternately oppressive and illuminating aspects of this are immediately obvious. Second, the fact that the plays encourage the reader/audience to think about the horrible things that happen does seem to us, once again, to be close to Freud's idea about what analysis is good for. Here, Beckett's literary success is in the evolutionary shift from use of the reader as container of hostile projections to an opportunity afforded to the reader/audience to think (or not). Third, the plays have a slapstick or vaudeville quality that mediates the despair, an action something like modification of an unbearable projection. Finally, the person of the other does not fade from the mind, for either character or reader, in Samuel Beckett's work, baffling and tormenting as he might be; he remains to contemplate, wrestle with, weep over. To this extent, it might be said to reflect the experience of being in a painful analysis with an analyst who remains with the sufferer, however unpleasant the experience.

Samuel Beckett represented the Patient Zero of postmodern psychoanalysis because Bion's work with him brought the absurdist and painful nature of interpersonal communication to the forefront of the mind of a young trainee who was able to stay with these issues and develop them into a metapsychology. More confrontingly, Bion apparently experienced Beckett as profoundly entangled with himself.

Wilfred Bion and Samuel Beckett were brought into the private, intimate, and non-intrusive contact that is psychodynamic psychotherapy early in their respective careers. They had similar personalities, not least of which was the capacity to experience the full horror of everyday life. The ways that Beckett's works embody and explicate Bion's most abstruse ideas, and vice-versa, shows that the relatively brief contact between them resonated deeply with their creative impulses and formed their later, mature work. For Bion, the Beckett effect merged with his own deepest conflicts—his Indian childhood and his experience at the Western Front—to shape his development of Kleinian theory. For Beckett, the experience of the London torture gave him an experience of an adversary who provided support through endurance, would not fight and would not run away: the opening lines of *Waiting for Godot* embody this.

VLADIMIR: . . . So there you are again.

ESTRAGON: Am I?

VLADIMIR: I'm glad to see you back. I thought you were gone forever.

Together with the assimilation of elements of psychoanalytic technique within literature, the idea of being able to think about destructive cruelty while stuck within it, and the comic absurdity of that position, is a profoundly hopeful one, and shows one of the most valuable lines of evolution from Freud through Klein and the post-Kleinians to twentieth-century literature. Beyond the thinking comes action, and the freed action that is the structural change in psychotherapy, as one human becomes more capable of appreciating and engaging with the other, might be therapy's highest yield. It is Beckett, rather than Bion, who gives this dramatic voice, in *Endgame's* final moments. Mindful of Nagg's sadistic cruelty to him earlier in his life, Hamm obliges the old man. He cries out for his father, in generous gratification of Nagg's desire. He says to Clov, "He doesn't realize, all he knows is hunger, and cold, and death to crown it all. But you! You know what the earth is like, nowadays. Oh, I put him before his responsibilities!" (Beckett, 2006c, p. 153).

Hamm's act is the child's good enough provision to his parent, the meeting of need with another's ability to fulfil it. Despite the pain Hamm has suffered from his father, his own life has allowed him to transcend his pain and to extend himself, in care, because he can.

This is Beckett's demonstration of action dependent upon the discernment of what, for the mature Bion, is a psychological "sense of truth":

> experienced if the view of an object which is hated can be conjoined to a view of the same object when it is loved, and the conjunction confirms that the object experienced by different emotions is the same object. (Bion, 1962, p. 310)

Beyond thought to action, and in the face of destruction and inhumanity, Beckett demonstrates the moral yield of psychoanalysis with early childhood anguish resolved, allowing the adult choice in loving human conduct, even including forgiveness of the failures of parents and therapists.

Conclusion

Samuel Beckett's precocious 1930 monograph, *Proust*, presents a blueprint for his radical use of literature as a vehicle expressing psychological process. This work, meant to set him up for a donnish life in Dublin, has two identities. One is conventionally *avant-garde*: just cool enough to make the writer look like the edgy young man of letters, quite scholarly enough not to frighten the academy. The other identity is unimaginable from the vantage point of 1930: it nods at an uninvented future where the writer will win the Nobel prize for literature for mind-boggling representations of psychological modernity, writing in French and translating it unidiomatically back into his native language. Beckett did not do Proust as the literary critics do, and he was not to do psychotherapy as either therapists or patients typically do. He was to take his experience of Proust, Bion, and psychoanalytic writing and psychotherapy and transform it utterly, making it an entirely new enterprise.

In *Proust*, Beckett's metapsychology focuses on thought as the continuous, involuntary stream underlying human consciousness and action. Necessarily, the composition of thought changes from moment to moment. Beckett equates this progressive loss with death: the death of the individual in one moment in transition to the individual's becoming in the moment to follow. Thought is always partial—integrating different aspects of the individual's fuller range of perception. And, in thought, the positive and negative acts of others endure as more trenchant, instrumental, and enduring than their earlier enactments in actual real time.

Against the dread of future indifference, the self's indifference to its former interests and individuals' interpersonal indifferences to one another, we act defensively. Habit ensures our security, but resists the necessary currents of ongoing change. Enduring this continuous dying—as catastrophic and jarring as the shift between emotional tranquillity and panic—requires courage and endurance. Involuntary memory does not enlighten. Rather, emotional contact, the capacity of the other to contain or to hold meanings, is what sustains us.

As a very young man, Beckett recognised in Proust's writing the radical use of the reader as a participant in the writer's work, enduring frustration and anger in order to apprehend the writer's meaning. This understanding reflects his experience in relation to Proust; it also provides his own warrant, as writer, for the expanded use of the reader. The idea of the reader's emotional "apprehension" of the writer's meaning, staked out in *Proust*, frees the author from several relational conventions between writer and reader. First, the author is freed from the need to pace his writing to ensure the reader's integration of coherence. Next, the author is freed from the convention of ensuring the goodwill of the reader, necessary for the act of reading to continue to its end. Instead, the indeterminate relationship of reader and writer, spanning a range of possibilities between necessity and indifference, expands the context of storytelling to enactment of a temporary relationship.

Within the action of psychotherapeutic experience, Beckett locates a resource that conforms to the radical model suggested in *Proust*. The patient, however undecided about the therapist's caring, remains fairly certain of receiving a fair hearing. The dyadic structure presents a battlefield for what Bion later terms the "emotional storm" generated in the meeting of two strangers, each with different psychologies. Because it generates each and any mixture of love and hate, contextualised by the rhythms and sounds of word and silence, the verbalised action of psychotherapy conforms to the written action anticipated by Beckett in *Proust*.

Beckett's experience of psychotherapy, together with fieldwork at Bethlem and extensive reading in psychoanalytic theory, become his literary resources in shaping the forms of relatedness between writer, character, and reader. The novellas, written both after Beckett's work with Bion and after the author's experiences of the Second World War, reflect a form of direct address between narrator and reader that, in both rhythm and sound, suggests the free associational technique of psychoanalysis. Unlike psychoanalysis, where the analyst's listening and interpretation create the linkage of feedback to the patient, the direct address in writing is unidirectional. The reader's experience cannot be clarified in feedback to narrator or author. Neither is the reader free to address the narrator concerning the affects that have been induced for containment through the projective actions of narration. Instead, Beckett pushes beyond Proust. His narrator might depend on the reader's attention and count on his willingness to contain frustration, but he also feels free to antagonise and even to punish the reader.

Beckett's written word, animated through the act of reading, becomes propulsive, an affective missile. For example, the narrator fairly spits at the reader in *First Love*, emphasising awareness of their differing psychologies, mirrored in aesthetic preference, "leave me my graveyards and keep—you—to your public parks and beauty-spots" (Beckett, 1995a, p 27). While seeking the reader's attention, the narrator also claims, through antagonism, his distancing space. Thin-skinned, wary of possible attack, he has faith in his unquestioned omniscience. Free to act on his privileged belief in knowing the other's mind, he attacks both presumptively and pre-emptively: "were you to inquire, as undoubtedly you, itch" (p. 32). Failing to threaten sufficiently, he dismisses violently, contemptuously, his thoughts "better not wasted on cunts like you" ((p. 33). His prickly insistence resembles a patient's telling of personal hurt from within the context of his own psychic suffering. Often in hateful display, it is presented to the attuned ear of the reader as if therapist, upon whom he relies for non-judgemental listening without retribution. Recognisably, it is also Beckett's marshalling of his own capacity for fury, as when, in his correspondence, he turns from Nuala Costello's dismissal with the cutting, if original, derogation to MacGreevy that she is "unclitadorian".

Beckett's use of the free associational form within literature is brilliant. The degree to which his fiction suggests issues actually encountered within his own therapeutic work is irrelevant. Indeed, the psychological contents of his narrators' rants might themselves be deduced from Beckett's extensive psychoanalytic reading, such as Jones' *Treatment of the Neuroses*. Rather, his fictional portrayal, in writing, of a speech form replicating a particularly difficult psychoanalytic patient is stunning. While the narrator's own reflections on the writing of characters, within his novels, mirror the encouragement he heard from Jung on 2 October 1935, using the author's own inner voices pragmatically, Beckett's characters construct a hall of mirrors between writer, narrator, and reader.

Beckett's fictional ramblings ring true as verbalised thought. He depicts an internal world from which the author's narrator declares:

> All these Murphys, Molloys and Malones do not fool me. They have made me waste my time, suffer for nothing, speak of them when, in order to stop speaking, I should have spoken of me and of me alone. But I just said I have spoken of me, am speaking of me . . . They never suffered my pains, their pains are nothing, compared to mine, a mere tittle of mine, the tittle I thought I could put from me, in order to witness it. ((Beckett, 2006b, p. 297)

It is not only the reader's necessity and insufficiency that enrages within Beckett's writing, but also the failure of his very characters to articulate fully and accurately the emotion-imbued thought of their original thinker/creator, authorial thought. Instead, a continuous narrator of multiple identities fiercely articulates narcissistic hurt in awareness of experience never to be apprehended or contained fully either by self or other. In *Texts For Nothing*, he writes,

> what is it, this unnamable thing that I name and name and never wear out, and I call that words. It's because I haven't hit on the right ones, the killers, haven't yet heaved them up from that heart-burning glut of words, with what words shall I name my unnamable words? And yet I have high hopes, I give you my word, high hopes, that one day I may tell a story, hear a story, yet another, with men, kinds of men as in the days when I played all regardless of nearly, worked and played. (Beckett, 1995a, p. 125)

Within Beckett's own experience of empathic auditors there was always Thomas MacGreevy, a constant reader and listener of flesh and blood, supporting him before, during, and after Beckett's psycho-therapy with Bion, as audience for written rants and confessions. Mac-Greevy seems to have been the prototype for the clinical model introduced by Bion of the listener, joined in contemplation with Beckett as narrator of his changeable mental contents.

MacGreevy, of course, received only one version of Beckett's continuously searching thoughts. Similarly, Bion probably remained unaware of what was split off from therapy—whether in the contents of letters to confidantes or in Beckett's relationships with MacGreevy and Geoffrey Thompson. Still, even within its singular forms, Beckett's provision of his thinking to others was generous. He made himself known to others, and well. The problem was in self and others' perfect apprehension of the general, the whole:

> For the particulars, if you are interested in particulars, there is no need to despair, you may scrabble on the right door, in the right way, in the end. It's for the whole there seems to be no spell. Perhaps there is no whole, before you're dead. (Beckett, 2006b, p. 23)

Beckett is similarly generous in his provision of particulars to the reader through his multiple narrators. Pursuing the whole, Beckett is nothing if not repetitive in his inculcation of detail "to ensure our dying every second". In this, Beckett establishes within the reader an emotional parallel to the anxious, often incoherent mutterings of his narrators. Reading Beckett, as Beckett found reading Proust, is not always easy. Still, a conception is embedded in the reader of a recog-nisable character: razor sharp, inwardly focused upon entrapment within his own mind, often contemptuous and intolerant, at turns obscenely derogatory and genuinely humorous, sometimes despair-ing to the point of self-destruction, but recovering to continue on, and, above all, damaged and hurt from his engagements with others.

A formal shift occurs between the novellas and the "trilogy", not simply in length but also in the manner of psychoanalytic telling. The novellas suggest a series of linked sessions, reflections on different moments of a singular narrator's past. Story elements such as the cyanide calmative, a small potted plant, and expulsions from the dependent security of multiple homes bind these tellings. They demand the reader's rapt attention because their timeframes often confuse. They also demand that the reader endure the narrator's cruelty in direct address.

With the "trilogy", the narrator seems to relax his confrontational testing of the reader. It is as if the narration itself has settled into a trusting dyad. The narrator seems more focused on the multiple iterations of telling a life. In the process, he reveals a long and recurring process of working through his relationship to a primary object. This is his auditor, an intrusive presence imposing his alien interpretative forms on the narrator's experience. Not unlike a patient's changing manifestations of transference to a psychoanalyst, knowable to Beckett in his own attitudes toward Bion, the transit from *Molloy* to *The Unnamable* depicts a shift in the other's significance to the narrator as well as clarification in pursuit of his life task, or "pensum".

Remarkably, where the novellas enact a field of projective identification wherein the narrators' unwanted bits are located harshly in the reader, Beckett reclaims the projections for his own use, his own ability to "witness" in the "trilogy" as a process of working through.

Beckett slowly and meticulously demonstrates the indirect and exhausting catastrophe beyond Proust's voluntary and involuntary memories through his narrations' repetitive iterations of both thought and enactment. A kind of hope resides in the persistence of this action, which, as in the "trilogy", sometimes achieves clarifying moments within the particulars and complexities of internal experience. From the retrospective of his metapsychological blueprint in *Proust*, Beckett's written depiction of human thought in its attempt to understand itself and to link with others is both successful and tragic.

His achievement also achieves a reflexive capability, extending Beckett's own range—as in the shift from the novellas to the "trilogy" as from free association to working through. Indeed, almost as if an empirical proof, the fruit of working through facilitates a different form of relatedness between both author and reader and between narrator and mental objects. The intense dyadic relationship with the reader mapped in the novellas relaxes through the narcissistic preoccupations of the "trilogy". It is released in Beckett's formal shift to drama with *Waiting for Godot*. Here, the intense burden of the reader is relieved. The reader becomes one of many in an audience, free to focus on any aspect of the enacted drama before them. While kindness and cruelty are depicted on stage, the multiple levels of relationship— the dyadic, triadic, quadratic, and more—are explored under constraints of dramatic coherence and time. The *bon mot* that in *Godot* nothing happens twice reflects the pressures under which the dramatist must labour in conformity with audience tolerance and demand.

Having explored the radical extension of his Proustian experiment in the relationship of author to reader, Beckett had achieved sufficient confidence in his own message and words to separate from his adhesion to the other's necessarily rapt attention. This is detailed in *The Unnamable* through the narrator's internal relation to the variously named Basil, Beckett's proxy for Bion. Achieving a redefinition of his life's work in the pensum, paralleling the author's own consolidation of adult identity, the narrator writes of Basil's transferential power,

> And still today, as he would say, though he plagues me no more his voice is there, in mine but less, less. And being no longer renewed it will disappear one day, I hope, from mine, completely, But in order for that to happen I must speak, speak. (Beckett, 2006b, p. 303)

Thematically, the rejecting and neglectful image of mother also changes in Beckett's writing after the trilogy. Notably, the mother who is remembered as telling her small son to "fuck off" in *The End* is softened to reflect her own personal inadequacy and anxiety in *From An Abandoned Work*. It is suggested that the author's own experience of psychological recognition is mirrored in his creative work, just as Beckett's own working through of resistances to knowing culminated in his recognition of the toxic danger to him of his mother's own "savage loving", years earlier.

Mental recovery, according to the psychoanalyst Paula Heimann, depends on conscious elaboration and understanding of the psychological conflicts uncovered by Freud, "through the medium of the patient's emotional relation with his analyst" (Heimann, 1956). In this sense, the consciousness embodied in Beckett's written word, ultimately related to the (fictional) patient's emotional relation with his analyst, in all the permutations of his identity, similarly travels a psychoanalytic path to "mental recovery". Two relational anchors secure this fictional enterprise. The first is the narrator's relationship to an internalised transference object. The second is the author's implicit and changing relationship to the reader through the narration of his characters, his "puppets" of fragmentary personalities.

Just as for Beckett, Richard Aldington's Bim and Bom surveying an English playing field in the aftermath of the First World War echoes in the repartee of Vladimir and Estragon, so Beckett's terror of Proustian indifference resonates in Bion's catastrophe. Bion's own "Catastrophic change", written in 1967, well after his former patient achieved extravagant celebrity, articulates Bion's own well-worn path from catastrophic war experiences through his awareness of Beckett's *Proust* and the permutations of their personal engagements to Bion's later theoretical and experiential contacts with others, including his own analysts and patients. Both Beckett and Bion observe minutely the shifts in thought, projected outward, of the searching soul. And there is congruence in the catastrophe they detail. Bion observes theoretically that

> The patient feels imprisoned in the state of mind he has achieved, and unable to escape from it because he feels he lacks the apparatus of awareness of reality which is both the key to escape and the freedom to which he would escape. The sense of imprisonment is intensified by the menacing presence of the expelled fragments within whose planetary movements he is contained. These objects, primitive yet complex, partake of qualities which in the non-psychotic personality are peculiar to matter, anal objects, senses, ideas and superego. (Bion, 1957, p. 269)

This clarity of observation could stand as a commentary on Beckett's "trilogy". Indeed, had Beckett functioned for Bion as "Patient Zero", the remembered physical sensations, confusions, and impasses of that therapy would clarify through Bion's later psychoanalysis and study with Klein. Beckett's own post-therapy writing, becoming available as Bion's own theoretical interests solidified and became publicly available, would dramatically resonate with Bion's evolving theoretical model. It would stand as external corroborating evidence, together with clinical theory and patient observation, that Bion was on the right track. Of course, as literary depiction, its contribution would be anecdotal only, and lost in the abstraction of Bion's clinical arguments. In this sense, just as Beckett suggests the working through of transference to Bion in the mufti of Basil, Mahood, and Worm, unknowable to the general public, so Beckett's shadow occupies Bion's "Imaginary twin" and subsequent papers, unattributed but present. Whether or not the two actually read each other's work, it is hard to imagine that they were not aware of the other's growing celebrity, and we also imagine that a sort of pride, perhaps a feeling

of having had a very lucky encounter so early in the professional journey, might have further freed and strengthened the ability to use the
memory of the other so freely.

Beyond their creative and creatively "ruthless" use of one another,
there is another significant similarity and difference between Beckett
and Bion. Each articulates the subjective experience of dwelling and
emergence from within the schizoid and fearful positions, common to
us all, within the broad spectrum of human psychological experience.
Bion's articulation instructs the professional. Beckett's creatively
presents this human condition to the reader/audience, subjectively
placing the reader in the privileged position of the professional. Bion,
in this sense, directs his energies to describing the feel of the unconscious, but, in doing so, he produces beautiful, sparse, stripped-down
prose, brimming with densely poetic phrasing that stays in the mind.
Beckett consciously transforms that unconscious into the other's direct
awareness, but, likewise, documents mental suffering with almost
diagnostic precision.

Beckett's brilliance in documenting the vagaries of the mind's
activity, first in French, his second language, and then self-translated
back into carefully stilted English, is that his writing represents his
own conscious activity. In this, while documenting a swirling and
planetary world of anal objects, senses, ideas, and superego judge-
ments, Beckett stays with thought and its representation, rather than
expressing them through explosive expulsion. The filter of the double
linguistic distancing provides extra control: a sort of sterile space in
which to bring two personalities together, a spectacularly literary
equivalent to the first rule of psychoanalysis. The triumph of Beckett's
accomplishment, in articulating through conscious observation and
literary expression what Bion recognises as a paradigm for psychotic
process beyond or before thought, is nothing other than brilliant.

Were Bion to have located psychoanalytic process within Beckett's
post-war writing, he would have been correct. Bion, of course, is the
internalised Basil–Mahood–Worm (not Jones!) of *The Unnamable*. This
unique variant of psychoanalysis, wherein both former patient and
former therapist employ literature as a transitional space to understand and work through their enduring memories and internalised
representations of the other, occurs privately for each. It occurs
without explicit consensual agreement, and under thick darkness.
Initially knowable only through literary–critical intuition, unpacking

the historical details of the interaction became possible only with the recent publication of Beckett's extensive correspondence, suggesting the aesthetic idiom of their work together, and their creative lives' work, separately, and their long faithfulness to, and solitary recognitions of, the other and their work together.

REFERENCES

Ackerley, C. J., & Gontarski, S. E. (Eds.) (2004). *The Faber Companion to Samuel Beckett*. London: Faber and Faber.

Aldington, R. (1929). *Death of a Hero*. New York: Covici Fried.

Aldington, R. (1931). *The Colonel's Daughter*. Garden City, NY: Doubleday, Doran.

American Psychiatric Association (1994). *The Diagnostic and Statistical Manual of Mental Disorders* (*DSM-IV*). Arlington, VA: American Psychiatric Association.

Anzieu, D. (1989). Beckett and Bion. *International Review of Psychoanalysis*, 16: 163–169.

Bach, S. (1994). *The Language of Perversion and The Language of Love*. Northvale, NJ: Jason Aronson.

Bair, D. (1978). *Samuel Beckett*. New York: Simon & Schuster.

Bauman, Z. (1997). *Postmodernism and its Discontents*. Cambridge: Polity Press.

Beckett, S. (1931). *Proust*. New York: Grove Press.

Beckett, S. (1970). *More Pricks Than Kicks*. New York: Grove Press (originally published, 1934 by Chatto & Windus).

Beckett, S. (1984). *Disjecta*, R. Cohn (Ed.). New York: Grove Press.

Beckett, S. (1992). *Dream of Fair to Middling Women*. New York: Arcade.

Beckett, S. (1995a). *The Complete Short Prose 1929–1989*. New York: Grove Press.

Beckett, S. (1995b). *Eleutheria*. New York: Foxrock.

Beckett, S. (1996). *Nohow On (Company, Ill Seen, Ill Said, Worstward Ho)*. New York: Grove Press.

Beckett, S. (2006a). *The Grove Centenary Edition. Volume I. Novels*. New York: Grove Press.

Beckett, S. (2006b). *The Grove Centenary Edition. Volume II. Novels*. New York: Grove Press.

Beckett, S. (2006c). *The Grove Centenary Edition. Volume III. Dramatic Works*. New York: Grove Press.

Bion, F. (1995). The days of our years. *The Journal of the Melanie Klein & Object Relations Journal, 13*(1). http://www.psychoanalysis.org.uk/days.htm, accessed 8 March 2013.

Bion, W. R. (1957). Differentiation of the psychotic from the non-psychotic personalities. *International Journal of Psychoanalysis, 38*: 266–275.

Bion, W. R. (1958). On arrogance. *International Journal of Psychoanalysis, 39*: 144–146.

Bion, W. R. (1959). Attacks on linking. *International Journal of Psycho-analysis, 40*: 308–315.

Bion, W. R. (1961). *Experiences in Groups*. London: Tavistock.

Bion, W. R. (1962). The psycho-analytic study of thinking. *International Journal of Psychoanalysis, 43*: 306–310.

Bion, W. R. (1963). *Elements of Psycho-Analysis*. London: Heinemann.

Bion, W. R. (1967). *Second Thoughts*. London: Karnac, 1984.

Bion, W. R. (1982). *The Long Weekend: 1897–1919 (Part of a Life)*, F. Bion (Ed.). Abingdon: The Fleetwood Press.

Bion, W. R. (1985). *All My Sins Remembered and The Other Side of Genius*. Abingdon: Fleetwood.

Bion, W. R. (1988). Notes on memory and desire. In: E. Bott Spillius (Trans.), *Melanie Klein Today, Developments in Theory and Practice, Volume 2*. New York: Routledge.

Bion, W. R. (1989). *Two Papers: The Grid and the Caesura*. London: Karnac.

Bion, W. R. (1990). *Brazilian Lectures*. London: Karnac.

Bion, W. R. (1994)[1987]. Making the best of a bad job. In: *Clinical Seminars and Other Works* (pp. 321–332). London: Karnac.

Bion, W. R. (1997). *War Memoirs 1917–1919*, F. Bion (Ed.). London: Karnac.

Bléandonu, G. (1994). *Wilfred Bion, His Life and Works 1897–1979*. New York: Other Press.

Bollas, C. (1987). *The Shadow of the Object: Psychoanalysis of the Unthought Known*. New York: Columbia University Press.

Bollas, C. (2006). Perceptive identification. *The Psychoanalytic Review*, 93(5): 713–717.

Britton, R. (1992). Keeping things in mind. In: R. Anderson (Ed.), *Clinical Lectures on Klein and Bion* (pp. 102–113). Hove: Brunner-Routledge.

Britton, R. (1999). Primal grief and petrified rage. In: D. Bell (Ed.), *Psychoanalysis and Culture: A Kleinian Perspective* (pp. 27–47). London: Karnac.

Burnett, F. (1910). *The Secret Garden*. Serialized in *The American Magazine*.

Casement, P. (1990). *Learning from the Patient*. New York: Guilford Press.

Chaudhuri, N. (1988). Memsahibs and motherhood in nineteenth-century colonial India. *Victorian Studies*, 31(4): 517–535.

Conci, M. (2011). Bion and his first analyst, John Rickman (1891–1951): a revisitation of their relationship in the light of Rickman's personality and scientific production and of Bion's letters to him (1939–1951). *International Forum of Psychoanalysis*, 20: 68–86.

Connor, S. (1988). *Samuel Beckett: Repetition, Theory and Text*. Oxford: Blackwell.

Craig, G., Fehsenfeld, M., Gunn, D., & Overbeck, L. (Eds.) (2011). *The Letters of Samuel Beckett vol. 2, 1941–1956*. New York: Cambridge University Press.

Dewey, J. (1910). *How We Think*. Boston, MA: DC Heath.

Díaz de Chumaceiro, C. L. (2003). On Rudyard Kipling's loss of Ayah. *PsyArt: A Hyperlink Journal for the Psychological Study of the Arts*, article 030802. http://www.clas.ufl.edu/ipsa/journal/2003/diaz01.htm.

Dicks, H. (1970). *Fifty Years of the Tavistock Clinic*. London: Routledge & Kegan Paul.

Duffell, N. (2000). *The Making of Them: The British Attitude to Children and The Boarding School System*. London: Lone Arrow.

Dupont, J. (Ed.) (1988). *The Clinical Diary of Sandor Ferenczi*. Cambridge, MA: Harvard University Press.

Erikson, E. (1959). Identity and the life cycle. *Psychological Issues Monograph 1*: 1–173.

Erikson, E. (1970). Reflections on the dissent of contemporary youth. *International Journal of Psychoanalysis*, 51: 11–22.

Fairbairn, W. R. D. (1952). *Psychoanalytic Studies of the Personality*. London: Routledge & Kegan Paul.

Fehsenfeld, M. D., & Overbeck, L. M. (Eds.) (2009). *The Letters of Samuel Beckett v.1, 1929–1940*. New York: Cambridge University Press.

Feldman, M. (2006). *Beckett's Books*. London: Continuum.

Ferenczi, S. (1919). On the technique of psycho-analysis. In: J. Rickman (Ed.), *Further Contribution to the Theory and Technique of Psychoanalysis* (pp. 177–189). London: Maresfield Reprints, 1980.

Ferenczi, S. (1926). Present day problems in psycho-analysis. In: *Final Contributions to Psycho-Analysis*. New York: Brunner/Mazel, 1980.

Ferenczi, S. (1930). Notes and fragments. In: *Final Contributions to Psycho-Analysis*. New York: Brunner/Mazel, 1980.

Ferenczi, S., & Rank, O. (1923). *The Development of Psychoanalysis*. Madison, CT: International Universities Press, 1986.

Ferro, A. (1993). The impasse within a theory of the analytic field: possible vertices of observation. *International Journal of Psychoanalysis, 74*: 917–929.

Freud, A. (1936). *The Ego and the Mechanisms of Defense*. New York: International Universities Press.

Freud, S. (with Breuer, J.) (1985d). *Studies on Hysteria. S.E., 2*. London: Hogarth.

Freud, S. (1900a). *The Interpretation of Dreams. S.E., 4–5*. London: Hogarth.

Freud, S. (1905c). *Jokes and their Relation to the Unconscious. S.E., 8*: 3–249. London: Hogarth.

Freud, S. (1908c). On the sexual theories of children. *S.E., 9*: 205–226. London: Hogarth.

Freud, S. (1909d). *Notes upon A Case of Obsessional Neurosis. S.E., 10*: 212–318. London: Hogarth.

Freud, S. (1910). Wild psychoanalysis. *S.E., 11*: 219–228. London: Hogarth.

Freud, S. (1912e). Recommendations to physicians practising psycho-analysis. *S.E., 12*: 109–120. London: Hogarth.

Freud, S. (1913c). On beginning the treatment. *S.E., 12*: 121–144. London: Hogarth Press.

Freud, S. (1914g). Remembering, repeating, and working through. *S.E., 12*: 145–156. London: Hogarth.

Freud, S. (1921c). *Group Psychology and the Analysis of the Ego. S.E., 18*: 65–133. London: Hogarth.

Freud, S. (1933a). *New Introductory Lectures on Psycho-analysis. S.E., 22*. London: Hogarth.

Gladwell, M. (2000). *The Tipping Point*. New York: Little, Brown.

Gray, A. (1994). *The Ego and Analysis of Defense*. Northvale, NJ: Jason Aronson.

Gutheil, T. G., & Gabbard, G. O. (1993). The concept of boundaries in clinical practice: theoretical and risk-management dimensions. *American Journal of Psychiatry, 150*: 188–196.

Heimann, P. (1956). Dynamics of transference interpretations. *International Journal of Psychoanalysis, 37*: 303–310.

Hunneybell, D. (2009). Some thoughts on the men's boarding school survivors workshops. http://www.boardingrecovery.com/images/Men_Boarding_School_Survivors_wkshp.pdf, accessed 8 March 2013.

James, W. (1981). *The Works of William James, Volume 1: The Principles of Psychology.* Cambridge, MA: Harvard University Press.

Jones, E. (1948). *Papers on Psycho-Analysis* (5th edn). London: Balliere Tindall & Cox.

Jones, E. (1963). *Treatment of the Neuroses.* New York: Schocken Books.

Joyce, J. (2003). *Portrait of the Artist as a Young Man.* Harmondsworth: Penguin Books.

Jung, C. G. (1968). *Analytical Psychology.* London: Routledge.

Kafka, F. (1948). The metamorphosis. In: *The Penal Colony, and Other Stories* (pp. 191–230). New York: Schocken, 1995.

Kernberg, O. F. (1988). Psychic structure and structural change: an ego psychology-object relations theory viewpoint. *Journal of the American Psychoanalytic Association, 36S*: 315–337.

Klein, M. (1935). A contribution to the psychogenesis of manic-depressive states. *International Journal of Psychoanalysis, 16*: 145–174.

Klein, M. (1975). *The Writings of Melanie Klein, Vol. 3: Envy and Gratitude and Other Works 1946–1963.* New York: Free Press.

Knowlson, J. (1996). *Damned to Fame.* New York: Simon & Schuster.

Knowlson, J., & Knowlson, E. (Eds.) (2006). *Beckett Remembering Remembering Beckett.* London: Bloomsbury.

Kris, E. (1956). Some vicissitudes of insight in psychoanalysis. *International Journal of Psycho-Analysis, 37*: 445–455.

LeJuez, B. (2008). *Beckett Before Beckett.* London: Souvenir Press.

MacGreevy, T. (1931). *Richard Aldington.* London: Chatto & Windus.

McDougall, W. (1918). *An Introduction to Social Psychology.* Boston, MA: John W. Luce.

Meltzer, D. (1992). *The Claustrum.* Strathtay, Perthshire: Clunie Press.

Miller, I. (1987). William James and the psychology of consciousness. *Contemporary Psychoanalysis, 23*: 299–313.

O'Brien, E. (1986). *The Beckett Country.* Monkstown, Co. Dublin: Black Cat Press.

Ogden, T. (1982). *Projective Identification & Psychotherapeutic Technique.* Northvale, NJ: Jason Aronson.

Poirier, S. (1983). The Weir Mitchell rest cure: doctors and patients. *Women's Studies, 10*(1): 15–40.

Reich, W. (1928). On character analysis. In: *The Psychoanalytic Reader V1*. New York: International Universities Press.

Reisenberg-Malcolm, R. (1999). *On Bearing Unbearable States of Mind*. London: Routledge.

Rey, H. (1994). *Universals of Psychoanalysis in the Treatment of Psychotic and Borderline States*, J. Magagna (Ed.). London: Free Association Books.

Rickman, J. (2003). Number and the human sciences. In: P. King (Ed.), *No Ordinary Psychoanalyst* (pp. 109–116). London: Karnac.

Robertson, B. (2002). Plenary panel on postmodern psychoanalysis. *International Journal of Psycho-Analysis, 83*: 468–472.

Segal, H. (1988). *Introduction to the Work of Melanie Klein*. London: Karnac.

Segal, H., & Britton, R. (1981). Interpretation and primitive psychic processes: a Kleinian view. *Psychoanalytic Inquiry, 1*: 267–277.

Shengold, L. (1975). An attempt at soul murder—Rudyard Kipling's early life and work. *Psychoanalytic Study of the Child, 30*: 683–723.

Simon, B. (1988). The imaginary twins: the case of Beckett and Bion. *International Review of Psychoanalysis, 15*: 331–352.

Sodré, I. (1999). Death by daydreaming: *Madame Bovary*. In: D. Bell (Ed.), *Psychoanalysis and Culture: A Kleinian Perspective* (pp. 48-63). London: Duckworth [revised and reprinted London: Karnac, 2004].

Souter, K. (2009). The war memoirs: some origins of the thought of W. R. Bion. *International Journal of Psychoanalysis, 90*: 797–808.

Steiner, J. (1993). *Psychic Retreats*. London: Routledge.

Stephen, K. (1933). *Psychoanalysis and Medicine: A Study of the Wish to Fall Ill*. New York: Macmillan.

Sterne, L. (1962)[1759]. *The Life and Opinions of Tristram Shandy, Gentleman*. New York: Harper Brothers.

Strachey, J. (1934). The nature of the therapeutic action of psychoanalysis. *International Journal of Psychoanalysis, 15*: 127–159.

Synge, J. M. (1982). *Collected Works II. Prose*, A. Price (Ed.), Washington, DC: Catholic University of America Press.

Thompson, G. (1976). RTE radio interview with Proinsias Ó Conluain on Beckett's 70th birthday.

Waelder, R. (1976). The principle of multiple function. In: S. Guttman (Ed.), *Psychoanalysis: Observation, Theory, Application*. New York: International Universities Press.

Winnicott, D. W. (1953). Transitional objects and transitional phenomena—a study of the first not-me possession. *International Journal of Psycho-Analysis, 34*: 89–97.

Woodworth, R. S. (1931). *Contemporary Schools of Psychology*. New York: Ronald Press.

INDEX